AMPHIBIANS:

Their Care and Keeping

Amphibians

Their Care and Keeping

STEVE GRENARD

FEATURING PHOTOGRAPHS
BY
BILL LOVE

HOWELL
BOOK
HOUSE

Howell Book House
A Simon & Schuster Macmillan Company
1633 Broadway
New York, NY 10019

Macmillan Publishing books may be purchased for business or sales promotional use. For information write: Special Markets Department, Macmillan Publishing USA, 1633 Broadway, New York, NY 10019.

Macmillan is a registered trademark of Macmillan, Inc.

ISBN: 0-87605-137-9

Library of Congress Cataloging-in-Publication Data
Grenard, Steve.
    Amphibians: their care and keeping/Steve Grenard: featuring
    photographs by Bill Love.
      p. cm.
    Includes bibliographical references and index.
    ISBN 0-87605-137-9
    1. Amphibians as pets. 2. Amphibians. I. Title.
SF459.A45G74   1998   98-38068
639.3'78—dc21   CIP

Manufactured in the United States

Book design by Nick Anderson

Contents

Acknowledgments

My early interest in amphibians came about as a result of my parents' absolute unwillingness to allow me to have a snake in the house. My father, therefore, spent more time than he was entitled trying to talk me into pursuing an interest in frogs, toads and salamanders. What finally convinced me was contained in a five-dollar box of "assorted frogs" that arrived from a dealer in Quito, Ecuador. Inside this box was a gravid female Marsupial Frog that delivered 92 fully formed tadpoles from her pouch. I soon learned that this was the first time that this was observed in a marsupial frog in the United States and that another hobbyist in England had almost simultaneously experienced a similar joyful occasion. John Walker wrote up his observations in the *British Journal of Herpetology,* and I was encouraged by the late Charles M. Bogert, Curator of Herpetology at the American Museum of Natural History, to do the same in an American science journal called *Herpetologica.* This fortuitous occasion gave me access to a number of experts, mandated by Bogert, to assist with the preparation of my paper. I will forever be grateful to Bogert; his assistant curator Richard G. Zweifel; his lab assistant Carl Herrmann, with whom I became good friends; James A. Oliver, Curator of Reptiles at the Bronx Zoo; Ray Cummins of the same zoo; and a host of others for guiding me, especially because I was 13 years old at the time!

I especially want to thank Lenny Flank for referring me to Howell Book House and my editor, Amanda Pisani, for her superb and professional handling of this project.

Amphibians are not always found in the most charming or hospitable of locations and, as a result, it is necessary to thank my wife, Vanessa, and my son, Kevin, who have, over many years, endured countless hours of swatting mosquitoes while tramping through mud and avoiding venomous snakes, alligators and other dangers…they deserve the amphibian medal of honor, if there is such a thing.

S.G.

Introduction

Of all the land-loving, four-legged vertebrates roaming the earth today, amphibians represent the most interesting and varied of creatures. An intermediate between totally aquatic fishes and land-dwelling, egg-laying reptiles and birds, the amphibians represent the first great leap out of primordial seas, developing the anatomical and functional assets to enable them to colonize land. If some great disaster or even a minor bend in their path to terrestriality had befallen them, it is reasonably certain that either they never would have evolved or their evolution would have been delayed by millions of years. This delay would have included the appearance of humans, who stand at the apex of this fascinating evolutionary tale.

The amphibian story is remarkable in other ways. It began some 350 million years ago during the Devonian period and although their evolution is not yet over, man can stand back and survey what has happened thus far. Today, the amphibians are noted not just as pioneering colonizers of land, but also as the most numerous of all living vertebrates, with some 4,500 species and subspecies known to science. Their diversity, in terms of their relationships with the envi-

ronment, is mind-boggling. Amphibians have adapted to virtually every climatic and geographic locale, save for full-strength sea water. Their differing modes of reproduction and life history exceed those of any other class; their shell-less eggs and free-living larval stage provide the means by which embryologists and developmental biologists can solve the mysteries of life itself in addition to furnishing a dynamic, living laboratory for the freshman biologist.

The future of amphibian biology is filled with the prospects of exciting new discoveries. More work needs to be done on the amphibian's unique ability to regulate its internal water balance and exchange gases through its permeable skin. Studies of amphibian reproduction, tolerance of environmental extremes and metabolism are continuing apace, as are discoveries of new biochemicals found within amphibian organs as well as secreted by their glandular skin structures. Many of these substances hold medical promise as painkillers, as antibiotics and as therapeutic and diagnostic drugs useful for the study and treatment of cancer, heart disease and AIDS. These kinds of studies, with few exceptions, require the maintenance and propagation of amphibians in a captive environment. Hobbyists have contributed greatly to the storehouse of knowledge required to successfully breed, rear and maintain amphibians outside of their natural environs.

And while such studies may be of significance in furthering human knowledge of amphibians, this same research can often benefit these animals in their natural homes as well. The study of amphibian diseases, for example, is still in its infancy, but it may well be a discovery made in the captive environment that provides an important clue to the decline or extinction of amphibians in their natural habitat. The same is true for amphibian responses to environmental pollutants, to toxins and, as has recently been theorized, to increased ultraviolet radiation (due to the ozone layer hole) and acid rain. Mysterious amphibian extinctions stand as one of mankind's most salient warnings that our environment may soon be unfit for either man or beast. So while many people do not mourn the loss of a whole population or species of frog or salamander, others are baffled, as well as terrified, by such occurrences.

The word *amphibian* is derived from two Greek words—*amphi,* meaning "both," and *bios,* meaning "life." Thus the word means "two lives." This term may actually refer to one or both of two different aspects of amphibians. It describes an animal that spends part of its life in the water, as an egg and as a free-swimming larva or tadpole, and part on land, which it does after metamorphosing into the adult form. However, it can also mean an animal that spends part of its daily life in the water and part on land, in trees, buried beneath the substrate or leaf litter or just hanging around an embankment. Although this describes most amphibians, it doesn't exactly fit every member of this group. In reality, there are some amphibians that spend their entire lives in the water (fully aquatic); and there are other types that are bred, born, grow up and live on land or in trees and never enter the water, even to breed or lay their eggs. Amphibians employ so many different reproductive strategies and adaptations to their environment that no one model truly describes them all. In short, they adhere to few rules and their life histories are truly a never-ending parade of exceptions, especially where frogs are concerned.

Before starting to read this book it may also be useful to understand a few things about the terms *salamanders, newts, frogs* and *toads.* All newts are salamanders, although the term *newt* does apply as a common name to a group of somewhat more aquatic but still amphibious species of salamanders. A few salamander groups are also strictly aquatic and never leave the water, even as reproducing adults. Moreover, all animals commonly referred to as toads are also frogs.

The term *toad* implies a predominantly land-dwelling species, whereas frogs are more amphibious than most toads. There are exceptions, such as the fully aquatic species known as the Surinam Toad, which is nothing like most land-living toads. Now that you are completely confused, take heart: Because common naming conventions have no scientific basis, it is necessary to consider the terms *salamander, newt, frog* and *toad* as common names that have "stuck" on a species and do not attribute any particular lifestyle to an animal. In other words, just accept them and don't dwell too deeply on the ambiguities or contradictions that occur where common names are concerned.

PART I

What Is an Amphibian?

Evolutionary History • *Basic Biology* • *Ecology* •
Taxonomy and Classification

CHAPTER 1

Evolutionary History

The prehistoric ancestors of the amphibians descended from a group of bony fishes known as the Osteichtyes. There are three different types of such fish: 1) the Actinopterygii or ray-finned fish, 2) the Dipnoi or lungfish, and 3) the Actinistia or lobe-finned fish.

It is now generally agreed that today's amphibians most probably descended from the lobe-finned fish, although controversy over this issue still exists and the subject is hotly debated by paleontologists and scientists who study evolution.

The earliest amphibians tended to lead a more aquatic, fish-like existence than the modern amphibians. And although some still lead a strictly aquatic lifestyle, they nonetheless differ markedly from fish. The most important advance amphibians made over fish was the development of legs, four of them to be precise. This is a condition known as tetrapody, and all four-legged creatures are known as tetrapods. The development of legs obviously gave amphibians the ability to haul out of the water and walk upon the land. Some fish are capable of such behavior on a limited basis. These include the walking catfish (*Clarius sp.*), which can walk over land for short distances to a new body of water should its current home dry up. Another type of fish, known as the mudskipper (*Periophthalmidae sp.*), can scoot around on mud flats, in an inch or less of water, with its head and prominent eyes protruding above the surface, breathing air. While the walking catfish and the mudskipper (the most amphibious of all fish) are evolving, each in its own way, neither has quite made it yet as an amphibian.

The mudskipper, a type of fish, is just a hop, skip and a jump away from evolving into an amphibian.

The first amphibians were a group of creatures called Labyrinthodonts, a name that refers to the maze-like pattern seen on their teeth. These animals are believed to be the first to have crawled out of the water and to have succeeded on land, thus truly leading the dual existence for which amphibians are aptly named. The earliest species of amphibians discovered to date is called Icthyostega, believed to be the link between the lobe-finned fish and the true amphibians. Ichthyostega literally means "fish-stage." And while Ichthyostega is the oldest known amphibian fossil ever discovered (in Greenland, from the upper Devonian era), scientists continue to debate whether it was the lobe-fin or lungfish that represent the ancestors of today's amphibians. Labyrinthodonts were huge (16 feet long), short-limbed crocodile-like amphibians with fins on their tails.

So while the lobe-fins had the fleshy lower fins that could evolve into four limbs for walking on land, the mudskipper and lungfish had the right equipment for exchanging gases out of the water. Marine fossils dating to the early Devonian era provide evidence of the early existence of lungfish and five species still exist today in Africa, South America and Australia. Lungfish have dual means of gas exchange: gills like fish, and lungs like land animals.

The three modern amphibian groups representing the salamanders, frogs and toads and cecillians (*var:* caecilians) are members of a larger assemblage or subclass known as the Lissamphibia. The Lissamphibia, both fossil and modern, were and continue to be found in tropical and temperate parts of the world. They do not reside in the most torrid deserts, Antarctica or the Arctic Polar ice caps, although some species are found at latitudes that range into the Arctic Circle. They are also absent from a few rocky, sparsely vegetated oceanic islands (mainly in the South Pacific) characterized by an absence of continual natural freshwater or rain. Although most amphibians are aquatic or semi-aquatic, modern amphibians do not tolerate full-strength sea water. They are thus not found in the oceans and seas, although a few species may be found near and have adapted to an estuarine or brackish (partly salty) habitat.

The earliest known fossils of the modern salamander date from the Upper Jurassic period (in North America and Eurasia) and extend through the Pleistocene period. There are eight living and three extinct families known from North American specimens, with one modern family extending to South America. There are five living and three extinct families known from Eurasia.

The secretive, burrowing group of amphibians known as the cecilians or apoda, a term that literally means "footless" or "legless," are

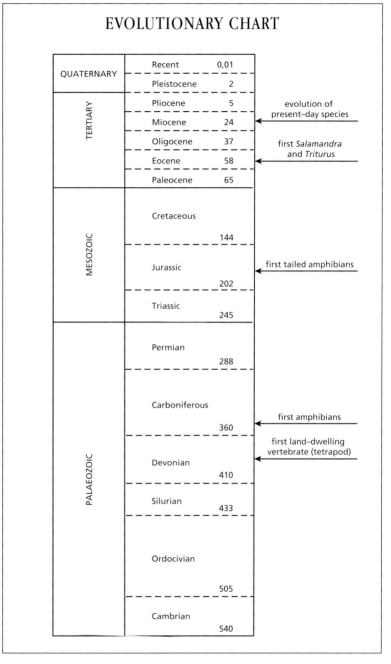

A graphic depiction of the evolution of amphibians. The numbers represent the beginning of the different periods as millions of years before the present.

Although all living frogs are tailless, some extinct species of frog had a short tail (*Bufo guttata*).

rare in the fossil record. They are represented by about 35 genera and 162 species. Prior fossil evidence of cecillians was restricted to just two vertebrae, one from the Brazilian Paleocene era and another from the late Cretaceous period in Bolivia. A recent fossil find, an extensive series of early Jurassic cecillians, indicates that at least some of the extinct families of cecillians may indeed have had small feet and legs. This amazing find was made at Gold Spring, Coconino County, Arizona. What's more, this find is much older than the earliest known salamander fossils (Middle Jurassic) but younger than the earliest known frog pro-anuran fossils (Late Triassic). This discovery, which was announced in 1993, promises to substantially alter the way scientists believe amphibians have evolved.

The earliest frogs and toads including extinct species are also considered poorly represented in the fossil record. The earliest known fossils *recognizable* as modern frogs were discovered in the Jurassic period in Europe, North America and South America. Fossils were found through the Pleistocene era. The frogs and toads have more species than any other living amphibians. Interestingly, while all living frogs and toads are virtually tailless, some extinct species did possess a short tail. The oldest order of amphibians, known as the pro-anura, had many frog-like traits. They are known from a single tiny fossil fragment dating to the Lower Triassic era. This fragment was found on the island of Madagascar, and it is believed to represent an animal that was highly aquatic. This early frog-like amphibian was called *Triadobatrachus* and lived some 200 million years ago. The earliest fossil that definitely represents a frog is that of

Vieraella herbstii, discovered in Argentina; it is approximately 160 million years old and bears the closest resemblance to modern frogs and toads.

The sheer magnitude of the amphibian accomplishment—invasion of the land—cannot be overemphasized. It paved the way for the reptiles, birds and mammals, and in the 120 million or so years since the first amphibian was believed to have emerged from its watery environment, these animals have been among the most successful of all land-living vertebrates. Today amphibians exist in virtually every topography earth has to offer, some even at altitudes of nearly 20,000 feet in the Himalayas and Andes Mountains.

All prehistoric amphibians were predacious carnivores. They preyed not only on each other, but on fish and a host of invertebrates including arthropods such as insects and shellfish. Although their larvae may be exclusively herbivorous, omnivorous or carnivorous, the modern adult-stage amphibian remains a predator of anything small enough to subdue and swallow. Remarkably, however, adult-stage frogs that may be both plant and meat eaters have recently been discovered, and this may also change the way scientists look at amphibian evolutionary history and amphibians themselves.

Basic Biology

The majority of salamanders are vaguely lizard-like, four-legged elongated creatures that walk with bellies slung close to the ground. They have smooth or rough glandular skin and a backbone that extends past the cloacal vent—which is another way of saying they have a tail. They range in size from the diminutive Mexican pygmy salamanders (*Thorius sp.*)—some just 1.5 inches from snout to tip of the tail—to the huge, fully aquatic Giant Chinese (*Andrias davidianus*) and Japanese Salamanders (*Andrias japonicus*), which reach lengths of 5 feet. A few species have greatly reduced appendages and one aquatic group, the Sirens, have small rear legs only.

Unlike the frogs and toads, species diversity of salamanders in the Northern Hemisphere is greater in temperate zones. Only one large family, the lungless salamanders, or Plethodontidae, are found in any numbers south of the equator. This family contains about 250 species, approximately half of all the known species of salamanders. Although frog species

The family of lungless salamanders contains about half of all known species of salamander (Slimy Salamander, *Plethodon glutinosus*).

are plentiful in Australia, salamanders are absent from down under altogether. North America and the Americas in general have more salamander species than the rest of the world put together.

Frogs and toads are tailless as fully metamorphosed adults (tadpoles have tails that disappear when they change to adult forms). They

have squat bodies that are, in many cases, only slightly longer than they are wide. They have no discernible neck, although one group of African frogs (*Phrynomantis sp.*) have what appears to be a distinct neck.

Once you recognize one kind of frog or toad, you will have no trouble identifying any other creature as one. They rest on all four limbs, some species with head up and rump down (on an angle that makes them look like tiny ramps), whereas others rest squat on the ground with head and rump at the same level. The front legs are shorter than the hind legs, which are usually more heavily webbed (if they are webbed at all). They have large, prominent eyes, as vision is an important sense among these animals in espying prey and predator alike. They have either thin, moist, smooth skin or thick, dry, warty and glandular skin. Land-dwelling bufonid toads, which represent the majority of dry thick-skinned species, have thinner,

The vast majority of frogs have no discernible neck (Black Spotted Walking Toad, *Melanophryniscus stelzneri*).

smooth skin on their undersides. This helps them to absorb water more effectively and affords them the ability to absorb moisture and exchange electrolytes with the environment through ventral surfaces that remain in contact with the damp ground. Frogs and toads range in length from less than $1/_2$ inch for the Cuban Toad (*E. limbatus*) to about 1 foot for the African Goliath Frog (*C. Goliath*) found in Cameroon and Equatorial Guinea.

The cecillians are secretive, burrowing or fossorial worm-like amphibians about which little is really known. They have either a very short tail or no tail at all, have no limbs and range in length from 3 inches to about 2.5 feet. Some species have embedded dermal scales, which are not found in other amphibians. These scales seemingly have no useful purpose, but their presence is curious and may be an evolutionary precursor to scales in reptiles and birds or a throwback to the scales of fishes. Aside from these scales, their skin is thin and moist. Cecillians have tiny, lidless eyes that are covered by bone or skin. Vision is a useless asset in their underground habitat. In some species, the eyes may respond to differences in light intensity but are certainly incapable of any other meaningful type of vision.

Cecillians have a pair of retractable tentacles on their front

The tiny eyes of cecillians are not a disability—as underground dwellers, they have little use for vision (*Amphibaena alba*).

snouts that are sensitive to tactile stimuli. These tentacles may well have other sensory functions, such as detecting odor, heat or movement, and would be of value in not only navigating but in locating prey. Cecillians may be found burrowed in loose, damp soil or in rotted wood on the forest floor as well as in murky aquatic environments. They are widely distributed in the tropics but are unknown in the more temperate and northern climates. What little is known about their reproduction and life history will be discussed later.

Amphibian Skin

The skin of amphibians is an elaborate and highly organized anatomical structure that contains a variety of cellular and noncellular components. In addition, the skin between the larval and adult forms of amphibians often differs markedly. Amphibians that never metamorphose and reach "adulthood" while still in their fully aquatic larval state often retain the characteristics of larval skin as well.

All amphibians possess more or less the same sort of thin, moist, water- and gas-permeable skin. The number of different functions served by amphibian skin reveals its highly dynamic and complex nature, and no other class of animal skin has as so many critically important attributes:

1. Protects the animal against abrasion and infection from environmental pathogens.

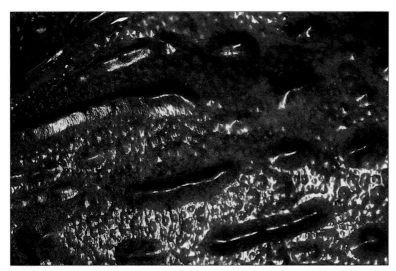

The skin of amphibians is both gas and water permeable (close-up of skin of African Burrowing Bull Frog, *Pyxicephalus adspersus*).

11. Liberates alarm substances in members of a population when one or more is attacked, thus alerting others to the presence of danger. Other odors associated with larval amphibians are said to allow them to recognize their siblings as well as their birthplace.

12. Presence of coloration is designed to permit sexual recognition in some species.

13. Skin distensibility or elasticity permits prodigious feats of jumping, leaping, and even "flying" and landing without injury, often from substantial heights.

2. Permits the exchange of respiratory gases (oxygen and carbon dioxide).

3. Permits absorption and secretion of electrolyte ions, thereby serving as an adjunct to the kidneys in maintaining correct electrolyte balance.

4. Permits absorption and release of water, thereby serving as an adjunct to the kidneys in maintaining correct water balance or hydrostasis.

5. Permits temperature regulation by lightening (reflecting heat) or darkening (absorbing heat) in some species.

6. Permits the animal to camouflage itself against its background in many species.

7. Brightly colored skins serve to warn potential predators of defensive noxious or even fatal glandular skin secretions in a number of species.

Many of these substances are finding value in medical and other scientific research.

8. In some species, the mucous membranes and specialized skin adaptations permit conservation of water during periods of aridity and inactivity; some even produce a mucoid "shroud" that forms a shell over the body which serves to retain water.

9. Serves sensory functions: chemoreception, mechanoreception or tactile sensibility; and electrodetection in some fully aquatic species that retain lateral line organs in their skin.

10. Protects against cutaneous external and internal wound infection through the secretion of peptide antibiotics in some species (see Chapter 13).

Because the skin of all three groups of amphibians (salamanders, frogs and cecillians) is alike, it was considered by early scientists as the marker that required the grouping of these animals in a single animal class, the Amphibia. As such, it also implies a common origin or evolutionary ancestor for this group, although cecillians are unique in having dermal scales that are not found in frogs or salamanders. Cecillian scales are embedded in the dermis within folds between their skin furrows. In some cecillian species, however, they are either not present or are poorly developed and greatly reduced.

Skin Glands

There are five types of glandular cells that have been identified in amphibian skin. They include mucus-secreting cells, granule-producing cells (that produce most of the poisons including peptides and alkaloids), mitochondrial cells, myoepithelial cells and duct cells. In addition, embryonic frogs have hatching gland cells (first reported in fish embryos) that contribute to the development of the egg. Leydig cells are found in the skin of larval salamanders and cecillians, and while their function is unclear, they disappear after metamorphosis in species that change to an adult form.

Lipid- or wax-secreting gland cells are found in some tree frogs and frogs that live in semi-arid environs. Such frogs are more prone than others to dehydration during normal activities. These glands secrete a fatty or waxy substance that insulates against water loss through the skin. Remarkably, the frogs that have this asset spread the secretion over their bodies using their limbs—in a manner reminiscent of a person rubbing on skin lotion!

Skin Coloration

Skin coloration in amphibians is produced by a number of specialized pigments. Melanin, a dark pigment (browns and blacks), is found in melanophores, a specialized grouping of pigmented cells. Xanthophores produce yellows, erythrophores reds and iridiophores reflective coloration, causing whitish/bluish or silvery coloration. Green, a common frog color, is produced by the effect of the iridophores creating light-scattering blue overlaid by the yellow-pigmented xanthophores.

Melanin movement is triggered by hormones that are involved in two types of color changes in amphibians. One is seen in larval amphibians that lighten in color when in the dark, as a result of pineal gland hormonal (melatonin) stimulation. The second is utilized in crypsis or camouflage, which enables an amphibian to blend in with its environmental background, thus escaping detection by would-be predators. This occurs as a result of a melanophore-stimulating hormone (MSH) released by the pituitary gland.

Amphibians that do not engage in crypsis or camouflage are often brightly colored—flashing reds, yellows, golds, oranges or bright blues. These species, more often than not, are endowed with noxious or poisonous skin secretions. Their bright colors ward off would-be predators and serve as a reminder to predators who mouthed them once before and were treated to a foul taste or unpleasant physical response as a result of their attempt to prey upon such species.

The brightly colored European Fire Salamander can, amazingly, forcibly eject its poisonous glandular secretions (salamandrine) as a spray against a predator. So while predators that pick up amphibians or bite them, liberating their noxious poisons into their oral cavity, are properly classified as being "poisoned," some objects of the fire salamander's defenses may more accurately be referred to as "envenomated." In this respect, the salamander is similar to a venomous snake, employing defensive actions not unlike the well-known behavior of the spitting cobras. The fire

Amphibians that are brightly colored, such as this dart poison frog, generally produce toxic skin secretions. The colors ward off predators that learn to avoid them (Strawberry Dart Poison Frog, *Dendrobates pumilio*).

salamander may be unique among amphibians in being capable of voluntarily and forcefully squirting its poison at a potential threat.

Skin Shedding

Amphibians cast off their outer layer of epidermis or *stratum corneum* (often in pieces) on a regular basis. In some species, shedding may occur virtually every day, while in others it occurs less frequently. In most frogs, the outer layer of skin splits down the back and is sucked into the mouth and eaten. Salamander skin breaks around the mouth. The salamander then pushes forward, constantly pushing the old skin down toward the chest area. At this time, the front legs are pulled free and then the old skin is moved back-

Lungless salamanders tend to eat their skin after shedding. Although this is unappealing to us, the shed skin is quite nutritious (*Plethodon yonahlossee*).

ward on the hind legs. The hind legs are then pulled free of the skin, after which they are used to move the cast toward the tail. By now the old skin is pretty well clumped, and it is eventually scraped off the end of the tail or may be pulled off and eaten by some species of salamander, particularly the Plethodontid or lungless salamanders. Recycling cast-off skin by eating it is a beneficial source of fluids and nutrients, but not every species engages in this behavior.

Amphibian Respiration

While there are many unique features of amphibians, certainly one of the most intriguing is the num-

ber and variety of means by which they breathe, exchanging gases with the atmosphere in order to support internal respiration and cellular metabolism. No other group of vertebrates has as many different ways to accomplish this same task.

Most adult amphibian species breathe by means of exchanging gases either via functional lungs or through the skin. Larval or tadpole amphibians, as well as amphibians that never metamorphose (a condition known as neoteny, or retention of juvenile traits throughout life), use three different means to accomplish respiration: gills, skin and lungs. The chief respiratory gases are oxygen (O_2) and carbon dioxide (CO_2). Oxygen is required for metabolism and energy production, so it must be obtained, whereas carbon dioxide is produced as a waste product of cellular metabolism and must be eliminated. In a sense, oxygen is exchanged for carbon dioxide (or vice versa, depending on point of view), and this is the ultimate purpose of breathing, or respiration.

The method of breathing used depends on different factors among different species. For example, the large group of lungless salamanders rely almost solely on their skin to exchange gases. Breathing through the skin is impossible for frogs that waterproof themselves by secreting a waxy coat or encasing themselves in a thick coat of mucous, so lung breathing assumes a position of prominence. Fully aquatic salamanders, neotenous salamanders, larval frogs and toads rely almost entirely on gill breathing, much as fish do. These three examples represent extremes, and many amphibians use a combination of breathing methods. For example, in the majority of amphibians that employ both skin and lung breathing, skin breathing provides about 65 to 75 percent of the total carbon dioxide elimination and about 25 to 35 percent of the oxygen intake. The residual balances are met by lung ventilation.

The act of breathing in frogs, and to some extent in salamanders, appears to be enhanced by throat pulsation and a type of air intake referred to as buccalpharyngeal respiration. It is often referred to as "frog-breathing," and a variation is taught to people with paralyzed or impaired intercostal and/or diaphragmatic muscles to enable them to inhale air without having to rely on a mechanical ventilator (respirator). These pulsations cause the flow of air or water over the highly vascularized lining of the mouth and throat. And while some researchers doubt that the pulsations have much significance for air intake to the lungs or water through the gills, it is true that amphibians have no diaphragm or true intercostal muscles to help

them effect mechanical inward movement of air for lung breathing. In the lungless salamanders, the pulsations may serve to provide some additional respiratory surfaces for gas exchange to take place. Studies linking increased temperatures to greater rates of throat pulsation also suggest a respiratory function for this type of action. As temperatures increase in ectotherms, metabolism also increases, and increased metabolism dictates the need for greater intake of oxygen and faster expulsion of carbon dioxide.

On land, most amphibians use the motion of the throat not only to transport air in and out of the oral/throat or buccalpharyngeal cavity, but also to push air into the lungs. They breathe with the mouth closed and control air flow by taking in air via their valved nostrils. Because they have no diaphragm, they use the motion of the throat as a substitute. When

the throat is lowered, it increases the size of the oral cavity and causes a pressure drop or partial vacuum much the same way a diaphragm muscle works in animals that have this structure. As a result of the pressure gradient created by the throat motion, air moves in through the nostrils. The reverse occurs as a result of the throat elevating or contracting while the nasal valves are opened, thus allowing exhalation to take place. The exhaled air moves out of the lungs as a result of the elastic recoil of these structures. The muscles of the body wall in some species may also assist in exhalation. This entire affair is known as the "buccalpharyngeal pump." Its efficiency will vary with the size of the oral/pharyngeal cavity. This pump is also involved in obtaining air to produce vocalizations in frogs and toads.

Frog and toad tadpoles, salamander larvae and neotenous

Tadpoles and salamander larvae breathe by the use of gills (larval newt).

salamanders that remain aquatic for their entire lives breathe by the use of gills. When tadpoles and salamander larvae metamorphose or transform into air-breathing, adult-stage organisms, these gills are lost and the lungs take their place. Water flows over the gills as a result of the aforementioned throat pulsations. When the throat is lowered, increasing the size of the oral cavity, water enters through the mouth or nostrils, passes into the pharynx and gills and exits through a slit known as the spiracle on each side of the head in anuran tadpoles.

Gas exchange between the blood and the inspired water takes place as a result of intimate contact with the gills' highly vascularized surfaces. They are so filled with blood, in fact, that in many species of salamander the external gills appear as bright red feathery structures that are readily observable.

The size and nature of amphibian lungs vary considerably with the importance they play in breathing. Because cold water holds more oxygen than warm water, smaller, cold-water aquatic species are apt to have need for smaller respiratory surfaces than larger, warm-water aquatic species. Similar distinctions exist among air-breathing land species. In bufonid toads, which have limited patches of skin available for cutaneous respiration, the lungs are apt to be larger and contain greater numbers of folds to increase surface area. Smaller, thin-skinned frogs can make do with smaller lungs as the area for cutaneous respiration is, relatively speaking, greater than it is in thick-skinned, leathery bufonids.

In contrast, pulmonary surface area reaches maximum levels in air-breathing mammals. If all the surfaces available for gas exchange in one pair of human lungs were laid out end-to-end, they would cover an area roughly equivalent to that of a tennis court. As one descends down the evolutionary ladder, the surface-area-to-size ratio of lungs in air-breathing organisms tends to diminish. The same is true of amphibians within their own grouping. Frogs and toads tend to engage in greater levels of activity and have higher metabolic demands for oxygen (and increased CO_2 elimination) compared to salamanders. As a result, their lungs are apt to be divided by ridges and folds or septae to provide a greater surface area, whereas salamander lungs of the same size are apt to have less surface area. Clearly, increased metabolic activity requires higher surface areas, and this trend is well documented among the amphibians.

Lungs, in addition to serving as respiratory organs for gas exchange, have another important purpose in some amphibians—that of hydrostatic organs, which help amphibians control their buoyancy or floating/diving abilities when in the water. By altering the volume of air in the lungs, an amphibian increases its ability to float at the surface, dive, sink to the bottom, swim or just hang at depths somewhere in between. The lungless salamanders, which rely almost entirely on cutaneous respiration to meet their metabolic requirements, are also almost entirely terrestrial, and if they enter the water it is in extremely shallow flats, never venturing into deeper locales. They would certainly suffer a deprivation of oxygen in oxygen-poor warmer waters if they were at all aquatic.

Heart and Circulation

In order to appreciate the heart and circulatory system of amphibians, it's good to have a basic idea of how these work in higher animals such as birds and mammals. Birds and mammals have four-chambered hearts divided into right and left sides. There are two upper chambers, the right and left atria, and two lower ones, the right and left ventricles. Blood perfuses the tissues of the body and returns to the right side of the heart via the veins and enters the heart through the right atrium. From here it passes downward through a valve into the right ventricle, which then pumps it into the lungs via the pulmonary arteries, where it releases carbon dioxide and exchanges it for oxygen. The blood, thus restored, returns to the left side of the heart via the pulmonary veins, first entering the left atrium and then passing down into the left ventricle. The left ventricle is the thickest-walled, strongest part of the heart, because it is from here that blood is pumped out to the body via a large artery called the aorta. From the aorta, the blood moves into smaller arteries, perfusing the tissues via a capillary network called arterioles. It is then picked up by similar draining capillaries called venules, which collect the blood and pass it back into the veins for return to the right side of the heart for the cycle to begin anew.

With an understanding of the above, it may be easier to comprehend the somewhat more complicated and varying means by which amphibians accomplish the same thing. Unlike birds and mammals, fish and almost all amphibians and reptiles have three-chambered hearts consisting of two atria or receiving chambers and a single, undivided or common ventricle. The exceptions to this among amphibians and reptiles are found in two species of aquatic salamander, the genera *Siren* and *Necturus,* and the crocodilians, which, alone among the reptiles, have four-chambered hearts. Some cecillians have extensive ridges or furrows in their single

Unlike the vast majority of amphibians and reptiles, salamanders of the genus *Siren* have four-chambered hearts (Greater Siren, *Siren lacertina*).

ventricle, which helps prevent mixing of arterial and venous blood. In the case of the four-chambered salamanders and cecillians, these adaptations help them to obtain higher levels of oxygenation given their difficult environmental conditions, either living in oxygen-poor waters or existing in underground burrows. Crocodilians are more closely related to birds than are other reptiles, and they clearly "paved the way" for internally regulated temperature and metabolism as exhibited by the higher vertebrates. A four-chambered heart may well have been the essential factor needed for endothermy (warm-bloodedness) to evolve in the birds and mammals.

For all the rest of the amphibians and reptiles, however, the single undivided ventricle provides a less-than-efficient means of obtaining oxygenated blood. This is readily countered by these animals' ability to thermoregulate or change their

body temperatures and consequently alter their metabolic rates as well. It is also useful to remember that many amphibians obtain oxygen and excrete carbon dioxide via their skin, a method that offsets their apparently less efficient cardiac arrangement. Blood that has perfused the tissues, low in oxygen and high in the waste gas carbon dioxide, returns to the right side of the heart and is passed into the undivided ventricle, pumped to the lungs or gills and then returned to the left atrium, down again to the left side of the undivided ventricle, where some mixing of oxygenated and unoxygenated blood occurs, and then pumped out to the body again. But by thermoregulating and engaging in cutaneous respiratory gas exchange, these animals function at optimal levels regardless of this arrangement. Without such abilities, no endothermic bird or mammal could operate optimally with a single-chambered ventricle, a congenital abnormality in human infants that must be surgically corrected for the baby to survive.

The Urogenital System

The urinary tract and reproductive system are closely related in amphibians. The kidneys in adult or metamorphosed amphibians are paired organs lying on the left and right sides of the descending aorta. They are long and slender in cecilians, extending almost from the level of the heart nearly to the cloaca. In some types of salamanders they are also elongated, but in most they are considerably shorter. In some genera of frogs and toads they are long and slender, but in most they are relatively broad. As in all vertebrates, kidneys function to produce urine by filtration of the blood, removing harmful metabolites or waste products while allowing other elements to be reabsorbed.

All amphibians, reptiles, birds and fish have a cloacal chamber (cloaca) and duct through which urinary and fecal wastes are excreted. This same structure is used to pass sperm from males and the ova of females outside the body. In salamanders practicing internal fertilization, this structure contains sets of glands and will be discussed in more detail in Chapter 9.

In addition, amphibians have a urinary bladder used to collect and store urine until it is necessary to pass it out of the body through the cloaca. Many amphibians release copious amounts of urine when threatened; they do this by relaxing the tension on the bladder sphincter. The amphibian urinary bladder is capable of great distention and can hold a significant amount of urine.

The gonads of amphibians consist of paired ovaries in females and testes, attached to the kidneys, in males. The testes produce sperm, used to fertilize the eggs, or ova, which are produced by the female. In most amphibians, fertilization of eggs by sperm takes place just outside the body in a carefully orchestrated and timed mating embrace termed amplexus. In some species of salamander, a packet of sperm is released in the water, picked up by the female and introduced into her cloaca, where its contents serve to fertilize her eggs before they are ejected. A few species practice internal fertilization, which will be addressed in Chapter 9.

Digestive System

The digestive system is similar in all three groups of amphibians, and begins with the buccal or oral cavity and terminates with the cloacal vent. Food is ingested through the mouth and may be partially or completely broken up by teeth.

As the food passes through the pharyngeal cavity, it is coated with mucus. A sphincter guards the entrance to the food tube or

AMPHIBIAN TEETH

Not all amphibians have teeth. The bufonid toads are completely toothless, and the occurrence of teeth varies considerably among other frog families both as to presence and type. All tree frogs, with the exception of a single genus, have teeth. Members of the aquatic genus *Xenopus* have monocuspid dentition, and a number of species have odontoid or recurved fang-like teeth capable of inflicting considerable trauma against prey and predator (and occasionally human handlers) alike. These fanged frogs include the popular South American Pacman or horned frogs (*Ceratophrys sp.*), the two species of African Bullfrog of the genus *Pyxiecephalus*, the Triangle Frog (*Ceratobatrachus guentheri*) and the horned tree frogs of the genus *Hemiphractus*. All salamanders have some sort of teeth, and these are mostly short bicuspids capable of inflicting little damage except in the particularly large, strictly aquatic forms. A few of the plethodontoid salamanders are an exception, and have longer, monocuspid teeth.

Some frogs have no teeth. Others, such as the horned frogs, have fang-like teeth capable of giving a nasty bite (*Ceratophrys cornuta*).

different enzymes and bile salts that break down fats. Trypsin further processes proteins and amylase digests carbohydrates, converting them to simple sugars. Lipase converts fats to fatty acids and glycerides to glycerol. Absorption of nutrients also occurs in the small intestine, whereas absorption of water and salts occurs in the large intestine.

Endocrine Glands

Amphibians have the same sorts of endocrine glands and hormonal production found in other vertebrates, including humans. In fact, much of the early research and the knowledge science has about endocrinology and hormones derives from studies performed on amphibians.

The Pituitary Gland

Located on the ventral surface of the brain, this gland produces the follicle stimulating hormone (FSH), luteinizing hormone (LH), prolactin, thyroid stimulating hormone (TSH) and adrenocorticotrophic hormone (ACTH), melanophore stimulating hormone (MSH), antidiuretic hormone (ASH) and arginine vasotocin. The pituitary is often referred to as the "master gland" for its many and varied roles in producing hormones that stimulate or affect functions elsewhere.

esophagus. Food is prevented from entering the respiratory tract by the closure of the glottis and the opening of the esophagus, a thin-walled tube that extends from the pharynx to the stomach. Glands in the esophagus provide additional mucus and the enzyme pepsinogen. The esophagus terminates at the entrance to the stomach, which as a rule lies just to the left of the midline. From here the digested or partially digested food matter passes into the intestines, a uniform tube except where it is broader as it changes into the large intestine. In cecillians the intestines are virtually identical throughout. Additional digestion and absorption of processed nutrients occurs principally in the intestines. Movement of food throughout the gastrointestinal tract occurs as a result of both muscular (peristalsis) and ciliary action.

Food is passed from the mouth to the esophagus as a result of the swallowing action of the tongue, although smaller bits of ingested matter may be swept along by cilia. In the stomach, the food matter is subjected to the action of hydrochloric acid, which kills any ingested prey animal that may still be alive. The low pH of the stomach helps to inhibit some kinds of bacterial growth and begins the breakdown of ingested bone minerals. Pepsinogen, in the presence of an acidic pH, is converted to pepsin, which breaks down proteins into amino acids.

Digestion is completed in the small intestine by a variety of

The Thyroid Gland

In amphibians, the thyroid hormone is responsible for metamorphosis. In human development, its absence as well as the absence of iodine-rich water or plant matter has been linked to developmental abnormalities in offspring. In fact, this is one of the reasons iodine has been added to virtually all the salt we humans use to spice up our food. Iodine is a necessary mineral for thyroid function and synthesis of thyroid hormone. Salamanders, such as the Axolotl of Mexico, that live in iodine-poor inland lakes do not metamorphose or develop into adult forms at all. A group of Axolotls brought to Florida by the author and placed in local iodine-rich ground water developed into adult salamanders in a matter of weeks. A control group kept in distilled (non-iodinated) water remained in their neotenous juvenile (larval) state. Iodine is an essential ingredient that the thyroid gland needs to manufacture thyroxin. Evidently when it is supplied to these normally neotenous salamanders, their thyroid gland is triggered and metamorphosis occurs.

The Parathyroid Glands

The parathyroid glands produce calcitonin and parathyroid hormone (PTH), which are involved in the metabolism of bone and tissues.

The Thymus

The thymus produces thymosin, a hormone that stimulates production of lymphocytes, a type of white blood cell involved in conferring immunity and helping prevent or counter infection.

The Pineal Gland

The pineal gland produces the hormone melatonin, which is involved in controlling skin color shade response to thermal cues but also regulates circadian rhythms, or day/night cycles.

Islet Cells of the Pancreas

These cells produce the hormone insulin, which enables the processing and assimilation of carbohydrates (sugars).

The Adrenal Glands

These glands, which sit atop the kidneys, have two portions that produce different hormones. The inner portion produces adrenaline and noradrenaline, which serve to increase or decrease heart rate, blood flow (through vasoconstricting abilities) and blood pressure. In the kidneys, the effect of noradrenaline is to decrease blood flow, but in the circulatory system it increases heart rate. Adrenaline increases blood flow to skeletal muscle, the liver and brain and increases heart rate. It is the emergency response or "fight or flight" hormone. The adrenal cortex (outer layer) produces corticosteroid hormones and in amphibians, they are also involved in facilitating metamorphosis.

The Male Gonads/Testes

The testes produce testosterone, which promotes sperm production and the development of male secondary sexual characteristics. In amphibians, these characteristics include protruberances (nuptial pads) on the feet used in enhancing amplexus, vocal abilities and, in some species, differences in coloration that can be used to distinguish males from females.

The Female Gonads/Ovaries

The ovaries produce the primary female hormones estrogen and progesterone. Estrogen initiates the formation of the primary egg follicles, and progesterone is involved in inducing the maturation of ova.

The Sensory (Nervous) System

Amphibians have the same sorts of heightened sensory abilities as most other vertebrates, including vision, smell (olfaction), taste, touch and hearing. Some aquatic amphibians and most larval-stage amphibians also have a lateral line organ, which enables them to detect motion as well as electric fields under water. Their heightened sense of olfaction also enables amphibian larvae in sniffing out food and identifying siblings. And the odor of an amphibian's birth pond is imprinted in its memory, permitting adults ready to breed to return to such ponds to perpetuate original populations.

Vision

Although there are wide differences in the degree of visual acuity enjoyed by differing amphibian species, it is an important sense in all but a few forms. Frogs have large, well-developed eyes that sit prominently at the sides and tops of their head, offering most species the ability to see in just about any direction. Experiments indicate that frogs have excellent depth perception and are able to easily differentiate between prey and predator. They can see for vast distances up to almost under their noses, at which point olfactory senses come into play.

Salamanders' eyes tend to be smaller and not nearly as versatile as those of frogs. Cecillians are virtually blind, as are some salamanders, and they use primarily the sense of smell and feel in locating prey or identifying predators. Some species, such as Bufonid toads and the majority of salamanders, have strong night vision, the time when they are most active.

The eyes of tadpoles and salamander larvae are located at the sides and tops of their heads and have less binocular vision than their adult counterparts. Olfaction clearly overrides vision as a more important source of sensory input in larval amphibians.

Loss of eyes and eyesight has occurred in a number of aquatic, cave-dwelling species, including the Georgia Blind Salamander (*Haideotriton wallacei*), the Texas Blind Salamander (*Typhlomolge rathbuni*) and the Adriatic/European Olm (*Proteus anguinis*). Some highly aquatic frogs such as the Pipids (*Pipa pipa* and *Xenopus sp.*) have extremely small eyes and may rely on other senses more than most frogs and toads. Whether those species believed to be blind are really blind is open to debate, as they have fully functional optic nerves and retinas. It is probable that they use what visual abilities they have to distinguish, at the least, between light intensities.

Based on such studies of amphibian eyes for the existence of cones in the retina, it has been determined that many amphibians have fairly good color vision. These determinations have been made not only by studying the retinal cones, but also by observing behavior in catching prey or mating between males and females that have distinctive color markings. Frogs, particularly aquatic species, seem to have a preference for blue light, an adaptation that probably aids such animals in determining their escape route, which is into the water. Terrestrial species and tree frogs move toward forested terrain, and plant-eating tadpoles seem to have a preference for green, the color of their food and shelter. In experiments with a number of species, it was determined that they have color perception about as great as that of humans—being able to distinguish between the eight basic colors: red, orange, blue, yellow, yellow-green, blue-green, green and violet—and

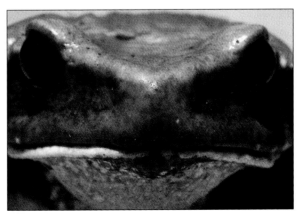

Bufonid toads are nocturnal and have strong night vision (*Bufo blombergi*).

were able to separate them from various shades of gray.

However, not all amphibians see all colors. In species where colors bespeak gender, there is often the ability to discriminate between these colors and little else. This has been observed in newts with an ability to discern red and blue, colors that advertise the male gender. Color vision in newts, therefore, is important both in finding a mate and locating suitable prey. Other amphibians have color vision that is largely restricted to the blue and green ends of the spectrum.

Underwater Vision

Because of their amphibious or aquatic and semi-aquatic lifestyle, amphibians must be able to see underwater as well as on land, although vision is not liable to be as accurate in both milieus. A land-dwelling salamander will become more farsighted in the water, and an aquatic species more myopic or nearsighted in air. Aquatic larvae may have a more spherical lens that flattens at metamorphosis in terrestrial species.

Distance/Depth Perception

Many amphibians are able to judge distances between objects, including themselves and prey or predators, with uncanny accuracy.

Obtaining prey with precision often involves excellent depth perception, even under conditions of very low light. One species of lungless salamander, the Italian Cave Salamander (*Hydromantes italicus),* is able to catch tiny bugs with the tip of its projectile tongue in total darkness. And Bufonid toads are able to target prey at very low light intensities, including at levels where higher vertebrates and humans cannot see at all.

Olfactory Senses

Amphibians have two basic organs for chemical olfaction or the detection of odors. One is the epithelium of the nose, and the other is the Jacobson's Organ, also known as the vomeronasal organ, located near the internal nostrils above the roof of the mouth. Airborne and aquatic odors are sensed mainly by the nasal or olfactory epithelium, whereas substances that end up in the mouth or on the tongue are sensed by the vomeronasal organs. In the lungless salamanders, however, these structures stretch from near the external nostrils back to the internal nares. The lungless salamanders have unique nasolabial grooves that they use to pick up particles from the substrate, which are then "tasted" by the vomeronasal system.

Cecillians possess a small hole on each side of the head between their eyes and nostrils, through which they pass a tentacle that also conveys airborne molecules to their vomeronasal organs. Although other vertebrates have tentacles and whiskers, these are used chiefly for tactile sensing. Cecillians alone have tentacles that are used in chemoreception.

Tadpoles and salamander larvae rely strongly on their sense of smell to detect danger and, in some species, to find food.

The sense of smell is generally well developed in all amphibians and after sight (in species with excellent vision), olfaction is the most important sense; in species with poor eyesight it is the most important sense of all. The sense of smell in amphibians has been linked to detection of breeding ponds, recognition of siblings, recognition of eggs, use in species and sex recognition and recognition of individuals. It is also involved in delimiting territories as well as enabling prey detection, especially in low-light or no-light situations. Thus olfaction is used in finding mates, avoiding enemies and helping amphibians find their way home, as well as getting a meal!

The olfactory senses are particularly important to larval amphibians. When a tadpole or salamander larva is attacked, it releases alarm substances that alert other larvae in the area of danger. The larval forms of some species also use their sense of smell to find food and to avoid predatory fish by detecting their odor.

Hearing, Voice and Communication

Frogs and toads, as highly vocal animals, are in need of a well-tuned auditory sense. Cecillians and salamanders have limited sound-making capability (some are known to click or squeak, usually when "attacked"), and their hearing is not apt to be as highly developed as that of the much more vocal frogs and toads (although there are exceptions).

Frogs and toads have well-developed ears—including an eardrum that is easily visible behind the eye (tympanum) in some species, a middle ear with sound-conducting bones and an inner ear where nerves provide the sensory input.

Frogs use their hearing mainly for one purpose: listening to and communicating with other frogs. Amazingly, frogs even have dialects. For example, when bullfrogs that communicate in the "bullfrog language" listen to bullfrogs from their own lake, they can distinguish them from other bullfrogs from a different lake, speaking the same language but with a different dialect. So while a New York bullfrog sounds just like a California Bullfrog to humans, the frogs themselves can tell the difference. This discovery astounded scientists.

Unlike frogs and toads, salamanders have no external eardrum, although they have internal ears that are used in maintaining balance and coordination as well as detecting ground vibrations. The vibrations are transmitted to the internal ear via the legs and shoulder bones to the inner ear. This ability is used mainly to detect predators that are nearby. The European Fire Salamander, however, is able to detect airborne sounds emitted from a loudspeaker that had no ground vibrations associated with them. Salamanders are basically mute and incapable of vocalization.

Frogs and toads communicate with each other by voice and in some cases by body language or movements. It is probable that frogs were the first vertebrates to communicate with each other by some sort of sound or speech (insects also do

If you hear a frog calling, it is generally a male in the mating season (Oak Toad, *Bufo quericus*).

it), but it is primarily the male of the species that has the best-developed voice. Females usually are mute. They are capable of making less robust sounds than males, as they lack the secondary sexual characteristic of well-developed vocal sacs and a larynx (voice box).

The frog call most commonly heard by people occurs during the mating season, when the males assemble in large choruses to advertise their presence to females. This is known as the mating call. Males also emit another type of call referred to as an advertisement call, but it can occur outside of the breeding season. It is frequently elicited by rain, although its purpose remains unclear. It may simply be a cry of joy (frogs love rain), or it may be one frog discussing the rainy weather with the others.

Another type of call is known as a release call. This distinctive call occurs when one male actually embraces another male instead of a female. The male is in effect telling the other to take a hike, saying, "Hey, I am not a female. Get lost." And while the aforementioned types of calls are made with the mouth closed, another type of call occurs with the mouth wide open: the distress call. It occurs when a frog is picked up or accosted by a predator and serves to startle the predator into dropping it, as well as to warn other frogs in the area that a dangerous situation exists.

Sound is produced by the voice box or larynx, a paired structure spanned by two vocal cords lying in the trachea or throat. It is controlled by two pairs of muscles that, in conjunction with the movement of air, cause it to open and close, producing the limited repertoire of sound that it does. In addition, most male frogs have vocal sacs that act as resonating or amplifying chambers. Some species have a single, large distensible or balloon-like sac occupying the entire submandibular (chin) region; others have two smaller balloon-like sacs, which, when inflated, protrude laterally or sideways and vaguely resemble puffy cheeks. Still other species have vocal sacs that are not externally visible. They are capable of making a substantial volume of sound, but the sacs inflate internally and are not readily apparent to an observer. And some species have no vocal sacs at all. Their calling repertoire is, therefore, not as loud or as boisterous as that of those endowed with these chambers.

When more than one species of frog or toad occupies an area, their distinctive calls are what sets them apart as well as indicates their presence. Their calls all operate at different frequencies, to which the listening frogs tune in. In fact, it is believed that because daytime airborne sound waves are so numerous in some areas, some species come aloft at night to call and breed when there is less competition from daytime sounds. And not to be outdone by competing sounds, some species even vocalize underwater to potential mates also swimming below the surface.

The din produced by frogs during the mating season is so loud in some areas it keeps people awake at night, although many people soon learn to appreciate its purpose and fall asleep in its presence. The noise produced by French frogs in the summer of 1789 is said to have precipitated the fall of the Bastille (July 14th) and the French Revolution. The aristocracy, apparently kept awake by the frogs, ordered their servants into the ponds in the middle of the night to silence the frogs by splashing around in the water. This humiliating exercise was the last straw, or so it is reliably believed—Dickens refers to the frog shushing in *A Tale of Two Cities*.

Body Language

Some frog species have been observed waving their arms around in what certainly looks like some sort of signal, greeting or similar form of communication. Curiously, this behavior was first observed in the small Australian frog *Taudactylus eungellenis*. According to observers it appeared as if these frogs were actually waving at each other. Notably, a similar behavior has been observed in another Australian species, a lizard known as the Bearded Dragon (*Pogona sp.*), that also lifts either of its front limbs and slowly and deliberately waves it in a circular fashion. If they were holding a small piece of cloth, these frogs could be put to work wiping down a window pane. The purpose of such behaviors is not clear. It may simply be a muscle-stretching exercise, or it may be some form of communication behavior or signal. It clearly resembles the hello/goodbye waving of people, and this makes it all the more mysterious. Some researchers believe that in the lizards, the waving is an appeasement signal. Did early man learn this form of communication by mimicking lizards or frogs?

Electroreception

The larvae of newts and salamanders, as well as strictly aquatic adult salamanders, have clusters of skin cells sensitive to water currents, changes in pressure and electric fields or low levels of electric currents that may be present in the water. These cells are collectively known as lateral line organs. They are also present in fish and in some strictly aquatic adult frogs (Pipids), as well as in larval frogs. The lines are distributed along the sides or back of the animals and are numerous on the head, where they can also be plainly seen. For amphibian larvae, they serve to detect underwater movements of potential predators and other threats (such as swimmers, divers and boats). They

Some frogs actually seem to wave as a form of communication—a behavior also seen in the Bearded Dragon, a popular reptile among herpers (*Pogona vitticeps*).

can function only underwater, and in animals that leave the water they cease to function and degenerate.

The source of electrical currents detected by electroreceptors in aquatic newts and salamanders is believed to be low-level currents generated by prey items such as snails, daphnia and aquatic worms. Increasing electrical fields around Axolotls, other larval salamanders and even adult Alpine newts increases prey-searching behavior. Axolotls are even stimulated to start snapping in the presence of increased electric fields, suggesting a feeding or defense-related purpose for this sense.

Water Regulation

Few amphibians drink water as other animals do. They absorb it through their skin. On land, amphibians lose water unless the air is highly saturated with moisture. Such losses are rapidly compensated for by either entering the water or finding a damp place on land from which water can be absorbed. In an arid environment, some amphibian species can become desiccated (dried out) and die; others have adaptations to help them weather such environmental extremes. In the water, amphibians have the opposite problem— absorption of too much water.

The process by which water is absorbed is known as osmosis. The

Leaf-Frogs secrete a waxy substance that they smear over their bodies to insulate them against evaporative water loss (*Phyllomedusa sauvagii*).

water moves from a region of low solute (electrolyte/salt) concentration, such as a freshwater pond, stream or lake, to an area of higher concentration (that of the amphibian's body). Osmosis occurs in fresh water. In water with a high salt content, the reverse occurs. Water moves from the amphibian's body out into the surrounding environment, which is why sea water cannot be tolerated by these animals. In fresh water, however, excess water must be eliminated, and this is usually accomplished by the kidneys by generating significant amounts of urine.

A number of arid land species have evolved special adaptations for coping with the absence of environmental water. These include wrapping themselves in a cocoon of dead skin or becoming virtually encapsulated in hardened mucus secreted by their dermal glands. Others reabsorb precious water while excreting a thickened, urate-filled whitish urine. Still others seek underground shelter from harsh weather conditions at the surface and do not reemerge until they hear rain pattering on the substrate above.

One group of frogs, known as urocotelic frogs, excrete practically no water at all, and their urine consists almost entirely of urea. The Leaf-Frog (*Phyllomedusa sauvagii*), a member of this group, has wax-glands that secrete a fatty or waxy substance onto their skin. The frogs smear it over their bodies using their both their front and hind feet. This insulates them against evaporative water loss.

CHAPTER 3

Ecology

Ecology is the study of the relationships between an animal or group of animals, such as the amphibians, and their environment. How amphibians evade predators, how they find food, how they thermoregulate and adjust their metabolism, how they manage both biological and nonbiological threats (such as chemical pollutants), their place in the food chain and how and why they benefit the environment are all part of amphibian ecology.

Ecologists also study the different kinds of habitat suitable for a particular species. Amphibians, with a few notable exceptions, almost always have one common requirement: the presence of fresh water, or at the very least, moisture or dampness. Amphibians are found in rivers, waterholes (temporary and permanent), drainage ditches, ponds, lakes, streams, forests, rain forests, jungles, cloud forests, montane rain forests, mountains, trees and low-lying shrubs or vegetation, as well as on the ground or under it. Dry plains and desert species, although rare, burrow into the substrata to find moisture and if that doesn't work, they use a variety of biological means to conserve what little water they have.

For frogs, a refuge, or hiding place, is also important. Researchers found that in northern Australia, the most important human-made frog refuges were public toilets. In fact, a great number of one species, an Australian tree frog known as *Litoria splendida,* have been found not in trees but in, on, or beside toilets! Scraps such as tin sheets discarded over damp or wet ground and even discarded tires that retain water also make ideal refuges for

Almost all amphibians live in or near fresh water (Southern Leopard Frog, *Rana utricularia*).

many species. Thus, even some types of garbage and similar blights on the landscape can have an ecological benefit under the right circumstances.

Thermal Regulation

Fish, amphibians and reptiles have no internal means of controlling or setting their body temperatures. A number of terms have been advanced over the years for this condition: cold-blooded, pokilothermic and ectothermic. All but the last have been dismissed as inappropriate. None of these animals can truly be considered cold-blooded, because they can find the means to heat themselves up or cool themselves down whenever they want. Pokilothermic means "of varying temperature," and is also inaccurate because these animals, through behavioral and other means (such as skin shade lightening and darkening) can maintain fairly constant body temperatures.

Thus the most accurate term is "ectothermic," which means they are dependent on outside (*ecto-*) conditions to maintain their body temperature. Birds and mammals, in contrast, are said to be endothermic, having an internal means of regulating or setting their body temperatures.

By and large, amphibians prefer cooler temperatures. Even in the steamy tropics many species are nocturnal, or only active at night, when temperatures drop. Frogs, toads and salamanders thermoregulate by moving from warmer to cooler locations and back again. A few species will try and warm up by basking, although this behavior is more common in reptiles. Aquatic species may move from warmer to cooler levels in the water and tree frogs may do the same high above the ground. As mentioned elsewhere, amphibians also can absorb or deflect light and heat by lightening or darkening their skin color.

Dark colors absorb light and heat; light colors deflect them. However, the most common methods used to escape unfavorable temperature conditions are to burrow into the substrate or to avoid activity at times of the day when temperatures are either too hot or too cold. Some species cool off by taking a quick dip, using the principle of evaporative cooling to help them achieve an optimal temperature. In captive situations, such behaviors may not always be possible, so it is important that keepers maintain temperature and humidity at optimal levels.

Overheating an amphibian can cause it to become stressed and inactive and to stop feeding. Providing too much heat is a common mistake many novice amphibian keepers make, and their animals die as a result. Conversely, tropical species of frogs will die, and temperate species will become inactive, if environmental conditions are too cold (below 60 degrees F) and if an adequate means to burrow into the substrate to stay warm are not provided. Moreover, thermal and other kinds of stresses in the captive environment may compromise immunity and leave animals open to attack by infectious microorganisms.

Remarkably, amphibians and reptiles with infections have been observed inducing fevers in themselves by seeking out and staying in warmer surroundings or basking in the sun for longer than usual. In mammals, a serious infection frequently provokes fever, which is produced internally. It is now recognized that such fevers help to fight off infections. (Of course, it is important to keep them under control to prevent seizures and brain damage.) Apparently amphibians and reptiles "knew about" the value of a low-grade fever to fight off infection before mammals, including man, were even around. No definite scientific work has been accomplished on how to best utilize these observations with sick captive specimens. However, one should consider providing a hot spot for a captive specimen that comes down with an infectious disease, which it may utilize if it is so inclined.

Food and Feeding

Amphibians are both prey and predators. Most amphibians feed on live animals and identify prey visually by the movement of potential food. They also may use their olfactory senses to tell if they are in close proximity to a prey organism, and some amphibians will taste and spit out prey that they find not to their liking. Although most amphibians prey on invertebrates, insects and crustaceans, arachnids or spiders, larger species will eat newborn or small vertebrates such as young rodents or even newly hatched bird fledglings. Nature photographers have caught bullfrogs in midair as they leap out of

Amphibians thermoregulate by moving to cool and warm areas as needed. Here, a frog enjoys the sun (*Hemiphractus proboscideus*).

the water and snap up small, low-flying birds as they pass overhead. And many amphibians are not above cannibalism, preying upon smaller versions of themselves.

Cannibalism is not uncommon among tadpoles and larval salamanders. Carnivorous and omnivorous frog tadpoles can frequently be found feeding on the dead remains of their siblings, thus validating the old adage that "you are what you eat." Or rather, in this situation: "you eat what you are."

Amphibian dietary preferences are often related to the availability of certain prey items in their environment. Thus aquatic salamanders such as Sirens (*Siren sp.*) forage for aquatic invertebrates and fish. The Mexican Burrowing Toad (*Rhinophrynus dorsalis)* specializes in ants and termites. A few amphibians feed on inanimate or dead food items—including dead animals (carrion), amphibian eggs (either their own or those of other species), relatively immobile insect pupae and even human-food scraps. At least one species of Brazilian tree frog, Izecksohn's Tree Frog (*Hyla truncata),* eats small fruits, the seeds of which germinate on being excreted (pre-fertilized) with their feces. This species may be instrumental in providing seed dispersal for the fruits it eats. A number of amphibians incidentally or deliberately feed on grasses and leaves, particularly if they are wafting in the wind (moving), or if they are providing a surface area for an insect that the frog will gobble up along with the veggies. Larger bufonid toads eat raw and cooked garbage, rotting lettuce and other vegetables, feces and dog food. Tiger Salamanders (*Ambystoma tigrinum*) and other abystomatid salamanders also eat rotting meat as long as it is fairly odiferous.

Thus, although the majority of adult phase amphibians are carnivorous and eat primarily animate prey that they detect by vision, more and more discoveries indicate that this is not true of all species and that many notable exceptions exist. Clues that some frogs ate vegetable matter were found nearly five decades ago when a scientist discovered two large Green Frogs (*Rana clamitans*) with stomachs filled with elm seeds that they had consumed from a stream as the seeds floated by on the water's surface. In 1955, Marine Toads (*Bufo marinus*) that were introduced onto Hawaii were discovered to suffer a fatal epidemic every season by gobbling up the falling blossoms of strychnine trees.

The overwhelming propensity for amphibians to eat insects has no doubt held insect populations in check for millions of years. Insects are the most numerous of all living animals, but their numbers would surely overrun the earth were they not such a convenient and nutritious source of food for higher animals such as amphibians, reptiles and some birds and mammals.

Although insects are the food of choice for most amphibians, some frogs, such as the Green Frog (*Rana clamitans*), may eat vegetable matter accidentally.

Many homes in the tropics have several resident frogs standing watch, snapping up insects either on their way in or on their way out. One couldn't ask for a more natural or effective exterminator. It doesn't take a frog long to figure out that the light on your porch is attracting bugs, and this is where you are apt to find your exterminator at the same time and place every night.

Frogs and salamanders have fleshy protrusible tongues, which are their most important organs involved in the capture of food. Most food is swallowed whole, but the teeth may incidentally crush some larger articles of food. In truth, frogs don't chew their food, but use their teeth mainly for gripping a prey item once it is drawn into the oral cavity. Many frogs and some salamanders may use both their fore and hind limbs to restrain prey and push it into their mouths. Frog tongues contain many taste buds, and they use their sense of taste to reject undesirable prey items.

Generally, the smaller an amphibian is, the smaller its prey must be. Tiny arrow poison frogs, for example, have difficulty eating full- or even half-grown crickets, so they must be presented with new-born crickets or insects of comparable size (such as fruit flies). Smaller species consume not only smaller prey but relatively large

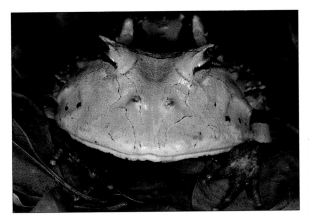

A large horned frog is likely to consume fewer, larger meals than a smaller species (*Ceratophrys cornuta*).

numbers of such prey compared with larger species, which take bigger meals in smaller numbers and much less frequently. Accordingly, a large horned frog (*Ceratophrys sp.*) might eat a single, small mouse once a week, but a tiny cricket frog (*Acris sp.*) consumes hundreds of pinhead-sized crickets in that same period of time, perhaps as many as 50 to 100 or more insects every day. When buying food for captive amphibians, remember that the size of the prey must fall within your pet's gape size.

Newts and salamanders have been carefully studied with respect to their feeding and prey capturing abilities. The most significant factors in this behavior include:

1. **Orientation movement**—Turning the head toward prey, which occurs when a salamander first notices a potential food item.

2. **Approach movement**—Some salamanders and newts just move forward a small distance and pounce; others can detect prey several inches away and stalk it over a somewhat longer distance.

3. **Olfactory (smell) test**—Newts in particular point their heads downward and virtually nuzzle the prey with their nostrils before ingesting.

4. **Fixation**—A final reorientation period, which occurs prior to snapping at the prey.

5. **Ingestion**—The prey is secured and swallowed by a rapid opening and closing of the mouth. As the throat is lowered, it causes a negative pressure in the oral cavity favoring the inward movement (sucking-in) of the prey item.

These five stages occur more or less in varying degrees according to species.

In contrast to frogs and salamanders, cecillians are so-called "jaw-feeders." They seize their prey directly in a strong bite without any use of the tongue. Many cecillians have sharp, hinged teeth that slant

Newts are known to "nuzzle" their prey with their nostrils before they eat (Ribbed Newt, *Pleurodeles waltl*).

It requires the same amount of effort for the average frog to eat a large fly as it does to eat a small one, so it is no wonder they would opt for the bigger portion when given the opportunity to do so.

Defense Against Predators

Frogs, toads, newts and salamanders as well as their larvae and externally deposited unshelled eggs have numerous natural enemies or predators. Because they are, for the most part, soft-bodied and thin-skinned, they are incapable of mounting any real defensive battle, although a few larger salamanders and frogs can inflict moderately severe bite wounds. Amphibians have, however, evolved many anti-predator devices and behaviors. These include adopting specialized postures and liberating toxic glandular skin secretions (some of which are fatal or nearly so). Others defecate or urinate when accosted by predators, causing such a smelly mess that the predator drops them and while it fusses with the indignity of being excreted upon, the amphibian often can escape. Others secrete such copious amounts of mucus that it sticks to predators like glue and can actually immobilize them long enough for the amphibian to abscond.

backward toward the gullet. The more the prey struggles to escape, the farther back it is snagged. Once prey is caught, cecilians often return to their burrows, swirling around rapidly like a corkscrew in the process. This unique behavior results in any prey animal left hanging out of the mouth being literally sheared down to jaw-width size, making it simple for the cecilian to gulp it down.

A few amphibians lure their prey. The horned frogs (*Ceratophrys sp.*) wiggle their toes, attracting the attention of small frogs wandering by who perceive the wiggles as something good to eat but are soon gobbled up themselves. Few frogs fall for this trick and survive. Other species may engage in similar luring tricks.

Diet

Salamanders, newts, frogs and toads can be rather indiscriminate feeders and will consume a wide variety of food items that are available and are within their prey-catching abilities. Amphibians will spit out unpalatable items, and a few do specialize in locally available prey such as the Asian/Filipino Crab-Eating Frog (*Rana cancrivora*). In order to pursue its favorite delicacy, this frog has adapted to estuarine or low-salinity environments.

Under experimental conditions, many amphibians exhibit an awareness that trying for a larger fly when smaller ones are also present is a better deal, thereby demonstrating a preference where energy expenditure versus gain (by ingesting a particular prey item) is concerned.

WHO LIKES TO EAT AMPHIBIANS?

Nearly any carnivorous mammal, bird or reptile relishes an amphibian meal if it is available. Some animals "specialize" in amphibians; these include the unusual Frog-Eating Bat, Water and Garter Snakes, Cottonmouths and other venomous snakes, Hognose Snakes and even human gourmets who enjoy the legs of larger frogs sautéed in lemon and butter. (Yes, it tastes a little like chicken.)

Hognose Snakes make a good living by eating Bufonid toads and are immune to the effects of the toad's poisons. Some birds that are not immune have even learned to eat such toads by turning them onto their backs and eating them from the belly side, thus avoiding any contact with their dorsal poison glands. Water frogs and salamanders are at the mercy of smaller alligators, crocodiles and mammals, such as otters and muskrats. A few species of salamander possess deadly toxins, and these are safest from predation but not from attack. Big fish will eat smaller frogs and aquatic salamanders, and smaller fish will dine on their eggs and larvae.

Of course, many carnivorous amphibians will prey on their own kind. Frogs and salamanders are neither at the bottom nor the top of the food chain, but somewhere squarely in between.

Even dart poison frogs (among the most toxic, even deadly, of the frog world) have their problems with predators. A large group of South American snakes, the Amazon Ground Snakes (*Liophis sp.*), prey upon dendrobatids and have been observed eating even *Phyllobates terribilis*, the most dangerously poisonous of all these frogs, with no ill effect whatsoever. Nobody knows why these snakes seem to be immune to the poisonous secretions of these frogs, but obviously they have developed a means to counteract their toxins.

Postural behaviors are among the most fascinating anti-predator defenses exhibited by amphibians. The California Slender Salamander (*Batrachoseps attenuatus*) actually coils itself around the back of a snake's neck to prevent it from biting and swallowing it. The salamander winds itself around the part of the head/neck precisely where a human handler might also hold a snake to avoid being bitten.

The unken reflex (named after the German word for *Bombina* frogs, "unken") is a defensive posture in which the animal arches its spine and rear while remaining motionless, almost in a "death trance." It was first observed and is most prominent in the frog species of the genus *Bombina*, but it is also seen in some bufonid toads. Some salamanders also arch their bodies, placing their mouths on their tails, forming a ring. These postures are designed to make their shape and size more difficult for a potential predator to manage.

Death feigning, lying still and motionless, is another form of postural defense also known as thanatosis. A number of amphibians engage in this motionless behavior. By lying still and inanimate, they are less likely to attract a predator's attention. There are, moreover, some predators that prefer live to dead prey. Species with prominent, enlarged parotoid glands

Even the highly toxic dart poison frogs are occasionally subject to predation (Dyeing Dart Poison Frog, *Dendrobates tinctorius*).

tend to adopt postures that present these glands first toward a predator. The glands liberate toxic substances when bitten into (by a predator), and thus a predator's first nibble is likely to liberate the disagreeable, bitter and potentially fatal secretions of these glands. Other amphibians will inflate themselves with air or adopt postures that make them look much bigger than they really are, thereby deterring gape-limited predators. The Cuyaba Dwarf Frog (*Physalaemus nattereri*) has rear-end, inguinal glands. This species turns and presents its backside to a predator. The glands look like two huge eyes, and appearance alone may scare off a predator. Biting into them will liberate a poisonous secretion if a predator is not otherwise deterred.

Voice may also be used as a defensive measure. On being accosted, some frogs will emit a loud, shrill alarm call that often deters inexperienced predators. On the other hand, some species will become immediately silent when a predator nears, realizing that their calls may be attracting danger rather than deflecting it. Other species produce disagreeable odors that may be used to deter or occupy a potential predator.

Biting back, the ultimate defense mechanism, is an ineffective option for most amphibians. A few species, such as the horned frogs (*Ceratotophrys sp.*) and the African Bullfrog (*Pyxiecephalus adspersus*), have sharp teeth and strong jaws and can deliver a fairly substantial bite. Some of the larger aquatic salamanders can do likewise. Other species, such as the Horned Tree Frog (*Hemiphractus fasciatus*), will threaten a severe bite by engaging in wide-mouthed gaping postures. Such behaviors also tend to make the species look larger than they really are, and therefore more difficult to grab and swallow. Some African grassland frogs of the genus *Ptyachadena* are actually capable of fighting back. They possess a sharp spine that is a modification of the third toe—a good kick by this frog can result in a painful laceration.

For amphibians, the liberation of noxious secretions and poisons from skin glands represents their best and most effective defense against a wide variety of predators. Cecillians, salamanders, frogs and toads have a wide variety of toxins available to deter, or even kill, predators that dare to mess with them.

A few other defensive measures are worth noting. These include a concept known as "aposematic coloration." Amphibians with toxic secretions tend to have aposematic colors or patterns: bright yellows and oranges, bright metallic blues and greens and reds that serve as warnings to would-be predators. A predator that once found a colorful species distasteful or problematic when placed in the mouth may soon learn to avoid amphibians with such colors again. Other, quite edible amphibians have evolved warning colors that mimic those of their more toxic relatives. This strategy may have been designed to fool predators into thinking that they were dealing with the real thing. However, the concept of mimicry is a controversial one among scientists. The reasons for and the precise means by which mimicry occurs remains a subject of perpetual debate.

Only a few amphibians can effectively bite back in self-defense, but the African Bullfrog is equipped with sharp teeth and a strong jaw (*Pyxiecephalus adspersus*).

CHAPTER 4

Taxonomy and Classification

The science (and art) of taxonomy is to provide every natural object on earth with a scientific name that is not duplicated for any other object. Every living species of plant and animal, including bacteria and viruses, as well as nonliving objects such as chemicals, is subject to taxonomy. The science of systematics then compiles all named objects and classifies them by placing them in a hierarchical group of related objects. In the case of living plants, animals and microorganisms, such classification is based on evolutionary lines in addition to the similarities of basic properties including appearance, blood and tissue proteins and, more recently, studies of mitochondrial DNA. Notably, there are numerous controversies and debates among scientists on whether an evolutionary or a biological basis should be used to classify all living things.

Taxonomists are forever changing the scientific names of living objects in order that such naming conventions fall within the basic rules of their field, which is known also as nomenclature (or naming). Systematists or scientists that classify living objects are constantly moving species, genera and families of living things around based on new discoveries or, on occasion, even intuition, in order to fit their idea of placement on either evolutionary or biological grounds.

Some scientists, known as "lumpers," believe that there are too many species and subspecies and that some are duplicative. They contend that a species should not be "divided up" into subspecies and would prefer that they were all lumped together under a single species name. Those with an opposing point of view are called "splitters." Splitters feel that there are sufficient grounds for according different names, either on the species or subspecies level, to various animals or plants because of dissimilarities among them. In short, splitters want a more complex system of assigning scientific names, while lumpers are content with a simpler set of nomenclatural rules. Arguments are passionate on both sides of this fence.

All amphibians, including cecilians, salamanders, newts, frogs and toads, belong to a higher classification of animals known as a class. It is called the Class Amphibia. There are believed to be about 5,000 different species of amphibians alive in the world today, but no one is certain how many exist, as new species are being discovered at a rate that boggles the mind. Moreover, some species undoubtedly disappear or become extinct before they are discovered. While discovery of a new bird or mammal species is usually a momentous event, similar discoveries among amphibians, fish and insects is almost a routine, everyday occurrence.

Animals and plants are classified as members of a kingdom (plant or animal), class, order, family, genus (plural, genera) and then species and subspecies. A subclass for amphibians was devised in 1866 called the Lissamphibia, which includes prehistoric (Triassic) to present-day amphibians. All animals and plants have one and only

Scientists believe that there are approximately 5,000 different species of amphibians alive today (Malagasy Pudge Frog, *Scaphiphryne brevis*).

one species name, which is composed of two parts. A subspecies' name has three parts. The first part of the name is the genus, the first letter of which is usually capitalized. The second and third parts of the name are the species and subspecies names, respectively. These are written all in lower case. As such names either are derived from Latin or Greek or are Latinized forms of non-Latin names, they are technically a foreign language and appear in the printed literature as italicized or underlined to denote this fact. Classes and orders, while also Latin nouns, are not italicized; however, order and family names may appear in boldface.

Orders of the Class Amphibia

1. The Order Gymnophiona was previously called Apoda, and it includes the cecilians or limbless amphibians.
2. The Order Caudata are the salamanders and newts or tailed amphibians, previously called the order Urodela.
3. The Order Anura are the frogs and toads or tailless amphibians. An earlier name for this order was Salientia.

Each of these orders is further divided up into families by systematics specialists:

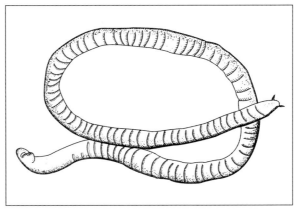

Cecillians have tiny eyes and segmented bodies.

Order Gymnophiona— Cecillians

This order is divided into six families:

1. Family Caeciliaidae— the common cecillians
2. Family Ichthyophiidae— the fish cecillians
3. Family Rhinatrematidae— the beaked cecillians
4. Family Scolecomorphidae— the tropical cecillians
5. Family Typhlonectidae— the aquatic cecillians
6. Family Uraeotyphilidae— the Indian cecillians

Cecillians are elongated worm-like limbless amphibians highly adapted for burrowing or a fossorial existence. Their bodies are segmented by grooves, and some species have small patches of scales. A tail, if present, is short and pointed and is defined by vertebrae that extend past the cloacal vent. The eyes are small, covered by skin or bone, and may only be sensitive to light intensities and not useful for true vision. Cecillians are basically tropical animals and inhabit Southeast Asia, Borneo, the Philippines, the American tropics, tropical sub-Saharan Africa and the Seychelles Islands. They are unknown elsewhere. Of the three orders of amphibians, they contain the fewest species.

Family Caeciliidae— Common Cecillians

The Caeciliidae are found throughout Central and South America, in wet tropical forests, in sub-Saharan Africa, in India and on the Seychelles Islands in the Indian Ocean. There are 24 genera with some 88 species, and it is the largest of all the cecillian families.

Family Rhinatrematidae— Beaked Cecillians

Members of the Rhinatrematidae family are found only in South

America, where they occur in two genera (*Epicrionops* and *Rhinatrema*) with nine known or recognized species. The Ichthyophiidae are old-world cecillians widespread in Southeast Asia, including India and Sri Lanka, Sumatra and Borneo and ranging to the Philippines. There are two genera (*Caudacaecilia* and *Ichthyophis*) with 35 known species.

Family Scolecomorphidae— Tropical Cecillians

Members of the Scolecomorphidae family are relatively large cecillians found in sub-Saharan Africa. Two species are known from Cameroon and three species from Malawi and Tanzania. There are a total of seven species in one genus (*Scolecomorphus sp.*).

Family Typhlonectidae— Aquatic Cecillians

The Typhlonectidae are completely aquatic cecillians found mainly in northwestern South America in the Amazon, Orinoco and Magdalena River drainages. Several species are also known from the La Plata drainage in Argentina and Brazil. There are four genera and 19 species known.

Family Uraeotyphilidae— Indian Cecillians

The family Uraeotyphilidae is known only from a single genus (*Uraeotyphlus sp.*) with four known species, all of which are found on the southern peninsula of India.

Order Caudata— Salamanders and Newts

The order Caudata is divided up into 10 families as follows:

1. Family Ambystomatidae— the mole salamanders
2. Family Amphiumidae— the amphiumas
3. Family Cryptobranchidae— the Asian giant salamanders and American Hellbenders
4. Family Dicamptodontidae— the American giant salamanders
5. Family Hynobiidae— the Asian salamanders
6. Family Plethodontidae— the lungless salamanders
7. Family Proteidae— the European Olms and American Waterdogs (or Mudpuppies)
8. Family Rhyacotritonidae— the Olympic (or Mt. Olympus) salamanders
9. Family Salamandridae— the newts and fire salamanders
10. Family Sirenidae—the Sirens

Family Ambystomatidae— Mole Salamanders

The family Ambystomatidae, or mole salamanders, are widespread throughout North America from southeasternmost Alaska and Labrador to the southern rim of the Mexican plateau. These are typical four-legged terrestrial and semi-aquatic salamanders. The largest member of this family is the Tiger Salamander (*Ambystoma tigrinum*).

The Spotted Salamander is a familiar North American member of the Ambystoma family (*Ambystoma maculata*).

The larvae of the Mexican sala-mander (*Ambystoma mexicanum*) remains in its juvenile or larval state throughout life and breeds in this condition. This is known as neoteny, which means retention of juvenile characteristics. Through the administration of thyroid hormones or if kept in iodine-salt-rich waters, the Mexican salamander can be arti-ficially forced into changing into its adult form. The larval form of this salamander is known by the Aztec name "Axolotl." Axolotl was a god with a variety of mythical responsi-bilities including resurrection of the dead. In Aztec, the name literally means "water dog." There are only two living genera within this family: *Ambystoma* (mole salamanders), with 26 living species, and *Rhyacosirendon,* with four living species. All four species of the latter genus are found exclusively in the mountainous streams and lakes of central Mexico, where they also pursue a neotenous life, rarely meta-morphosing to land-stage animals.

Family Amphiumidae— Amphiumas

The Amphiumidae family are rep-resented by only three known living species in one genus, *Amphiuma.* Amphiumas, as they are also com-monly known, are large, eel-like, strictly aquatic amphibians that are found exclusively throughout the waters of the coastal plain of the southeastern United States, from Virginia to Louisiana. They are also known from the Mississippi River drainage north to Missouri. They reach lengths of nearly 40 inches. The three species are defined by the number of toes pre-sent on their greatly reduced fore-limbs. There is a one-toed amphiu-ma, a two-toed and a three-toed species. The amphiumas are some-times referred to locally as Congo or "Conger Eels."

Two-toed amphiumas are also known as Congo Eels (*Amphium means*).

Family Cryptobranchidae— Asian Giant Salamanders and American Hellbenders

Cryptobranchidae is a small family of strictly aquatic salamanders with two extremely large (in fact, the largest of all salamanders) species found in China (*Andrias davidi-anus*) and Japan *(Andrias japonicus)* and one species in North America (*Cryptobranchus alleganiensis),* known as the Hellbender. There are two subspecies of Hellbender in North America, an Ozark subspecies and an eastern subspecies. The Chinese Giant Salamander reaches lengths of nearly 5 feet, and the Japanese representative just short of that. American Hellbenders are the largest of all North American sala-manders, reaching lengths of 2.5 feet and, on occasion, somewhat longer. Fossil specimens of sala-manders identified as *Andrias* mea-sure about 8 feet in total length.

Family Dicamptodontidae— American Giant Salamanders

The family Dicamptodontidae are found in the coastal Pacific and mountainous regions of the north-western United States, from Washington State (and adjoining Canada) southward to northern California and Idaho. They are semi-aquatic, broad-headed and heavy-bodied salamanders 6 to 8 inches in length. There are just four species in one genus (*Dicamptodon*):

the Idaho Giant Salamander (*D. aterrimus*), Cope's Giant Salamander (*D. copei*), the California Giant Salamander (*D. ensatus*) and the Pacific Giant Salamander (*D. tenebrosus*).

Family Hynobiidae— Asian Salamanders

The family Hynobiidae are small- to medium-sized Asian salamanders. They are terrestrial, with well-developed lungs, spending their lives in damp woodlands and mountain ranges from Siberia west to the Urals and southwest to Turkestan, Afghanistan and Iran. They are also found to the southeast in China, Korea and Japan. There are 32 species in nine genera.

Family Plethodontidae— Lungless Salamanders

The family Plethodontidae, or lungless salamanders, are the largest family of salamanders, with some 250 species contained within two subfamilies and some 27 or so genera. Members of this family are found on the west coast and throughout the eastern half of the United States, with scattered populations in the plains and Rocky Mountain regions in between. They are also found throughout Mexico, Central America and the northern half of South America. They are the largest and clearly most wide-ranging family of salamanders, with some species

extending into Nova Scotia in eastern North America and extreme southeastern Alaska in western North America. Because of their lungless condition, they rely solely on cutaneous breathing and require a damp or moistened habitat to facilitate this type of respiration. Accordingly, they are absent from deserts and other dry areas.

Family Proteidae— European Olms and American Waterdogs or Mudpuppies

The family Proteidae is a strictly aquatic, gill-breathing group of salamanders with just one species in Europe, the Olm (*Proteus anguinus*) or European Blind Cave Salamander, and five species in eastern and southeastern North America

(*Necturus sp.*), known as Waterdogs or Mudpuppies. The Olm is restricted to subterranean (cave) waters in a small area of southeastern Europe, along the eastern Adriatic coast.

North American Mudpuppies or Waterdogs grow to about 8 to 10 inches in length and are popular animals for comparative anatomy studies. They have four toes on each of four reduced limbs and small but normally sighted eyes. The Olm has degenerated eyes, is devoid of pigment (albino or leucistic) as a normal condition and has only three toes on the front limbs and two on its reduced rear limbs.

Family Rhyacotritonidae— Olympic Salamanders

The family Rhyacotritonidae, or Olympic salamanders, consists of

Strictly aquatic salamanders, Mudpuppies are noted for their short limbs (Lake Winnebago Mudpuppy, *Necturus maculosis ssp.*).

just three species (and two sub-species) in one genus, *Rhyacotriton*. These salamanders are found in the northwestern United States in mountainous regions of Oregon and Washington. At one time the species in this family were considered part of the family Dicamptodontidae; some experts may still refer to them as such.

Family Salamandridae—Newts and Salamanders

The family Salamandridae, to which the newts and fire salamanders belong, is the second-largest family of salamanders, with some 55 or so species in 15 genera. They enjoy a widespread distribution throughout Europe and Asia, from the British Isles and Scandinavia, east to the Urals and south to Spain, Turkey, Greece and some of the Greek islands. Salamandridae are found on Corsica and Sardinia and throughout most of western Europe, including throughout Italy. They extend eastward to central and eastern Asia, northern India, Burma, Thailand and Vietnam and then southeastward to Hong Kong and through many parts of eastern and south central China as well as throughout Japan. In addition, two genera extend from Europe southward to extreme northwestern Africa. Two genera are also found in North America, throughout the eastern half of the United States as well as along the

Fire Salamanders secrete toxins from their skin (Hi-Yellow Fire Salamander, *Salamandra sp.*).

Pacific coast. Clearly this distinguishes them as the most successful group of all salamanders.

While terrestrial or adult forms of this family are semi-aquatic, many of the members referred to as newts are either partially or wholly aquatic. Some change back and forth from land to aquatic stage. As a result, courtship and reproductive strategies vary widely. Salamandridae range in size from a few inches to as long as 5 or 6 inches in length. They all have well-developed limbs, and the strictly aquatic forms of newts have prominent dorsal and tail fins that help them swim. All have toxic skin secretions. Some of the newts, including the North American varieties, produce and secrete tetrodotoxin, a deadly poison identical to that of the puffer fish or Japanese Fugu fish. As a

result of this, many sport bright, aposematic colors that are either readily evident or are revealed during threat and defense displays. The European Fire Salamander is capable of forcefully squirting its toxin, known as salamandrine, from protuberant or swollen skin glands when threatened; other members of the genus may have similar capabilities.

Family Sirenidae—Sirens

The family Sirenidae is a small group of strictly aquatic, eel-like salamanders that consists of four species, with several subspecies in two genera (*Pseudobranchus* and *Siren*). All living representatives of this family can be found in the southeastern United States, along the Atlantic coastal plain as far north as Maryland and south to northeastern Mexico. Members of the genus *Siren* may reach lengths of 1 foot or more, while those of *Pseudobranchus* (the dwarf sirens) rarely exceed 5 inches. The limbs are small. *Pseudobranchus sp.* has three toes on each foot, whereas the genus *Siren sp.* have four.

Order Anura—
Frogs and Toads

The Order Anura (frogs and toads) is divided into 27 families, a number of subfamilies and more than 4,500 species and subspecies.

Taxonomic and classification experts have published different schemes for the classification of the frogs, but for the sake of simplicity each family will be listed in simple alphabetical rather than taxonomic order. The term *anura* derives from a Greek word meaning "tailless" but obviously does not take into account the tailed larvae of frogs.

Frogs and toads are most species-diverse in the tropics. In one small valley in Ecuador, scientists discovered 56 different species in a single evening. Eventually, 81 species were found in this locale, about the same number of frog and toad species in the entire United States. Throughout the tropics it is not unusual to find 40 or more species of frogs in a swath of rain forest no larger than several square kilometers.

The 27 families of frogs and toads are:

1. Family Allophrynidae—Turkeit Hill Frog
2. Family Arthroleptidae—screeching frogs
3. Family Ascaphidae—Tailed Frog
4. Family Bombinatoridae—fire-bellied toads
5. Family Brachycephalidae—saddleback toads
6. Family Bufonidae—true toads
7. Family Centrolenidae—glass frogs
8. Family Dendrobatidae—dart poison or arrow poison frogs
9. Family Discoglossidae—midwife toads and painted frogs
10. Family Heleophrynidae—ghost frogs
11. Family Hemisotidae—shovelnose frogs
12. Family Hylidae—tree frogs
13. Family Hyperoliidae—African reed frogs
14. Family Leiopelmatidae—New Zealand frogs
15. Family Leptodactylidae—tropical/robber frogs
16. Family Megophryidae—Asian lazy or spadefoot toads
17. Family Microhylidae—narrow-mouthed toads
18. Family Myobatrachidae—Australian froglets/toadlets
19. Family Pelobatidae—spadefoot toads
20. Family Pelodytes—parsley frogs
21. Family Pipidae—African clawed frogs and Surinam "toads"
22. Family Pseudidae—harlequin swimming frogs
23. Family Ranidae—"true" frogs
24. Family Rhacophoridae—flying frogs
25. Family Rhinodermatidae—Darwin's frogs
25. Family Scaphiophrynidae—web-foot or rain frogs
26. Family Sooglossidae—Seychelles frogs

Family Allophrynidae—
Turkeit Hill Frog

This family is represented by a single species, *Allophryne ruthveni* or the Turkeit Hill Frog, which is found in a small area of northeastern South America (Guyana).

Family Arthroleptidae —
Screeching Frogs

This group of frogs is found throughout sub-Saharan Africa. It is represented by six genera and some 50 species. Among this family is the well-known but seldom-seen Hairy Frog (*Trichobatrachus robustus*), which sprouts filamentous, hair-like skin appendages along its thighs during the breeding season. It is believed that this growth is to give the frog increased surface area for cutaneous respiration during this active period.

Family Ascaphidae —
Tailed Frog

The Ascaphidae family is represented by a single species found in the American northwest known as the Tailed Frog (*Ascaphus truei*). It is the only frog with an appendage that extends past the last vertebra, but it is not truly a tail—more amazingly, it is an extension of the cloaca and serves as an intromittant organ enabling the male frog to perform internal fertilization. The female of the species does not have this extension. The Tailed Frog is protected as an endangered species in many but not all locales where it is known to live.

Family Bombinatoridae— Fire-bellied Toads

This is a small family of eight species in two genera. These frogs (they are not truly toads, but then again, all toads are frogs…) are

It's easy to see how the Fire-Bellied Toad got its name (Oriental Fire-Bellied Toad, *Bombina orientalis*).

noted for their noxious secretions and the bright yellow or fire-red bellies that they flash as a warning to predators. They are also noted for engaging in a defensive posture known as the Unken reflex that makes it difficult for predators to pick them up, swallow them and even decide "which end is up." The two members of the genus *Barbourula* are found on Palawan, the Philippines and northern Borneo. Members of the genus *Bombina* have an enormously widespread distribution ranging from western Europe through Turkey, western Russia and eastern Asia to China, Japan and Korea.

Family Brachycephalidae— Saddleback Toads

The Brachycephalidae is a small family of just three species, two in the genus *Brachycephalus* and one in *Psyllophryne*. They are found along the wet coastal regions of southeastern Brazil and the forests of the state of Rio de Janeiro, respectively. Eggs are deposited on land, in a damp environment to prevent dessication, and develop directly into froglets, bypassing the aquatic free-living tadpole (larval) stage.

Family Bufonidae— True Toads

The Bufonidae is a huge family of some 30 genera and more than 350 species and subspecies widely distributed throughout the world.

Bufonid toads are found throughout North, Central and South America, sub-Saharan Africa and across Europe, the former USSR, Asia including China, Japan and Korea, and south through the Austral-Indonesian archipelago. They are absent in Australia save for a single species, introduced artificially in 1935, known as the Cane or Marine Toad, *Bufo marinus*. This giant tropical species is rapidly expanding its range throughout Queensland, New South Wales, and north to the Northern Territory of Australia, and is wreaking havoc on native wildlife, which it either out-competes for food resources or gobbles up itself. Moreover, the toad has no natural enemies to hold it in check. The government of Australia has gone to great lengths to get the toad population under control including bounties and toad-hide tanning schemes, and it has even considered introducing a toad virus to kill them off.

Traveling far and wide is nothing new for this species. It has been accidentally, deliberately or secretly released in many locales outside its natural range since before 1844 and as recently as 1976, when some escaped confinement in Thailand. Sometime before 1955 it made its first appearance in Florida, and it is well established in the more tropical parts of the state at the present time. In fact, the

Bufonid toads are found throughout the world (Western Toad, *Bufo boreas*).

founding toads brought to Australia, ostensibly to control an insect pest known as the sugar cane beetle, were transported there from Hawaii, where it was deliberately introduced a few years before, also for pest control.

Many *Bufo* toads are known for their enlarged parotoid glands on the head behind the eyes, around the shoulder area. These glands produce a dangerous toxin that is potentially fatal because of its effect on the heart. Most true toads deposit strings of black pigmented eggs in an aquatic milieu and have a free-living tadpole stage. A few species are believed to produce eggs that undergo direct development (bypassing the free-living larval stage). The eggs are retained internally and release fully developed tadpoles or fully formed toadlets.

Most toads are drab in color, but some have bright red or orange markings over an olive brown background. The exception to this are the highly toxic toads of the South American genus *Atelopus,* which are so brightly colored they have earned the nickname of "harlequin frogs." Atelopids are found from Costa Rica through Bolivia,

in the Guyanas and in eastern coastal Brazil.

Family Centrolenidae— Glass Frogs

This is a moderately sized family of about 85 species in three genera. They are found throughout moist regions from southern Mexico south to Bolivia and in northeastern Argentina. They are noted for their translucent ventral surface— held against a strong light, it is possible to see the shadows or outlines of their internal structures, egg clutch (in gravid females) and bones; it's almost as if one were looking at an X-ray picture. Glass frogs deposit their eggs on leaves or rocks near streams, and in some species, the males protect the nest.

Family Dendrobatidae— Dart Poison or Arrow Poison Frogs

Although all members of this family exude a toxic skin secretion, the

Glass frogs are known for their translucent surface.

The small, colorful dart poison frogs are popular among frog enthusiasts—but be careful, their skin secretions are very toxic (*Dendrobates imitator*).

secretions of a few of the more potent frogs are employed by native peoples to tip their darts or arrows in order to bring down game. It is likely that these poisons were also used by tribal peoples using arrows or darts in warfare, although this has never been confirmed.

This is a large family of about 125 species divided into seven genera. They are found throughout Central America from Nicaragua south along the northern Pacific slopes of the Andes, across the northern rim of South America and in isolated populations in southeastern Brazil and Bolivia. In Hawaii, there is also an introduced population of the Green and Black Dart Poison Frog, *Dendrobates auratus*, where it has been thriving for more than 60 years. The original frogs were obtained from Isla Taboga off the Pacific coast of Panama in 1932. Interestingly, the toxins secreted by the Hawaiian frogs differ from those of their Panamanian forebears, indicating that toxin production may somehow be linked to diet or environmental conditions, which differ between Hawaii and Panama. What's more, poison frogs born in captivity as well as wild-caught, long-term captives also have different toxin profiles than their wild counterparts and in some cases stop manufacturing the most dangerous of all toxins when fed a diet of cultured or captive-bred insects such as crickets and fruit flies. These diminutive, colorful species are extremely popular as terrarium animals and they enjoy a large following among frog enthusiasts. Even though such frogs may stop producing some toxins, captive animals should be treated carefully and with respect, as one can never really be sure. Careful handling is as important for the frog as it is for its human caretaker.

The majority of dendrobatids deposit their eggs in trees, on air plants (puddles on epiphytes or bromeliads), in pools of water in tree holes and the axils of bromeliads or in moist terrestrial nests. Males or females may attend the nest, and in one species the female returns periodically to her entrapped tadpoles (usually placed one to a puddle of water) and extrudes an unfertilized egg into their "container," which the tadpoles then eat. Other species carry their tadpoles to the water, where they are released to fend for themselves.

Family Discoglossidae— Midwife Toads and Painted Frogs

As their scientific name implies, the frogs of this genus have disk-shaped structures at the ends of their tongues. This is a small group with three species of midwife toad (*Alytes sp.*) and six species of painted frog (*Discoglossus sp.*). The midwife toads are distributed through western, central and southern Europe. One species, discovered by science as recently as 1979, is found in obscure mountainous regions on the island of Majorca. Another species is found within a small range in northwest Africa. The six species of Discoglossid are found throughout southern Europe, northwestern Africa, Israel and Syria. Species are also known from the islands of Corsica and Sardinia.

The midwife toads mate on land; eggs are extruded in strings, are fertilized, and then the male of the species thrusts his legs into the eggs until they stick to his lower back and thighs. He then wears the eggs, going in and out of the water to keep them moist and viable, until they are ready to hatch. He liberates the tadpoles into the water, where they develop as free-living larvae. The first midwife toad was discovered by scientists in 1768 and given the Latin name *Alytes obstetricans,* or Obstetrician Frog.

Family Heleophrynidae— Ghost Frogs

The Heleophrynidae family is a small group of six species, all of which are found in southern Africa. They deposit their eggs on rocks in rapidly moving streams in the highlands of South Africa. Tadpoles are adapted to life in such waters. They earned their common name from their habit of being heard but not seen, a common occurrence with numerous other species of frogs.

Family Hemisotidae— Shovelnose Frogs

This is a small family of seven or eight species in a single genus, all of which are found in tropical sub-Saharan Africa. Their common name suggests the shape of their snouts, which they may use to excavate or burrow head first—uncommon among frogs, which

usually burrow rear end down first, head facing front.

Family Hylidae—Tree Frogs

The tree frogs are a huge family of nearly 700 species in 40 or so living genera. Various genera are constantly being reclassified as members of the family, or are moved out of the group—it is difficult to say with certainty what the precise numbers are at any point in time.

In recent years, newly discovered frog species have frequently been deemed members of the hylid family. Their arboreal nature and presence high within the canopy of many tropical and subtropical forests is probably responsible for the constant spate of new discoveries.

Tree frogs are unique in having somewhat disc-shaped pads on

their toes, which are composed of interlocking columnar cells that act very much as Velcro™ does, enabling them to stick to rough surfaces upside down and sideways or to dangle by a single limb from a branch high above the ground like a circus acrobat. On smooth surfaces, mucus-producing cells produce a sticky substance that acts as an adhesive, also enabling them to walk on walls, even when they are as smooth as glass.

Although the majority of hylids lay aquatic eggs and have a free-living tadpole stage, a number of genera have specialized life histories. Notable among these are frogs of the genus *Gastrotheca* or the marsupial frogs, which are found in the Andean region of South America, in Ecuador and Colombia on the

Tree frogs have remarkable, sticky toes that allow them to walk on walls if necessary (Selva Tree Frog, *Hyla ebraccata*).

Pacific coast and from Venezuela to eastern Brazil and northern Argentina on the Atlantic side, as well as in Panama. The females of these frogs have dorso-lateral pouches into which they push their eggs following fertilization. Here they develop into either tadpoles or fully formed froglets (depending on species). When they are ready to emerge, the female uses the toes of her rear limbs to stretch open the slits of her pouch to allow them to escape. If she is carrying tadpoles, she releases them into the water. Species where the larvae develop inside the pouch are released either in shallow water or on land.

The gorgeous poster-frog of the save-the-rain-forest movement, the Red-Eyed Leaf Frog or Tree Frog (*Agalychnis callidryas*), is a member of this family. The tree frogs are widely distributed throughout North, Central and South America, Europe (but not the British Isles), in a narrow corridor eastward through the former USSR into China and Japan, on the island of Papua New Guinea and through a large area of Australia, as well as on many islands in the Caribbean and elsewhere. They are absent from Africa, India and southeast Asia.

Family Hyperoliidae— African Reed Frogs

This is a moderate-sized family of more than 200 species in 18 genera

known by other common names including banana frogs and running frogs. A single species in this family, *Alexteroon obstetricans,* the African Midwife Toad, engages in male parental protection of its eggs and tadpoles. This family of frogs is widely distributed throughout sub-Saharan Africa and along the eastern third of the island of Madagascar from north to south. One species is also found in the Seychelles.

Family Leiopelmatidae— New Zealand Frogs

This is a small family of just three species, all of which are indigenous to New Zealand. They are believed to be closely related to the American Tailed Frog (*Ascaphus truei*). They are noted for their tail-wagging muscles and ability to wiggle their rumps, although they have no tails. They deposit their eggs on land, in damp or moist locations, where they undergo direct transformation to froglets, bypassing the free-living tadpole stage.

Family Leptodactylidae— Tropical/Robber Frogs

The tropical or robber frogs are a very large family of some 800 or more species divided into more than 50 genera. They are found from southern North America and the West Indies through most of Central and South America. Several species have been introduced into Florida, and some primarily

Mexican species occur naturally in the extreme southwestern United States. They employ a variety of reproductive strategies, including depositing of eggs in foam nests; others have land-laid eggs that produce tadpoles that somehow move into the water to complete their development. Some species lay their eggs on land, which develop directly into froglets. The Puerto Rican Coqui Frog (*Eleutherodactylus coqui*) and the Cayey Robber Frog (*E. jasperi*) employ internal fertilization, which helps to insure that the greatest number of eggs produced eventually develop.

Family Megophryidae— Asian Lazy or Spadefoot Toads

This is a family of nine genera and nearly 100 species found from India through southeast Asia, China, Burma, Borneo, Malaya, Sumatra and Java, the Philippines and the Sundra Islands to Bali. They have aquatic eggs and free-living aquatic tadpoles. A group of these toads, known as the Asian spadefoot toads, are related to the American, European and African spadefoot toads.

Family Microhylidae— Narrow-mouthed Toads

This is a moderately large family of some nearly 300 species in some 62 genera. They are found throughout

There are nearly 300 species of narrow-mouthed toads (Paraguayan Narrow-Mouth Toad).

the south central and southeastern United States, Mexico, Central America and the northern two-thirds of South America. Members of this group are also present in the southern half of Africa, on the east coast of India, throughout southeast Asia and China and in the Austral-Indonesian Archipelago, including Papua New Guinea and northern Australia. Most members of this family deposit aquatic eggs that develop into free-living tadpoles. A few genera deposit eggs on land that develop directly into nonfeeding tadpoles that complete their development in the nest.

Family Myobatrachidae— Australian Froglets/Toadlets

The Myobatrachidae family is a group of small frogs and toad-like frogs, as their common name implies, found in Australia and Papua New Guinea. There are approximately 100 species in 21 genera. Because of the arid conditions in the habitat of many of these species, eggs are deposited in damp terrestrial nests and develop directly into adults. The male Pouched Frog (*Assa darlingtoni*) broods its eggs in a special brood pouch. Perhaps the most notable of all the Australian myobatrachids are the two species of Gastric Brooding or Platypus Frog: *Rheobatrachus silus* and *Rheobatrachus vitellinus*. Both of these species may well be extinct, but Australian scientists are not certain. The tragedy of any species' extinction is heightened here, as scientists hardly had a chance to discover much about these amazing frogs before they disappeared. *R. silus* was discovered in 1973 in

southeastern Queensland, and the second gastric brooder became known to science in 1984, when it was found in central coastal Queensland. The cause(s) for the disappearance of these amazing species is unknown.

Although never witnessed, females apparently extrude their eggs, which are then externally fertilized by the male. The female then swallows the eggs and gestates them in her stomach. The eggs develop into tadpoles that progress to fully formed froglets, which are then either regurgitated by the female, or, in another scenario, climb their way up through the esophagus and pop out of the female's mouth. Australian scientists have termed this process "oral-birth," and it is the only known instance of its kind. There has been little work on how the female gastric brooder turns her stomach into a womb for six weeks, shutting off her stomach acids and going without food while remaining active. In addition, the gut must become paralyzed so that the eggs or tadpoles are not excreted prematurely. Studies of *R. silus* note that portions of the wall of the stomach undergo radical alteration: dilating, becoming thin and nearly transparent. These changes do not occur in *R. vitellinus*.

Another fascinating member of this family is the Australian Sandhill or Dumpy Frog (*Arenophryne rotunda),* which was first described to science in 1976 from the sandhill environment of Shark Bay, western Australia. This frog exists in a habitat that is virtually devoid of fresh water almost year round and does so by living in the damper levels of the sandy substrate, which contain small amounts of fresh water that it absorbs through its skin. Unlike most other burrowing frogs, the Dumpy Frog dives in head first, tunneling at an angle of about 45 degrees. As the upper layers dry up, the frog just dives deeper and deeper and has been found at depths of 3 feet or more. The frogs mate underground in a ritual that to date has escaped scientific scrutiny. The eggs develop directly into froglets, bypassing a free-living aquatic tadpole stage. Under laboratory conditions, development takes about $2^1/_2$ months to complete. A related species, called the Turtle Frog because it resembles a shell-less turtle (*Myobatrachus gouldii*), also burrows with its hands rather than its feet and also deposits direct developing eggs in the absence of water.

Family Pelobatidae—
Spadefoot Toads

The spadefoot is a small family of 11 species divided into three genera: the European spadefoots (*Pelobates sp.*), the U.S. Eastern spadefoot toads (*Scaphiopus sp.*)

and Western spadefoots (*Spea sp.*). These frogs, known in the vernacular as toads, are widespread throughout the entire continental United States as well as from Spain north through all of western Europe, western Asia and extreme northwestern Africa. They are noted for the presence of special growths on their hind feet that enable them to burrow into the substrate backwards or rump first. They do so to escape temporary arid conditions at the surface and reemerge when they detect the patter of rainfall on the ground above them. At such times they feed, breed and lay their eggs in temporary pools. The tadpoles develop rapidly before their pools become dried out, and then they dig in again to await the next rainy season.

Family Pelodytes—
Parsley Frogs

This is a tiny family of two species in a single genus. They are alleged to exude a substance that smells like parsley. Parsley frogs are found in Spain and western Europe through the Caucasus Mountains of southwestern Asia. They lay eggs in water (ponds) and have a free-living aquatic tadpole stage.

Family Pipidae—
African Clawed Frogs and
Surinam "Toads"

The Pipidae is a small, primitive family of 28 species divided into five genera. They include the Dwarf African Clawed Frogs (*Hymenochirus sp.*) and the African Clawed Frogs (*Xenopus sp.*), all of which are found throughout sub-Saharan

Spadefoot toads are known for their ability to dig into the substrate rear first—hence the name (Couch's Spadefoot Toad, *Scaphiopus couchii*).

tropical Africa, as well as a single genus, *Pipa*, with seven species found in South America and adjacent Panama known as the Surinam "toads." They are strictly aquatic frogs, as are the clawed frogs, and never come up on land. Their flat, squat, almost pancake-like bodies and limbs are strictly suited to swimming or hanging about in the water. They are unable to move on land save for a desperate and inefficient type of "crawl." They deposit their eggs in the water and have a free-living aquatic tadpole stage. In the genus *Pipa,* the eggs are embedded in the dorsal skin of the female, where they hatch either into tadpoles or directly into froglets.

Family Pseudidae—Harlequin Swimming Frogs

The harlequin swimming frogs are a small group of five species in two genera found in tropical south America east of the Andes and in Guyana, as well as in the Magdalena Valley of Colombia. One species, the Paradoxical Swimming Frog (*Pseudis paradoxsus*), produces huge tadpoles that eventually develop into tiny adult froglets, hence earning them their common as well as scientific name as they develop or "grow" by shrinking in size! Although this phenomenon is nowhere more pronounced than in this species, most tadpoles do grow by shrinking, because as adult froglets they lose their tails, which contribute to much of their length as larvae.

Family Ranidae—"True" Frogs

It is difficult to say what a "true" frog is, since all frogs and toads are frogs. The only living frog or toad that wouldn't be a true frog is, well, a false frog, and such a creature doesn't exist. This is a huge family of more than 700 species and numerous subspecies divided into more than 50 genera.

Among the true frogs are the familiar common American Bullfrog (*Rana catesbeiana*) and Leopard Frog (*Rana pipiens*), the North American Wood Frog (*Rana sylvatica*) and the small, bright, colorful and toxic mantella frogs (*Mantella sp.*) of Madagascar, which resemble dart poison frogs. Ranids are widespread throughout the world, both naturally as well as through artificial introduction. The American Bullfrog, once found only in eastern North America, now extends from coast to coast wherever there are bodies of water for it to live and breed in. These giant frogs have also been introduced into Hawaii, and escapes from frog farming operations have resulted in the establishment of populations in Italy and Greece. Ranids occur naturally

The ranids are a diverse family, ranging from the visually dull (Carolina Gopher Frog, left) to the eye-popping (Golden Mantella, *Mantella aurantiaca*, right).

throughout North America, including inside the Arctic Circle (the Wood Frog); in Mexico, Central and the northern third of South America; throughout sub-Saharan Africa and along the northern coast of Africa and in the Middle East; in Scandinavia and all of western Europe, including England and Ireland; throughout the former Soviet Union, China, India, southeast Asia, Indonesia, Papua New Guinea, Japan and Korea; and on many tropical and oceanic islands where there is adequate habitat. While the Ranids are found almost everywhere, only one species is found on the east coast of the Northern Territory of Australia and the Cape York Peninsula: the Australian Wood Frog (*Rana daemeli*).

Ranids lay aquatic eggs and have a free-living aquatic tadpole stage, although a few Asiatic genera have direct-developing eggs that are deposited in terrestrial nests. Ranids are generally nontoxic and some of the larger *Rana* species, such as the American Bullfrog and Asian Tiger Frogs *(Rana tigrina)*, are the most common sources of edible frog legs. The latter species, in fact, became critically endangered when exporters collected millions of wild-caught frogs for the frog-leg trade, whereas bullfrogs are commercially farmed for this purpose. The largest frog in the world, the West African (Cameroon) Giant

Flying frogs have an extraordinary ability to "fly" with their webbed feet (Asian Flying Frog, *Rhacophorus nigropalmatus*).

Frog, is a ranid *(Conrau goliath)*. These frogs are robust, powerful jumpers and avaricious predators, gobbling up anything they can swallow.

Family Rhacophoridae— Flying Frogs

The Rhacophoridae family consists of some 200 species in 11 genera. Members of this family are found in the tropical rain forests of southern India and Sri Lanka, Asia, Indonesia and the Philippines; two species are found on Madagascar, and a number of species are widespread along the eastern third of Africa, with a narrow corridor stretching across the continent through parts of west Africa.

The Rhacophorids are known for their amazing ability to glide through the air and "land" in targeted areas with uncanny accuracy. They splay their bodies but use the extensive webbing between their fingers and toes as deflectors of gravity, or parachutes of a sort. Not all members of this family "fly," and a few genera are strictly terrestrial.

Arboreal species deposit their eggs in sticky foam nests on the undersides of leaves; the tadpoles wriggle their way out and drop into the water below them. A few species lay their eggs in the holes of trees and produce nonfeeding tadpoles that metamorphose rapidly into froglets. Some employ the standard amphibian practice of external fertilization, water deposition of eggs and a free-living aquatic tadpole stage.

THE HISTORY OF CLASSIFYING AND NAMING PLANTS AND ANIMALS

The first person to place all animals and plants in a systematic classification was a Swedish botanist, Carl von Linne, who latinized his own name to *Carolus Linnaeus*. His book, *Systemae Naturae*, published in several editions during his lifetime (1707–1778), laid the foundations of modern animal and plant classification. However, von Linne did not invent the idea of giving all animals two names (or three, in the case of subspecies). The system of naming all plants and animals is called binomial nomenclature, and the idea was devised by Caspar Bruhin in Switzerland and John Ray in England about 100 years before von Linne published his classification.

The American Bullfrog, *Rana catesbeiana*, was named for Mark Catesby, an early American naturalist.

Latin was chosen as the language in which all species are officially named, but latinization of Greek nouns, and nouns or descriptors (adjectives) in other languages, are also widely used. For example, the American Bullfrog is named *Rana catesbeiana*. Its species name, *catesbeiana*, is a latinized version of the name of the early American naturalist Mark Catesby. A species can be named in honor of a person, as in the case of Catesby, or after its geographic location, its color, habits, behaviors or other traits perceived by the scientist giving the official description (and having the honor of choosing the name). Sometimes a species that was previously identified and named is overlooked by a scientist who finds this same species, believes that he or she has found a new species and gives it another name. When this event is discovered (and it frequently is), the new name is disqualified and the species' name reverts to the first or earliest name.

With so many different species to keep track of, the science of naming species is constantly in a state of flux. But because the same common names are often deliberately used for different species in different parts of the world (including through translation), it is important for scientists to have a system with rules that help them recognize an animal for what it is and not something else. Common names often cause confusion, but they remain useful for nonscientists who don't need precision in conversational use.

The classification of a single species, for example, Fowler's Toad (*Bufo woodhousii fowleri*), a subspecies of Woodhouse's Toad (*Bufo woodhousii*), reads as follows:

Kingdom—Animalia
Phylum—Chordata
Subphylum—Vertebrata
Class—Amphibia
Subclass—Lissamphibia
Order—Anura
Family—Bufonidae
Genus—Bufo
Species— woodhousii
Subspecies—fowleri
Designation: *Bufo woodhousii fowleri* **Hinckley 1882**

The phylum Chordata indicates that this species is a member of the group of all animals with a notochord or spinal cord. The subphylum Vertebrata indicates that additionally it is a member of the group of all animals with a vertebral column or bony case around the spinal cord. In addition, in the scientific literature, all scientific names are followed by a person's name and date. This is the name of the person who first published a scientific description and scientific name for the species plus the date of that publication. If the name and date are enclosed in parentheses, this is a signal that the designation has been corrected or changed from an earlier mistaken identification, usually of a previously described and named species that the later scientist didn't know existed. In this example, a scientist named Hinckley is credited with publishing a description and choosing a name for the Fowler's toad, and he did so in 1882.

The species (Woodhouse's Toad) and subspecies (Fowler's Toad) are both named in honor of others (Woodhouse and Fowler). In theory, a scientist can name a species after his mother, his dog, a favorite sports figure, an actor or just about anything else. In South Africa there is a snake named after the *Cape Herald*, a newspaper.

Family Rhinodermatidae—Darwin's Frogs

The Rhinodermatidae family is small—three species in two genera, found in Mexico (one species) and in the rain forests of Chile and Argentina. These toads are noted for their unusual life history. On hatching, the tadpoles are ingested by the male and are ensconced in his vocal pouch, where they either develop into froglets (*Rhinoderma darwinii*) or are carried in the mouth to pools of water and released (*Rhinoderma rufum*).

Family Scaphiophrynidae—Web-Foot or Rain Frogs

The web-foot frogs are a small family of nine species in two genera, all of which are found on Madagascar. The Web-Footed Frog (*Paradoxophyla palmata*) lays its eggs in the water, where they develop into free-living aquatic tadpoles. Tadpoles of the other genus in this family, *Scaphiphryne*, have also been identified, but little is known of their breeding rituals.

Family Sooglossidae—Seychelles Frogs

This is a small family of three species in two genera, all of which are found on the Seychelles Islands in the Indian Ocean. They deposit terrestrial eggs that develop directly into froglets. In one species, *Sooglossus seychellensis*, the eggs hatch into nonfeeding tadpoles and complete their development on the back of the adult in a fashion similar to that of the Midwife Toad.

PRESENTATION OF SCIENTIFIC NAMES

All scientific names are technically a foreign language (Latin or a latinized noun or adjective). They are written in the printed literature in italics. In handwriting or typewriter text, they are underscored.

On modern computers and word processing programs, italics are readily available, and so underscoring is not used. The first letter of the genus name is always capitalized. The species and subspecies names are all in lower case (Bufo woodhousii fowleri **Hinckley 1882;** on a computer or in printed text, *Bufo woodhousii fowleri* **Hinckley 1882**). Because the names of the discoverers are important only to taxonomic specialists, they are frequently omitted.

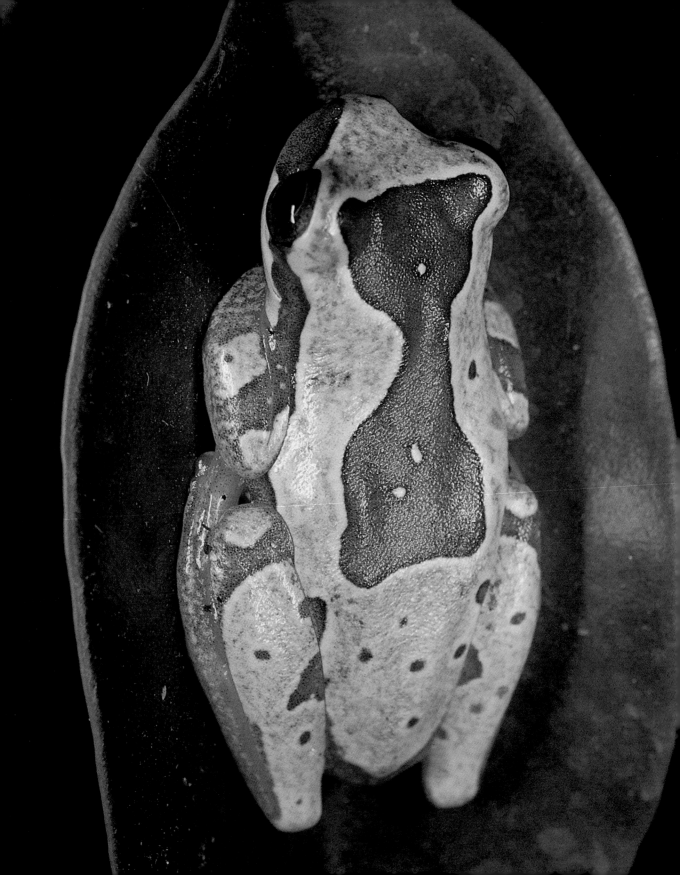

PART II

Care in Captivity

*An Amphibian for You · Housing ·
Handling · Feeding · Reproduction and Breeding ·
Health Care*

CHAPTER 5

An Amphibian for You

With so many thousands of amphibians to choose from, it may seem difficult to decide which you'd like to raise in captivity and possibly breed. In reality, the majority of the world's amphibians are not commonly available for this purpose, so that narrows the hobbyist's choices from thousands to perhaps a hundred or so different species.

Before embarking on the acquisition, care and keeping of an amphibian, there are a variety of issues that you should consider. This section will endeavor to address these issues, based on the questions that future hobbyists most frequently ask.

Where Can I Get an Amphibian?

There are actually many sources for an amphibian pet, and it's best to be an educated shopper. Think about your concerns and needs, and then explore the following options.

Pet Shops

Your local pet shop is the first and most logical source for your first amphibian. If you are considering purchasing an amphibian at a pet shop, spend some time talking with the staff. Be confident that the personnel are knowledgeable about keeping herps. A friendly source of competent advice can be an advantage to purchasing your amphibian in a nearby store. The other advantages to buying an amphibian at a pet shop are that you can see and examine it in person and can purchase all the necessary equipment to care for it at the same location. Moreover, you get a steady source of live food, because pet shops must stock crickets, flies, mealworms, waxworms and other live foods to feed their own animals. Note, however, that pet shops that do not specialize in reptiles and amphibians are not likely to have a large selection from which to choose. If this is the case, and you wish to buy an animal first-hand at such a store, get out the Yellow Pages. With some research, you should be able to determine which shops in your vicinity have amphibians and the supplies needed to feed, house and otherwise care for them.

Swap Meets, Expos and Herp Shows

There are hundreds of herp events all around the United States and in many countries overseas. They may be held as frequently as monthly or one to four times a year. You can find the swap or expo nearest you by consulting the calendar of events appearing in the reptile and amphibian magazines mentioned in the resource section at the back of this book.

Swaps provide the advantage of a bigger selection of pets, supply and live food dealers, as well as the opportunity to examine your purchase in person. The major drawback of buying at a swap, however, is that you may not see your dealer again until the next event (perhaps for six months or a year), and if you have a problem a week later it may be difficult to resolve. Nonetheless, dealers at these events tend to be quite knowledgeable, and you will

At a herp expo, some breeders will bring photographs of their frogs mating to show that they are in fact captive bred (*Ceratophrys ornata*).

undoubtedly receive good advice and assistance should you shop at one. In addition, most of these events allow the sale of only captive-bred animals, which increases the likelihood that you will be getting a healthy pet. To substantiate the representation that their animals are captive bred, some breeder/dealers bring along photos showing their frogs or salamanders mating and their tadpoles developing and metamorphosing, as well as pictures of how they cared for the eggs.

Herp Society Meetings and Shows

There are some 50 or more local hobby herpetology associations in the United States and many similar clubs overseas. These organizations hold monthly meetings and are a good place to obtain information as well as find sources for animals and related supplies and foods. There is no better way to learn than by garnering the experience and knowledge of those who have done it before.

You can find a local herp society by asking around at pet shops, schools, your nearby zoo or animal control center. *The Guide to North American Herpetology* also lists such groups with contact information or see the resources chapter in the back of this book. In addition, there are a number of national and international groups that specialize

in amphibians; they are also listed in the resource guide. Joining one or more such groups provides a great educational opportunity, as well as a great way to locate private breeders and dealers in the specimens and supplies that you need.

Mail-Order Dealers and Breeders

There are innumerable importers and breeders of amphibians and reptiles throughout the world. You can find them in the aforementioned guidebook, in advertising in the pages of amphibian/reptile publications and society newsletters and on the World Wide Web. All legitimate mail-order suppliers will guarantee live arrival and unconditional satisfaction with your purchase.

The disadvantage of buying by mail is that you cannot examine the animal prior to purchase, and if for any reason you are unhappy with it, it is often not worth the

price of paying shipping charges both ways in order to obtain a refund or swap it for another. If you are going to do business this way—and, because of location, many people are forced to—it is wise to get on friendly terms with the dealers who are recommended by fellow hobbyists you meet at swap meets or at society/club meetings. Occasionally, someone has an unfortunate experience with a mail-order dealer or supplier, but the majority of dealers are trustworthy. Getting a referral or recommendation to a mail-order supplier who has been in business for at least several years is probably your best protection, but on occasion it is necessary to do business with an unknown dealer who has that special something no one else can provide. A disreputable dealer in this business doesn't last very long. I have seen a number of people who were dealing in these animals ripped to shreds by Internet

It's helpful to see the animal before you buy it. A healthy amphibian will be active and bright-eyed (*Hyla triangulum*).

discussion groups and at herp meetings. Hobby herpetology may have millions of adherents, but it is still a small world—scam artists become known very quickly.

Collecting Animals Yourself

Doing it yourself is a fun and educational way to obtain one or more specimens. However, in the United States and overseas there are many laws that govern such activities, and you should be up-to-date on the legality of collecting from the wild, lest you wind up on the wrong side of a court summons. *A Field Guide to Reptiles and the Law* by John P. Levell, which includes amphibians as well as reptiles, (see resources in the back of this book) is indispensable for anyone interested in field collecting. Your local herpetology society can also advise you what you can and cannot do in your jurisdiction when out collecting.

In addition to not disturbing or taking any endangered species you might be lucky enough to come across, there are limits as to the number of animals you can collect, as well as limits on the methods you can use. There are also certain aspects of field etiquette that everyone should obey; for example, you should leave the habitat undisturbed, reposition overturned logs or rocks and avoid littering or creating a fire hazard. In many jurisdictions, there are seasons when you can collect and seasons when

collecting or "hunting" of such animals is prohibited. Some states now prohibit the collection of any amphibians without a permit, which simply means that you have to take the time, trouble and expense of obtaining one. In addition, collecting amphibians or hunting or collecting any animal on Federal, state, county or city property may be a criminal act—so always be sure you are not violating the law when on public ground. If you are collecting on private property that you do not own, make sure you have the owner's permission to do so. If not, you are trespassing.

What Kind of Amphibian Do I Want?

Salamander, frog, cecillian…huge, little or medium-sized? Do I want a colorful pet, or will I be happy with a less flamboyant animal? These are all personal preference questions you need to answer yourself, but answer them you must, as they form the basis for your selection process. Reading up on the different kinds of amphibians (in this book and elsewhere) and studying them at the zoo, a friend's collection or at the pet shop may help you to form some opinion if you have yet to do so. Although the

tiny, colorful dart poison frogs are attractive, they are also challenging and expensive. Many keepers of these frogs will tell you they got their feet wet (no pun intended) with less costly, less exotic species that were easier to care for. Once they had some experience, they decided that they were ready to care for dendrobatids.

Is there any amphibian you don't want? Yes. First and foremost, you don't want any rare, endangered species unless it was captive bred and born and you have the documents to prove it. You may not want any species that is too large or that requires an extremely large and expensive habitat to set up and maintain (unless you have the time and money to devote to it). A huge five-dollar bullfrog requires an indoor setup that could cost hundreds of dollars to house comfortably and healthily. However, if such species are native to your area or you can confine them properly, you may want to put such animals up in a garden pond (see Chapter 6) on your own property, or perhaps in a custom-built pool located inside a greenhouse. Given the funds and the space, there is nothing you can't accomplish. For the majority of us, however, while such setups may be ideal, they are often not possible. In choosing any amphibian, be sure you understand its requirements and know the limits to

It is recommended that keepers new to amphibians start with a relatively low-maintenance animal. Exotic animals, such as the dart poison frogs, are both challenging and expensive (Green and Black Dart Poison Frog, *Dendrobates auratus*).

which you can go in order to provide them.

Choosing a Healthy Amphibian

If you have the chance to select your pet in person, it is important that you know how to assess it. Although there are no guarantees that some specimens, particularly wild-caught animals, don't have internal parasites or diseases, you can make sure that the skin is unbroken, free from blisters, sores or other suspicious-looking bumps, discoloration or scars. The most prevalent external parasites of amphibians are leeches. Even if you don't actually see them, you can tell if they were present recently because of the telltale marks they leave behind.

Make sure there is no fungus present on the animal. Fungi may appear as cottony hair-like tufts; most often it will be gray, white,

yellow or even brown. Definitely avoid any animals that exhibit these kinds of problems unless you are interested in running your own amphibian hospital.

You should elicit a statement from the seller that the animal is eating and, if possible, ask to see it eat as well as find out what it has been fed and whether such items are available to you. Animals that have stopped feeding are often sick and may be dying. Look for plump, active animals with clear eyes and a healthy escape reflex. If you gently prod all but a few very sedentary species, they should take off rapidly.

Always ask for captive-bred and captive-born animals—such animals tend to be in better health than wild-caught specimens. Also, because they were not removed from the wild, they do not contribute to the decline of wild amphibians being reported throughout the world.

Salamander or Frog— Aquatic or Not?

Your next decision involves whether you want a terrestrial (land-living), semi-aquatic (land- and water-living) or strictly aquatic (water-living only) species. There are pros and cons pertinent to each type of animal. Generally, aquatic and semi-aquatic species that need a lot of water to roam around in need elaborate habitats including the same sorts of accessories for filtration, maintenance of water quality and heating that aquariums require. The Pipid frogs, for example, must be kept in fully operational aquariums and require no landside whatsoever. But they need an efficient, high-throughput filtration system in order to prevent water pollution, which could build up in a matter of hours without it. The last thing you'd want in your living room is a deplorable stinky mess of an aquarium, and your frogs wouldn't appreciate it either.

Raising tadpoles also requires a fully operational and effectively filtered and aerated aquarium. For many types of herbivorous tadpoles, a good green algae growth, as unseemly as it may appear, can provide an excellent source of nutrition.

Salamanders are not nearly as popular or well-known as are frogs and toads. Frogs have served as test animals and anatomical models. We know them from ancient fairy tales—turning into princes and vice versa—and from their mystique as ingredients in witch's brews. More recent entertainment has brought us Warner Brothers' Michigan J. Frog and the late Jim Henson's Kermit. Finally, frogs have been featured in well-received Budweiser beer commercials. All of this "exposure" has produced far greater popularity for frogs than for salamanders. Although some readers will recall the accusation "She turned me into a newt!" from *Monty Python's Holy Grail,* witches are far better known for turning people (particularly princes) into frogs.

However, salamanders should not be cast aside. Although they are not as animated as frogs, and have no true voice, they can be just as interesting and rewarding to study and keep. Salamanders also fall into the same three classes where habitat is concerned: terrestrial, semi-aquatic and strictly aquatic. Because they are less commonly kept, less is known about their captive care and husbandry. In this respect, salamander keeping presents a true challenge. Hobbyists who dedicate themselves to salamanders are in a good position to help make rewarding new discoveries. And the majority of the world's salamanders are not being bred in captivity. This represents another uncharted area for the hobbyist bent on new challenges.

If you really want to delve into unknown territories, you may want to try your hand at a cecilian. These unusual amphibians are only occasionally available from specialty dealers, and they are the least known and least popular of all the amphibians because of their secretive habits. Due to their fossorial nature they are rarely seen, but this doesn't mean they are an endangered species. In fact, scientists don't really know the status of the cecilians' ecological welfare.

Okay, I Want a Frog—Which One Should I Get?

Fire-bellied Toads

These small frogs, which range in size from 2 to 4 inches, are frequently available at reasonable prices. They are semi-aquatic and require as much as or more water than land. A favorite setup is a half-filled, well-filtered fish tank with rock formations for them to haul out onto. They are colorful and emit a baleful wooing-like call that will entrance you the first time you hear it. Fire-Bellied Toads are hardy and will eat almost any bug you offer them as long as it moves. The most commonly available are the Oriental Fire-Bellied Toads (*Bombina orientalis*), the European Fire-Bellied Toads (*Bombina bombina*) and the Yellow-Bellied Toads (*Bombina variegata*). You may also happen upon a hybrid of *variegata* and *bombina* that has an orange-colored belly.

Bombinids eat any insect or invertebrate small enough for them to swallow. Note that their food

Yellow-Bellied Toad (*Bombina variegatus*, left), European Fire-Bellied Toad (*Bombina bombina*, right). These frogs prefer a half-water, half-land setup.

must be alive or animated. A multi-vitamin/mineral supplement with Vitamin A or carotenoids is recommended for these frogs to maintain their color. The Oriental Fire-Bellied does well in an aquarium filled with 4 to 5 inches of water plus plenty of rocks or other accessories jutting just above the surface so that they can haul out. Your pet shop can provide plenty of items to create floating islands or decorative rock formations suitable for this purpose.

As they are found throughout more temperate, nontropical climes, they prefer 60 to 75 degrees F and should be kept, at a minimum, in a 10-gallon tank for two to three bombinids. For five frogs, a 20-gallon tank would be appropriate. Include either a high-efficiency submersible filter or an undergravel filtration system or both. Because bombinids secrete a potentially harmful toxin, their tank should be completely drained and refilled weekly and kept well filtered between water changes.

These frogs mate and breed readily in captivity given proper stimulation. Like most frogs, they like rain, and an artificial rainmaker or a waterfall arrangement can encourage them to mate. Eggs are laid in water and should be carefully removed (dip-netted) and allowed to develop in a separate, well-aerated aquarium tank. Because they stick to vegetation and rocks, it may be

Large Bufos such as the Marine Toad will eat fuzzy mice as adults (Marine Toad, *Bufo marinus*).

easier in some cases to quickly remove these items to other tanks with the eggs intact.

Because larger bombinids will eat smaller ones, baby froglets need to be segregated.

True Toads

Many species from this large family of terrestrial, warty or dry-skinned frogs are readily available, and most make excellent and hardy captive specimens. True toads are so common that almost any area in the country is apt to be home to one of more species of bufonid toad—even the suburbs or the middle of some big cities.

The following are highly recommended as inexpensive starter species: American Toad (*Bufo americanus*), or its subspecies the Southern Toad (*Bufo terrestris*), Woodhouse's Toad (*Bufo woodhousii*) and numerous other bufo toads, all of which require basically the same kinds of care, feeding and habitat.

Larger species such as the Cane or Marine Toad can be fed large insects and, when fully grown, will eat fuzzy and hopper-stage mice. In a pinch, these frogs can be induced to eat cooked lean hamburger or even dog food. These latter foods should be avoided as a steady diet, as their fat content is apt to be high and this is not a normal dietary item for any amphibian.

Bufo habitat is always all terrestrial, with a small pond of water that reaches no higher than the frog's shoulder. Different Bufo species have different temperature preferences, but most do well between 65 and 80 degrees F. A 10-gallon aquarium can house one or two toads of 2 to 3 inches in length, but a larger tank would be appreciated by your pets.

Breeding these frogs in captivity is problematic. A large (at least 55-gallon) tank is necessary, which is then divided into two sides—a small land side and a longer water side in which the eggs are laid. The water should be about 3 inches deep. If you are thinking about breeding some of the really large species of toad, think again: Keep in mind that they can lay tens of thousands of eggs. Any indoor setup for this kind of operation needs to be huge and elaborate. Outdoor ponds or water-filled troughs inside a greenhouse are probably the only way to breed and raise this many frogs successfully.

If the species you choose to keep is not native to your area, make sure that none escape into your surrounding environs. Any nonnative species can cause ecological havoc if they establish themselves.

Dart Poison Frogs

Dart poison frogs are for advanced amateurs and experienced frog keepers. They tend to be expensive and require specialized conditions as well as small, live insects such as ants, wingless fruit flies, pinhead (newborn) crickets, termites and the like. If two days pass without food you are apt to see your frogs die, so it is essential to make sure you have access to a daily ration (even a twice-daily ration) of the right-sized bugs. Tadpole feeding is more problematic. The Strawberry Dart Poison Frog (*Dendrobates pumilio*) feeds her tadpoles an unfertilized egg, and breeders have tried feeding captive-born tadpoles a tiny drop of raw chicken egg yolk with some success.

A possible danger to dart poison frogs is the buildup of their secretions in their enclosure. It is therefore not a good idea to mix species or keep them with other types of amphibians that may not be immune to their toxins. Change water ponds daily or more frequently, and remove and replace the substrate at least once a month.

The habitat for these frogs is largely terrestrial, with a small pond or dish of water as indicated.

As tropical species, they prefer temperatures of 75 to 85 degrees, and most species enjoy a high humidity level. Thus, it is recommended that you provide a rainmaker or fogging equipment for dendrobads. Enclosures should be heavily planted with plenty of places to hide. Naturalistic small caves and rock formations are available in pet shops.

Although these frogs are small, it is a good idea to give them plenty of room. Two or at most three small specimens per 20-gallon enclosure is recommended, as they are territorial and may become stressed if overcrowded.

Most dart poison frogs lay eggs out of the water that hatch into tadpoles, which require special conditions to raise. In some species, the parent frogs lift the tadpoles on to their backs and carry them to water. Many breeders move each tadpole to a separate beaker of water and feed them individually, mimicking what happens in nature.

Midwife Toads and Painted Frogs

The members of this family are small, terrestrial frogs that are fascinating to keep and raise if you are lucky enough to come across them in the United States. They are found primarily in Europe, south to Spain and Majorca. The painted frogs are native to Spain, east to the Middle East.

Dart poison frogs should be housed separately from other amphibians due to the toxins that they secrete into their habitat (Green and Black Dart Poison Frog in "blue" phase, *Dendrobates auratus*).

The midwife toads eat all kinds of bugs small enough for them to swallow and are fairly hardy. They are recommended for advanced newcomers and advanced hobbyists. Their habitat is terrestrial with a small pond of water and as they come from temperate and more northern climates, they prefer temperatures in the 60-to-75-degree range. Moderate to little humidity is required, and they will soak to obtain water via cutaneous absorption. No more than two or three small frogs should be housed in a 10-gallon aquarium.

The other members of this group, the painted frogs, may require somewhat warmer (70 to 80 degrees F), terrestrial surroundings and do not exhibit the pattern of parental care exhibited by the midwife toads.

The Red-Eyed Tree Frog is a favorite with both hobbyists and calendar manufacturers (Red-Eyed Tree Frog, *Agalychinis callidryas*).

Tree Frogs

This is a large family of frogs that offer many different varieties suitable for captive husbandry and observation projects. Starter species include cricket frogs (*Acris sp.*), any one of a number of common tree frogs (*Hyla sp.*) and chorus frogs (*Pseudacris sp.*). For more advanced hobbyists the leaf frogs such as the Red-Eyed Tree Frog (*Agalychinis callidryas*), the Marsupial Frogs (*Gastrotheca marsupiata* and *Gastrotheca riobambae*) and the casque-headed tree frogs (*Trachycephalus sp.*) make interesting study subjects.

A favorite among hobbyists is White's Tree Frog (*Litoria caerulea*), an Australian and Indonesian species that is widely available as captive bred and born. While more exotic than most common North American hylids, it is a good starter species, as it is hardy and easy to care for. When stressed, however, it will exude a toxin known as caerulin from its skin gland that appears as beads of milk over the dorsal surfaces. Take care not to handle the frog with bare hands when such secretions are noted. After whatever stress is causing its liberation, pick up the frog with disposable unpowdered surgical gloves and rinse it thoroughly before handling it with bare hands again.

Marsupial Frogs are best kept by more advanced hobbyists (Marsupial Frog, *Gastrotheca marsupiata*).

In general, tree frogs do well in a well-planted, tall terrarium with plenty of branches and shrubs for them to climb. Many species, in the absence of such structures, will content themselves by adhering to the walls and corners of their enclosure. These are active species that need plenty of room, from the perspective of both height and area. A minimum of a 30-gallon aquarium should be used, but if you have space, tree frogs will enjoy an even larger tank.

All the species mentioned are live bug or worm eaters and need to be fed at least once daily. Mealworms, crickets, fruit flies and similar insect prey supplemented with a calcium and vitamin/mineral powder is best. As for any amphibian, vary the diet as much as possible.

There are two species and five subspecies of cricket frogs from the United States, mostly known by common names that reflect their origin, such as Northern Cricket Frog, Southern Cricket Frog, Florida Cricket Frog and Coastal Cricket Frog. Although classified as tree frogs, these frogs do not climb but will still benefit from plenty of low-lying shrubbery and hiding places.

The leaf frogs, including the well-known Red-Eyed Tree Frog (*Agalychinis callidryas*), are increasingly being bred in captivity and are often available in specialist shops and on amphibian mail-order price lists. These are relatively small species (about 3 inches in length) but in spite of their small size, they require a fairly large enclosure. Even a single trial specimen should be given the run of a 40-gallon high tank. Leaf frogs need height as well as vertical space. Only males vocalize, and sound is the best way to determine whether you have a male or female. Males also develop dark pads on their thumbs when reproductively active.

To accommodate these tropical rain-forest inhabitants, simulate the rain forest as best as possible in your terrarium. A pond of 6 to 8 square inches with about 3 inches of water is recommended.

Red-eyes will eat crickets, flies, mealworms…just about any fast-moving or highly animated small bug will be eaten. Vitamin D3 and calcium supplements are recommended at least once a week, although the frogs should be fed daily.

As these are active species, opt for as large an enclosure as possible. A 40- to 50-gallon tank for anywhere from one to six of these frogs is recommended. Clearly these frogs prefer foliage, and plenty of it. Branches should be strong enough to support their weight. Fogging or rain-making equipment can help provide humidity. They prefer temperatures in the 70-to-80-degree F range. Humidity should be moderate and not excessive, but it is required.

These frogs deposit their eggs on leaves overhanging water. The tadpoles drop off into the water below, so it is a good idea to provide a dish of water to serve as a pond under wherever the eggs are deposited. Cycling or raising and lowering temperature between day and night, as well as changing the length of the daylight period over a period of a few months during the winter, seems to induce reproductive behavior.

The White's Tree Frog is hardy and relatively easy to care for (White's Tree Frog, *Litoria caerulea*).

In South America, you can find Marsupial Frogs living in urban gardens, but a tropical rain forest is their habitat of preference (Marsupial Frogs, *Gastrotheca marsupialis*).

Another favorite group of tree frogs among hobbyists are the Marsupial Frogs of the genus *Gastrotheca*, a word that means "stomach pouch." This is somewhat of a misnomer, because the pouch in which the female Marsupial Frog gestates her eggs has its entrance on the lower back or dorsal surface although inside it extends around to the sides of the frog. In some species, eggs develop into tadpoles that are released, whereas in others the female retains the tadpoles until they are fully formed froglets.

Marsupial Frogs eat any insects and other invertebrates that are small enough to swallow. Although they are found in urban gardens in many large South American cities, they clearly prefer a tropical rain-forest habitat with a small pond of water. Females ready to release their tadpoles should be placed in a fully semi-aquatic habitat.

At least a 20-gallon terrarium for three or four specimens is required. The "litter" of some nearly 100 tadpoles can be raised in a green-algae-filled 30-gallon long tank and can be fed boiled lettuce and moderate amounts of green-leaf spinach (as it contains a significant amount of oxalic acid). Although from South America, these frogs do well at cooler montane temperatures ranging from lows of 65 to 70 degrees F at night to highs of 80 to 85 degrees F in the daytime. They require moderate to low humidity. Substrate can be sterile well-planted potting soil or sphagnum moss. When not breeding the frogs, a small soaking dish should be provided and the water should be changed daily.

After fertilization, the male may help the female insert the eggs into

YOUR HOBBY CAN CONTRIBUTE TO NEW DISCOVERIES

One of the first exotic frog species I ever obtained was a gravid, female Marsupial Frog *(Gastrotheca riobambae)*, which was collected in a backyard in Quito, Ecuador, and sent to me by airmail. Shortly after placing the gravid female into a semi-aquatic tank in Brooklyn, New York, she proceeded to release about 95 tadpoles into the aquarium side of the setup. This was in 1957, and no one in U.S. herpetology had ever witnessed it before. Tadpoles were given to zoos and museums all over the country for study and careful notes were taken of their feeding habits (they were vegetarian tadpoles). Finally, with the help of the late Charles M. Bogert of the American Museum of Natural History, I was encouraged to document the event and submit it to a scientific journal, *Herpetologica*, in which my paper was published in 1958. This is an excellent example of how a nonprofessional hobbyist can make an important contribution to science as a result of his or her hobby.

The common Green Tree Frog is an uncommonly beautiful pet (Green Tree Frog, *Hyla cinera*).

her brood pouch. When ready, the female, alone, uses her hind legs to open the entrance to the pouch to permit the release of either tadpoles into an aquatic milieu, or fully formed froglets into a terrestrial environment. It is truly an amazing spectacle to watch.

The common tree frogs of the genus *Hyla* are the largest group of all the tree frogs, and many notable examples are available for the terrarium. Included among these are the beautiful U.S. species Anderson's Tree Frog (*Hyla andersoni*), the common Green Tree Frog (*Hyla cinera*) and innumerable others, the care and keeping of which are all basically the same. Note, however, that different members of the *Hyla* genus prefer different temperatures and activity levels based on their geographic origins. Subtropical and tropical species will prefer more humid and slightly warmer conditions than temperate and more northern species. In fact, the more northerly species, such as

the Spring Peeper (*Hyla crucifer*), the Gray Tree Frog (*Hyla versicolor*) and Cope's Gray Tree Frog (*Hyla chrysoscelis*), are among the very few species that manufacture a glucose- or glycerol-based cellular "antifreeze." By doing so, they are able to survive the cold of winter months by almost totally freezing their bodies.

Both species of North American Gray Tree Frog (*Hyla versicolor* and *Hyla chrysoscelis*) make interesting terrarium specimens. They are active year-round in the southern parts of their range, and from April to October in the northern range. In the northernmost reaches of their territory, they may emerge in early spring and begin calling when nighttime temperatures reach at least 50 degrees F.

They are easy to sex: males can be identified by their dark throats, females by their light or white-colored throats. Both sexes call, and they can be loud and boisterous. If two males move too close to each other (about 30 inches or less), they emit antagonistic or aggressive warning calls that are loud and abrupt.

Gray Tree Frogs survive cold winter months by nearly "freezing" their bodies (Gray Tree Frog, *Hyla versicolor*).

Like most frogs, gray tree frogs will eat any insect or small arthropod small enough for them to subdue and swallow.

In the wild, Gray Tree Frogs live in forested woodlands. In captivity, they should be given plenty of sturdy branches and foliage to climb and perch upon. They are most active at 60 to 70 degrees F, but can tolerate lower temperatures into the 50s. They definitely prefer it on the cool side and become stressed at temperatures above 80 degrees F. Their enclosure should be as large as possible for one or two pairs, with a significant amount of water at one end if breeding and egg-rearing are contemplated. They are stimulated to call and breed by rain, so rain-making equipment may help in this area. Males are best given enough space to maintain territories that are at least 30 inches from each other.

Eggs hatch in less than three to five days, and up to 2,000 may be deposited by a single female. Tadpoles may take up to two months to transform into froglets. As in other fecund species, it is difficult to expect to hatch out and rear almost all the eggs that are deposited in captivity because there are so many. Due to predation and other factors in the wild, only a small percentage of such large clutches survive to adulthood.

Spring Peepers are tiny frogs with loud voices and will often begin calling even when there is still snow on the ground in the more northern parts of their range. Peepers eat small insects such as ants, termites, fruit flies and newborn to two-week-old crickets. They live in flood plains, woodland forests and meadows.

In spite of their small size these frogs are extremely active, so they should be given the largest possible enclosure in which to move around. Up to six specimens can be kept in a 30- or 40-gallon terrarium with a small pond of water. Although active at temperatures as low as 40 to 50 degrees F in some parts of their range, a preferred temperature for captives is from 60 to 70 degrees F. Enclosures should be well-planted and have some height, as these are active climbers.

Peepers breed for periods of up to two months or more after winter emergence; rainfall helps stimulate mating, so rain-making equipment may be of some value. These frogs can be very noisy during the breeding season and this should be taken into consideration if prolonged, loud calling is seen as an annoyance. Like all species that deposit their eggs in the water, these frogs mate in the water as well, and therefore a pond of 10 to 12 square inches and about 2 inches in depth should be provided. Up to 1,000 eggs may be deposited, usually on plants and in small clusters; they hatch within a week. Tadpoles take two months to metamorphose. These plentiful frogs are best bred outdoors or in larger facilities in greenhouses if one expects to try and rear a significant number of the eggs to adulthood.

The Australasian and Indonesian tree frogs of the genus *Litoria* provide at least two species and a number of color variants (including a jade green and an all-blue version) to the amphibian hobbyist. These are White's Tree Frog (*Litoria caerulea*) and the less commonly kept White-lipped or Australian Giant

In the wild, Spring Peepers are rarely seen, but often heard (Spring Peeper, *Pseudacris crucifer*).

Tree Frog (*Litoria infrafrenata*). Most of the specimens now in the hobbyist trade are from captive-bred stocks, although wild-caught animals are still exported from Indonesia at this time. Both Australia and, more recently, New Guinea have banned the export of all wildlife from their countries, so, unless smuggled illegally, one is not apt to get any recently caught wild specimens of either of these frogs. The Australian Giant Tree Frog is rarely seen (no exports are allowed) and only a few people have succeeded in breeding it in captivity.

Both of these large species eat insects, small arthropods and even small rodents such as newborn or fuzzy mice.

These frogs are found in a variety of habitats, but in captivity they do well in a basic terrarium with heavy, wide branches made of cured and cleaned driftwood, bamboo rods or similar material. A soaking pan is necessary.

As these frogs are rather sedentary, about one resident per 10-gallon aquarium is sufficient. The cage should be well ventilated, with moisture kept to a minimum. A substrate of plain white paper toweling is all that is necessary to maintain these frogs hygienically and adequately. As the frogs can be a little messy, clean the glass walls of the tank every few days with paper toweling and hot water. They endure temperatures down to 60

The White-Lipped Tree Frog and its cousin the White's Tree Frog are somewhat sedentary captives and don't require a particularly large tank (White-Lipped Tree Frog, *Litoria infrafrenata*).

degrees F at night to a high of 85 degrees F during daylight.

Eggs hatch within two days and tadpoles metamorphose into froglets in about four weeks. You can sex frogs by noting that males have darker-colored throats than females; in addition, males have nuptial or grasping pads on their thumbs. However, it is often difficult to recognize these characteristics except in adult frogs that are ready to breed.

Tropical Frogs

The tropical frogs (Family Leptodactylidae) originate in South and Central America, Mexico, many tropical islands in the Caribbean and the extreme southernmost United States. This family contains a number of species frequently

available for hobbyists, including some that are regularly bred in captivity, among them albinos: the Pac-Man or horned frogs of the genus *Ceratophrys*. These frogs are ferocious sit-and-wait predators. If accosted or approached by humans they may puff up, gape and even bite, snagging their caretaker with what can only be described as a fang (ondontoid tooth) as well as sharp, smaller teeth. They eat anything that moves, comes within range and is small enough to swallow. They are sedentary and obese and don't move far, but rather wait for food to come to them.

Some Leptodactids (horned frogs), have horn-like protruberances over both eyes, from which they get their common name. They are also known as *escuerzos*, in

Spanish. The most frequently seen species is the Chaco or Cranwell's Horned Frog, both in traditional coloring and as albinos. Its scientific name is *Ceratophrys cranwelli*. It was first discovered and described in the science literature in 1980, but less than 20 years later it has become one of the most popular frogs in the hobby. The largest species is the Brazilian Horned Frog (*C. aurita*), which grows to about 8 inches around.

Another popular species that is being bred in captivity is the Argentinean Ornate Horned Frog (*C. ornata*). It is indeed ornate with yellows, blacks, reds and browns. Females of this species are about 6 inches around.

Horned frogs are available as captive-breds year round. They are most economically purchased as juveniles and you can start them on mealworms and other small insects, gradually increasing quantity and size of food matter as they grow. Frequent handling at this early stage helps to condition them against trying to bite. Horned frogs will eat anything small enough to swallow, including full-grown mice for some species, while smaller species will enjoy smaller mice, ranging from newborn to fuzzy to small "hopper"-sized rodents. They will also eat giant mealworms, zoophobias, beetles…just about anything that crawls near their cavernous mouth.

Although found in tropical forests, these frogs require little more than a simple substrate, such as paper toweling and daily spray misting or a small tray of water to soak in when the spirit so moves it. Depending on the size of the animal, an appropriate terrarium would be from 10-gallon to 20-gallon in size. These are a sedentary species that remain stock still most of the time, so large areas for exercise are not required in spite of their large size. Pebbles and other particulate (substrate) matter that is accidentally consumed with food can cause intestinal impaction, so must be avoided. Horned frogs prefer 75 to 85 degrees F temperatures, and humidity should be held to a moderate, but not excessively high, level. Good ventilation is required for these frogs.

Heavy cloth or leather work gloves should be employed to handle the animal unless it is sufficiently conditioned not to try and bite when approached.

Narrow-mouthed Toads

A number of these frogs, from the Microhylidae family, are available to hobbyists on a regular basis, although most are believed to be wild caught rather than captive bred. A few very popular members of this group, such as the Malagasy tomato frogs, are protected now, and those available are generally born in captivity unless illicitly smuggled. The brightest red of these frogs and most distinctively

Horned frogs will consume almost anything they can fit into their mouths (Cranwell's Horned Frog, *Ceratophrys cranwelli*, left; Argentinian Ornate Horned Frog, *Ceratophrys ornata*, right).

The nocturnal Sambava Tomato Frog must be fed in low light conditions (Sambava Tomato Frog, *Dyscophus guineti*).

marked is the Sambava Tomato Frog (*Dyscophus guineti*). Active at night, these frogs should be fed in low light conditions. Not realizing this, early hobbyists could not get them to eat anything in daylight and the frogs would die of starvation, earning a reputation as "difficult to feed." Nothing could be farther from the truth. They should be fed a variety of live insects including crickets, flies, giant mealworms and even newborn mice. They tolerate a wide range of temperatures, but most activity occurs in the 80 to 90 degree F range. As they reach 3 to 4 inches in size, and are moderately obese, each specimen should be given a tank of at least 10 gallons in size. Found in the tropical forests of Madagascar, moderate humidity is all they require. The frogs can be sustained in a bare-bones aquarium with white paper toweling substrate or in more elaborate surroundings. A pond of water large enough for partial immersion is recommended.

The Malaysian Narrow-Mouthed or Painted Toad (*Kaloula pulchra*) is an attractive and commonly available microhylid and is readily bred in captivity. Captive care and conditions suitable for this animal are similar to those for the tomato frogs.

Spadefoot Toads

Spadefoot toads, of the family Pelobatidae, get their name from the dark brown growths or protruberances on the inner side of their hind feet. These growths permit them to burrow well into the substrate to avoid dry, harsh conditions at the surface. Spadefoots are small and rather pretty yellow and brown frogs reaching maximum lengths of about 3 to 3.5 inches. Males can be recognized by a dark patch on their throats during the mating season.

Spadefoots eat any small insect including crickets, flies, mealworms and the like. They are noc-

turnal, and so should be fed under conditions of low light intensity. Their habitats are variable—spadefoots are found in meadows, well-planted fields and forests, on dusty, dry plains and occasionally in desert-like conditions. They require about 10 gallons of space for each animal with a soil substrate several inches deep and a small pool of water. Although sedentary, they are territorial and must be given space to avoid excessive stress.

In nature, spadefoots lay up to 2,000 eggs in temporary ponds, some of which may be no more than puddles. In temporary bodies of water, eggs hatch in a day or so and tadpoles can metamorphose in a scant two weeks. Spadefoots with access to permanent bodies of water tend to have both longer egg-hatching periods and longer tadpole stages.

Clawed Frogs and Surinam Toads

These strictly aquatic frogs of the Pipidae family are aquarium favorites. Note that because of a presumed environmental threat posed by released captives, they are banned from some localities, including the entire state of California, where some of these frogs have already established themselves in the wild. Although nothing earth-shattering has occurred thus far, California officials are

Spadefoots are territorial and although not particularly active, they need a good deal of space in order to feel comfortable (Couch's Spadefoot Toad, *Scaphiophis* couchii).

concerned that if the frogs have no natural enemies and otherwise prosper, they could crowd out native amphibians and fish. These primitive, aquatic frogs share several features with fish. They have lateral line organs and are bereft of a tongue.

There are several different types of African Clawed Frog, including a dwarf genus, *Hymenochirus*. A number of species that get much larger are members of the genus *Xenopus*. *Xenopus laevis*, the common African Clawed Frog, is readily available. Both the Dwarf and common African Clawed Frogs are exported in large numbers from Africa along with tropical fish shipments; they are also readily bred in captivity, especially for scientific research (as in the case of *Xenopus laevis*).

As expected, these frogs relish aquatic live food worms such as tubifex, blood worms, brine shrimp and daphnia. Some will eat tropical fish flakes that are set in motion by water currents created by aerators or filter returns. Larger clawed frogs can be fed earthworms, better-grade dry aquatic

turtle food, feeder guppies and platys (but goldfish should be avoided, as they may be somewhat toxic to these frogs).

The dwarf species and young of the larger forms can be kept in a community aquarium so long as the fish are too big to be of any interest to the frog as food, and the frog is not fodder for the fish.

Clawed frogs do well at water temperatures in the 70- to 80-degree F range. Three to five dwarf specimens can be kept in every 20 gallons of water. Larger clawed frogs of the genus *Xenopus* should be limited to one pair to each 20 gallons. Although they survive quite well under crowded conditions in laboratory tanks, such facilities become quickly fouled and need constant attention. You can eliminate more frequent water changes by keeping fewer frogs in larger quarters.

A powerful filtration system and an accessory airstone are essential

Because African Clawed Frogs get quite large, you should keep no more than two in a 20-gallon tank (African Clawed Frog, *Xenopus laevus*).

equipment. If your home is kept at temperatures below 70 degrees F in the winter, a heater may be required, although the frogs seem to tolerate lower temperatures without too much difficulty.

The clawed frogs have a complex mating ritual that is difficult to miss. They move in an arc formation as they pair off, and the male fertilizes the female's eggs as they are extruded while the female is actually upside down in the water. They may do this repeatedly until all the eggs are expelled. Stimulation of these frogs occurs when colder water is added to their aquarium, although the precise mechanism for this is not clear. Tadpoles are carnivorous and thrive on small aquatic invertebrates such as daphnia and zooplankton.

The other genus of this family available to hobbyists is the strictly aquatic South American Surinam Toad. This large, flat, strange-looking frog defies description. The first time people see them, they think they are a slab of floating vegetation or wood! If you like odd, even ugly-looking animals, this fellow is definitely for you. Follow the above advice on care and feeding the African Clawed Frogs if you obtain a South American Surinam Toad. If you breed these toads, be aware that the female of this species carries the fertilized eggs on her back until they hatch.

True Frogs

There are many familiar and easy-to-maintain frogs among the ranidae family for both beginning and intermediate frog-keepers. Ranids are found throughout the United States, Europe, Asia and Africa. Some of the foreign species are also available occasionally to U.S. hobbyists, but there are many to choose from right at home. Care for all is basically the same for these medium to large semi-aquatic species.

True frogs will eat anything that moves, including invertebrates such as insects and other small arthropods; larger species may eat newborn or juvenile mice, and a few of the very big ones, such as the American Bullfrog, can be fed half-grown mice and even baby chicks.

These frogs love to jump and move around, so put very few in as large an enclosure as you can pro- vide. The habitat of most ranids is semi-aquatic. At least one-half to two-thirds of the enclosure needs to contain well-filtered water. Some hobbyists fill an aquarium about one-third of the way with water and place built-up rock formations within it to provide the landside. Some small species, such as wood frogs, are more terrestrial than aquatic and need a terrarium setup with a small pond of water. Because there are so many ranids with differing habitat requirements, be sure you research the needs of whatever one you are going to get before you acquire it. The same is true of temperature preferences, which depend upon the origins of the ranid(s) you keep. You must, therefore, familiarize yourself with climate conditions around the world. In general, most North American or temperate-zone ranids are active at temperatures in the low to mid-70s F. However, some northern North

American Bullfrogs grow to a formidable size, so give them plenty of room (American Bullfrog, *Rana catesbeiana*).

American species are active in the 60-degree F range and can tolerate temperatures in the 50s at night, making them ideal species for households that are kept cooler in the winter (but still well above freezing levels). Tropical species will prefer temperatures up to 80 degrees.

Among the ranid species recommended for beginners are Leopard Frogs (*Rana pipiens*), Wood Frogs (*Rana sylvatica*), Bullfrogs (*Rana catesbeiana*) and Green Frogs (*Rana clamitans*). The latter group's call sounds like a banjo, which you may (or may not) find appealing. Pig Frogs (*Rana grylio*) are also available—and yes, they grunt sort of like pigs. All of these are North American species.

The African Bullfrog (*Pyxiecephalus adpersus*) is also popular in the United States and is being captive bred. This giant frog, whose scientific name begins with *Pyxie* and is often popularly called a Pyxie frog, is anything but that. It is one of the largest frogs in the world, reaching over 8 inches in length. The origin of this name is the Latin *pyxis*, which means "small box," and *cephalus*, meaning "head." (The scientist responsible for naming it felt it had a head like a small box.) It also has a cavernous mouth; in fact, its head is nothing but a giant mouth and it has several sharp teeth, so take care to avoid

The Pig Frog actually grunts like a pig (Pig Frog, *Rana grylio*).

getting snapped and don heavy gloves when handling until the frog becomes accustomed to it. Buying these frogs as babies, and handling them frequently while raising to large size, helps to assure that your Pyxie Frog won't accidentally bite you.

Because of their sedentary nature (they are sit-and-wait predators like horned frogs), Pyxies don't need a lot of room to move around. A 20-gallon tank is sufficient for a single animal. Never keep more than two together if they are different sizes, as Pyxies are cannibalistic. They can be kept in a terrestrial setup (damp soil or sphagnum moss, which should be changed every two days as it becomes fouled with excretions) with a 1.5-inch-deep water dish of sufficient area to

allow the frog to soak. The water dish also needs to be cleaned and refilled, on a daily or even twice-daily basis if it becomes fouled.

What About Salamanders?

Although frogs and toads are the best known and most popularly

SAFE FEEDING TIP

When feeding larger mice to frogs, make sure the mice are eaten right away or remove them from the tank. Frogs that are not hungry can, in turn, be attacked by the mice. Obviously, this is a situation that you want to avoid at all costs.

kept terrarium amphibians, hobbyists shouldn't overlook salamanders. There are many personable, colorful and interesting salamanders that deserve further study and attention from hobbyists and scientists alike. One of the best books for getting people interested in salamanders is *Of Salamanders and Scientists,* a volume by the late professor Victor Chandler Twitty. He makes a strong case for the charm and fascination of these often neglected members of the ecosystem. Long out of print, if you can ever find a copy of this book, grab it and read it in small installments, savoring the wealth of information it provides.

Salamanders are found in a variety of habitats: on land (terrestrial), in the water (aquatic) or in both environments. There is at least one genus that climbs into low-lying shrubbery and trees (tree salamanders), and many are fossorial or burrowers, staying hidden either beneath the substrate or under leaves and other detritus on the forest floor. Some are found in caves, leading a sightless existence, and others can be found in the Alps in colder-than-expected environs. Newts adapt from an aquatic existence to a terrestrial life seasonally. Others remain strictly aquatic, remaining gill and lung breathers for their entire existence. The majority of salamanders prefer conditions of little or no light

and spend the daylight hours hiding from the sun. Salamanders found abroad in the daytime are often located deep in heavily forested areas where the canopy lets little light reach the forest floor.

Salamanders eat living matter almost exclusively—small insects such as crickets, termites, beetles, mealworm larvae and the like. Some of the strictly aquatic forms such as the cryptobranchids may eat carrion or dead animal matter; amphiumas are cannibalistic, and sirens eat small invertebrates such as freshwater crayfish and shrimp, as well as algae and other plant matter that is set in motion by water currents.

Mole Salamanders

The mole salamanders of the family Ambystomatidae are largely terrestrial salamanders (as their common name implies). They do, however, enter the water to soak as well as to mate, breed and deposit their eggs. Some forms remain in their larval state (which means they are strictly aquatic) for their entire lives. Notable among these is the Mexican species *Ambystoma mexicanum,* known in Aztec as the "Axolotl."

Axolotls are small, reclusive aquatic life forms that can be kept singly or in pairs in a 5- or 10-gallon tank that is filtered and lightly aerated. Some fanciers keep a solitary

specimen in a brandy snifter or globe-like goldfish bowl and clean it through partial water changes on a regular basis. Axolotls are tolerant of a wide variation in water and temperature conditions, and this makes them a favorite research animal. Several university-based Axolotl colonies in the United States and overseas provide large numbers of these animals for important scientific research. Surplus animals often find their way into the aquarium trade through dealers and pet shops, and this is where they (occasionally) may be found. If kept in an aquarium with other fish, it is important that no nippers be present among them, as these salamanders sport feathery, colorful, external gills that may appear as worms to be eaten by tropical fish.

All other ambystomids, including the land or adult form of the Axolotl if it can be induced to transform, are terrestrial animals that need a woodland habitat with a small dish of water. As many salamanders are cannibalistic, they should be segregated as to size. With some species, unless you are mating them, it is advisable to keep but a single specimen per small enclosure, as they can be fiercely territorial. Large Tiger Salamanders (*A. tigrinum*), Spotted Salamanders (*A. maculatum*) and Marbled Salamanders (*A. opacum*) are among the most commonly kept

It's easy to see how the tiger salamander got its name (Tiger Salamander, *Ambystoma tigrinum*).

and hardy varieties for the novice salamander-keeper. They need a terrestrial habitat and a small dish of water, and should be fed live food daily until they are full. They prefer cool, temperate-zone temperature levels, ranging from 60 degrees F to no warmer than 75 degrees F, with moderate to little environmental humidity.

Salamanders such as these are relatively sedentary and therefore don't need much space. They grow from between 3.5 to 5 inches, including the tail. A 10-gallon aquarium for one or a pair of such specimens is required. Terrestrial substrate can be nothing more than several folds of paper toweling, sterile potting soil or sphagnum moss, which must be removed and replaced two to three times a week to prevent decomposition. It can

be lightly misted once a day to provide a moderate amount of humidity. The mole salamanders should be given a dish of water in which they can, at least partially, immerse themselves. They will also drink from the dish. Accordingly, the water dish should be removed, rinsed and refilled on a daily basis, or more frequently if fouled by excreta.

Amphiumas

Species of the Amphumidae family are large (up to 40 inches in length by some accounts), eel-like, strictly aquatic salamanders that are best kept in a large, heavily planted, well-filtered aquarium with a pebble substrate and an undergravel filter. Make sure that the plants are well anchored so as to withstand being knocked about by these salamanders. To maintain high-quality water, about one-third of the water should be changed weekly, and a complete water change should be performed once a month. Water temperatures should be in the high 60s to low 70s. Auxiliary heating is rarely needed, but a tight-fitting screen cover is a must, as these salamanders can wriggle up over the sides and if they escape into the dry world, they will die if not found within a few hours and returned to their water.

Marbled Salamanders are hardy and make a good pet for the novice hobbyist (Marbled Salamander, *Ambystoma opacum*).

Amphiumas are strictly aquatic animals needing a well-filtered aquarium (Two-Toed Congo Eel, *Amphiuma means*).

Amphiumas eat small fish, fish foods that move in the currents of the aquarium's filtration or aeration system, tiny snails and other invertebrates they ingest by means of suction feeding, lowering the pressure in their oral cavities and sucking in the food matter. One can also try feeding live fish foods such as tubifex, blood and white worms, daphnia and brine shrimp.

Amphiumas should be handled with large nets, as they are impossible to grab with the hands. They have no gills and breathe by means of lungs at the surface. These species are not particularly colorful; they are generally a dark brown or charcoal gray.

Hellbenders

Hellbenders fall within the Cryptobranchidae family. Two of the three strictly aquatic species are protected by international treaty: the Chinese and Japanese Giant Salamanders. They are so large (5 feet or so) that one would need

hundreds of gallons of aquarium water to house just one specimen satisfactorily. Their American cousins, the Hellbenders, are also protected by state law in some areas, but specimens from unprotected resources and captive-breeding operations occasionally are available.

These too are large animals and are best housed alone. Although they are not as large as their Asian counterparts, you will need a 50-gallon aquarium to keep one or two of these animals. They need a tight-fitting, heavily weighted screen cover and plenty of vegetation to make them feel at home. Rock formations at the bottom to emulate large caverns or caves provide shelter for these salamanders in the daytime. They also require a powerful filtration system and regular water changes. They are not enormously popular with hobbyists, as they are drab and fairly grotesque in appearance, but some people find them interesting. They reach about 26 inches in length.

Hellbenders have no gills, but they do have open gill slits that

Extremely large (and rather unsightly), the Giant Chinese Salamander is protected by treaty—don't expect to find one to keep as a pet (Giant Chinese Salamander, *Andrias davidianus*).

may be lost or reduced on one side. They inhabit large, fast-moving streams and rivers in the northern and eastern parts of the United States, and so prefer water temperatures in the mid-50 to mid-60-degree F range.

Hellbenders are nondiscriminatory feeders, eating all manner of fish as well as a variety of invertebrates including snails, crayfish, freshwater crabs, aquatic worms and the like. They can be induced to eat dead food as well, including highly aromatic fish flakes or sticks that float on the surface and are swirled around by water currents. They are best bred in large outdoor ponds or troughs, as they lay some 400 or so eggs, which will hatch in about three months. The larvae take about 18 months to lose their gills and begin breathing air via their lungs, although they remain aquatic all their lives and never venture onto land.

Lungless Salamanders

Lungless salamanders of the Plethodontidae family are slim, semi-aquatic temperate forms that range from the United States into the northern half of South America. They prefer cooler temperatures, and their small size often makes them problematic feeders unless you can assure a steady supply of small wingless fruit flies or very small crickets. They can be kept in a woodland habitat with a small pond of water that should be kept very clean at all times. Lungless salamanders reach maximum lengths of 2 to 6 inches (including the tail), and several can be kept in a well-planted 20-gallon aquarium with plenty of places to hide or burrow.

These salamanders are fond of hiding under logs of rotting wood, rocks and leaf litter loosely scattered on the forest floor. They require damp but not overly humid conditions. Lungless salamanders must never be allowed to dry out, as they rely on their moistened skin to breathe. A few completely aquatic forms such as the Georgia Blind Salamander (*Haideotritoin wallacei*) retain their external gills as a consequence of their lungless but completely aquatic condition. This particular species was originally discovered from a 200-foot well in Albany, Georgia, and was first described in 1939. Other species of blind salamander have been discovered in deep wells and in underground rivers running through caverns.

Breeding patterns vary by species, but lungless salamanders generally deposit small numbers of eggs (15 to 30, some far fewer) in damp situations on land or in the water. In a number of species, the female may remain coiled around her eggs to protect them. In fact, the breeding habits of many species have yet to be described, so the study of these salamanders remains a fruitful area for meaningful scientific contribution.

The Olm and Mudpuppies (or Water Dogs)

The Olm is the only species of the Proteidae family found in Europe. Known also as the Blind Cave Salamander (*Proteus anguinis*), the Olm is found only in the Dinaric karst region from northeastern Italy through Slovenia to the River Trebisnjica in Herzegovina. Olms are strictly and permanently aquatic

Lungless salamanders rely on their moistened skin to breathe and thus must never be far from water (lungless salamander, *Plethodon jordani*).

salamanders, reaching lengths of about 8 to 10 inches. They are never seen in the pet trade in the United States and little is known about them, although there have been some successful attempts at captive breeding in Europe (where one may encounter such animals for sale). Olms require a well-covered and well-filtered 20-gallon aquarium with low light conditions. They prefer cool temperatures (from 50 to 70 degrees F). Olms will feed on small aquatic invertebrates such as baby snails and crustacea and have been noted to forage among detritus, undoubtedly for microscopic animals or zooplankton.

Captive animals have laid up to 70 eggs, attached to the underside of rock formations. The eggs hatch in two months. During this time, the female remains near her clutch. Little else is known about their habits or behavior in the wild, and both captive and natural studies are needed.

On the other hand, the familiar American Mudpuppies or Waterdogs (*Necturus sp.*) are known to generations of biology students, as they are a species that is frequently the subject of study and dissection in comparative vertebrate anatomy courses. They are both collected and raised in great numbers for scientific use and can be obtained from specialist dealers; however, they are not especially popular in the pet trade.

American Mudpuppies are permanently aquatic larvae with three pairs of bushy, red gills, but they also breathe by means of lungs. They range in size from 7 to 17 inches and require large, well-filtered and well-aerated aquariums with tight-fitting screen covers or hoods. They require temperatures in the 65-to-75-degree F range. Captives are apt to eat any kind of animate animal prey they are able to subdue and ingest, including fish, as well as a variety of aquatic invertebrates. Mudpuppies can also be induced to eat some types of tropical fish food that is perceived as animate as it is moved around by currents or falls through the water.

American Mudpuppies engage in amplexus and internal fertilization, after which the female places her eggs in a "nest" and guards them until the larvae hatch in about two months' time. (Hatching can occur earlier in warmer waters.) The larvae reach sexual maturity at about 8 inches in length and 8 years of age. Although there are a number of species, the best studied is *Necturus maculosus,* which is also the most widespread geographically.

Newts and Fire Salamanders

Newts, members of the Family Salamandridae, are the most likely salamanders to be found in pet shops. These colorful, popular salamanders are widely available and have been bred on fish farms and in indoor facilities for the hobbyist. They are locally very abundant in some areas and collecting for this trade, while threatening, does not at this time seem to have caused any overall decline in populations of the more common forms of this salamander.

Newts are found on both coasts of the United States. Rough-skinned newts of the genus *Taricha* are found on the Pacific coasts and Red-Spotted Newts (*Notophthalmus sp.*) inhabit the east. Both secrete small quantities of poisonous toxins, so care should be exercised in handling either of these species. Newts and other members of this family are the most diverse and commonly encountered species of salamander in Europe as well.

A number of domestic and foreign newts show up regularly in the pet trade. Included among these are members of the genus *Triturus* (Alpine and Crested Newts), *Taricha* (U.S. Rough-Skinned Newts), *Cynops* (Japanese Fire-Bellied Newts) and *Tylotriton* (Chinese Crocodile or Emperor Newts), as well as our common eastern U.S. Red-Spotted Newts of the genus *Notophthalmus.* The European Fire Salamander (*Salamandra salamandra)* is also a colorful (bright yellow or orange-and-black) member of this family that is a popular terrarium animal both in Europe and North America.

Amphibian fans at home and abroad are especially fond of the European Fire Salamander (European Fire Salamander, *Salamandra salamandra*).

newts move, on a seasonal basis, from a semi-aquatic or terrestrial existence to an aquatic one and then back again. Such newts need to be provided with a true aqua-terrarium. A deep-water (6 inches or more), well-filtered aquarium furnished with rock formations that jut above the surface is ideal for these species. No more than two newts should be housed in a 10-gallon tank.

Salamandrids eat the same sort of foods as most amphibians: small invertebrates, including insects and other arthropods that they are capable of swallowing.

Nearly all newts require a semi-aquatic existence, but terrestrial forms such as *Salamandra* require a predominantly terrestrial environment with a water dish sufficient to accommodate it. The Fire Salamander is a large, heavy-bodied species, with some forms attaining nearly 10 inches in length. There are fourteen subspecies according to some experts, encompassing a wide range throughout Europe, Asia Minor and parts of the Middle East and coastal North Africa. The Fire Salamander prefers shade, dampness or moisture, and places to hide such as caves and log or rock formations. Their water dish should be drained, rinsed and refilled with fresh water daily. A substrate of sphagnum moss over smooth water-worn pebbles or sterile potting soil

is acceptable. Sphagnum moss, if used, should be discarded several times a week to prevent buildup of salamandrine, a toxin secreted by these salamanders. Due to their toxic secretions, they should not be handled with bare hands, especially if the handler's skin is broken in any way. Use clean, unpowdered medical gloves or a net to move them around. The pores through which this toxin is secreted are quite large and are visible to the naked eye. For defensive purposes and under conditions of stress, these salamanders can actually squirt their toxins for short distances by contracting some of the muscle tissue surrounding the glands.

All members of this family prefer cooler temperatures, ranging from 60 to 70 degrees F. Some

Sirens

The sirens are a fully aquatic North American group of salamanders that are also eel-like in general appearance. They are members of the Sirenidae family, in which there are two genera—the Dwarf Sirens (*Pseudobranchus sp.*) and the common Sirens (*Siren sp.*). The Dwarf Sirens range from 5 to 8 inches in length, whereas some species of the common sirens, such as *Siren lacertina,* can grow to 3 feet in length. An aquatic salamander of such great size requires a 55-gallon aquarium fitted with a tight, heavily weighted screen cover. The tank should be well filtered and well aerated and special handling equipment may be necessary, because these animals are impossible to grasp and can inflict a painful bite if they are so inclined. For this reason, they are not recommended for the beginning, or even somewhat advanced, hobbyist, and may be more problematic in their larger forms than they are worth. They are drab in color and have no particularly striking features. Unless you fancy large snake-shaped, underwater eely creatures, they are best avoided.

Sirens eat all manner of aquatic live foods including the full complement of live tropical fish worms and small invertebrates, small snails, feeder platys and guppies, as well as some prepared foods. While they may uproot plants, aquarium-safe rock formations can be constructed along the bottom to provide hiding places for them. A substrate of water-worn pebbles over an undergravel filtration system, in addition to an outside power filter, is highly recommended. Sirens are active at and prefer water temperatures ranging from 60 to 70 degrees F over most of their range.

It is difficult to breed sirens, and breeding is not recommended to any but the most experienced herpers.

Are Cecillians Ever Kept by Hobbyists?

Actually, hobbyists do keep cecillians, but they are among the least known and most misunderstood of all the amphibians. They are not especially popular, because you don't see them most of the time. They even feed underground. Aquatic forms like to stay buried in the mud of their aquatic habitats, a difficult substrate to provide in an aquarium tank, although rock formations on a smooth pebble bottom can serve as a substitute.

However, cecillians can be exceptionally easy to care for. The terrestrial forms can be housed singly or in pairs in a wide-mouthed 1-gallon glass container such as can be obtained from a

laboratory supply house. It should be covered with netting, a screen or a lid with air holes punched in the top. A sterile soil substrate, some moss and a daily vial full of ants, termites, mealworms, slugs or small land snails serve as food that they will find underground. Most cecillians are from the tropics, and so the room temperature should be kept at around 70 to 75 degrees F. If you keep your home cooler than 70 degrees F, a small, thermostatically controlled heat pad such as those manufactured especially for reptiles and amphibians may be employed to keep substrate temperature at the recommended level. The soil should be misted once or twice a day, as cecillians like damp but not overly wet conditions.

If you have your heart set on a cecillian, you should know that they are rarely offered in the pet trade and are not bred in captivity at all. Most of the specimens in captivity are part of zoo-, museum- or university-based research projects, and the scientists involved often had to arrange collection of their specimens themselves. Occasionally a specialty dealer may have some of the more common cecillians on their price lists, so you need to monitor such dealers carefully as well as make them aware of your wish to obtain a cecillian (or two or three) should they ever come in.

Members of the eel-like Siren family tend to bite and are recommended for only the most accomplished hobbyist (Lesser Siren, *Siren intermedia*).

CHAPTER 6

Housing

Housing or caging for amphibians can take a number of different forms depending on several factors. Naturally, the most important consideration is the species being housed. You should not keep a tree frog in a terrestrial, toad environment without

If you have the space, a large walk-in cage can be quite attractive. Here, a White's Tree Frog shares a home with several lizards.

sort, especially during breeding season. Clearly, then, the best overall enclosure option is the all-glass, silicone-bonded aquarium tank; the second best option is a similar enclosure made of molded clear acrylic. Both types are readily available in any pet shop. Special sizes in all-glass aquariums can be built to order as well.

Security

All tanks housing amphibians need to be secured against escape. An amphibian that escapes its enclosure and is not retrieved quickly is apt to die in the unfamiliar habitat of a human house, devoid of moisture and adequate food supplies and perhaps even laced with insecticides and other dangers. Some amphibians are also apt to become injured during a sojourn through an environment designed purely for human habitation. Other pets,

such as cats and dogs, espying a frog or salamander along the floor are usually more than inclined to play with it, pick it up in the mouth and quite possibly eat it. This is *not* good for either the amphibian or the larger pet, who could easily die from the toxic secretions liberated by some amphibians.

For aquariums, the most secure arrangement is a screen cover that locks down or can be weighted by a lighting fixture. I use 2-pound dumbbell weights on each of the four corners of the screen cover when keeping particularly strong jumpers such as bullfrogs or sneaky tree frog species that crawl up the corners to the top and then try and work their way out by pushing up on the corners of the lid. If the walls of the enclosure are high enough (a minimum of 8 to 10 inches), some sedentary ground-living frogs and salamanders may

branches to perch upon; nor should you keep a strictly aquatic species in a dry, rocky habitat!

You should also decide whether you want the setup for your amphibian to be decorative or bare bones. Breeders don't bother with a lot of cage furniture or fancy substrates. They are not interested in aesthetics, so they often make their caging options as sparse and as easy to care for as possible. Because they may be housing large numbers of animals, their caging options are often restricted in terms of size as well.

Although a few amphibians do best in well-ventilated, low-humidity environments and use soaking dishes to obtain needed water via cutaneous absorption, almost all others require humidity of some

KNOW THE HABITAT OF THE SPECIES YOU PURCHASE

Always research the habitat needs of your intended amphibian purchase. Most, if not all, amphibians fall into a set number of categories: strictly aquatic, semi-aquatic, terrestrial, dry plains or desert, montane (mountain), arboreal (tree-dwelling) or fossorial (burrowing and cave-dwelling species). And some species, regardless of their natural habitat, do well in relatively sterile-looking environments, with paper toweling as substrate and plain water-dish containers. Thus, if you are going to buy a Siberian Salamander that prefers temperatures between 32 and 45 degrees F, think again—unless you are ready to set up a refrigerated exhibit for it! (That is if you can find a Siberian Salamander.)

be kept with no lid—but a lid is still a good idea to keep other pets and small children out.

Purpose-built small plastic boxes with locking screen hoods are also available, but only in a limited number of sizes ranging from very small to no more than 10 by 20 inches in area and only about 6 inches high. Breeders and wholesale dealers also use a variety of Rubbermaid™ boxes and clear plastic shoe/sweater boxes that come with lids. Air holes need to be carefully drilled into these containers, originally designed for purposes other than housing amphibians. Such bare-bones environments are temporary in nature and are used for utilitarian rather than aesthetic purposes. Note, however, that you might find such a container useful for temporary housing while you clean your amphibian's tank.

Sharing a Human Home with Amphibians

Thanks to a burgeoning industry with many specialty items designed for keeping and maintaining reptiles and amphibians, it is reasonable to believe that it is very possible to actually share your home with amphibians. My first Florida home boasted a screened-over atrium with a pond and a stand of tropical vegetation right in the middle of the house. It wasn't long before this unique feature was put to good use housing a variety of native amphibians, now close at hand for observation and study. But you don't need a tropical atrium in southern Florida to provide a nice home for amphibians.

Aquatic Environments

Strictly aquatic environments for amphibians are essentially identical to tropical fish aquariums. Frog tadpoles, salamander larvae, aquatic- phase newts and a variety of strictly aquatic salamanders—Sirens, Amphiumas, Mudpuppies, Hellbenders, Blind Cave Salamanders, Axolotls and other neotenous or nonmetamorphosing salamander larvae—all require such an environment.

A few types of adult frogs, including the African Clawed Frogs and Surinam Toads (family Pipidae), are also completely aquatic and are totally unable to navigate on land in any kind of effective or efficient manner. These frogs are designed purely for swimming.

The aquatic cecillians are also strictly aquatic, but the likelihood of them ever becoming popular (or even widely available) to the hobbyist or pet trade is debatable. However, they are sometimes imported in shipments of tropical fish where they are called freshwater eels or mini-eels. If you are

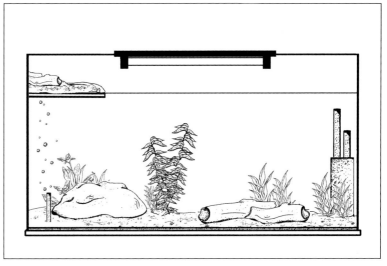

An aquarium similar to one for tropical fish is appropriate for tadpoles, as well as for fully aquatic species such as African Clawed Frogs and Hellbenders.

interested in them, you should inquire every so often at your local tropical fish store. To identify a cecillian, look for the presence of segments or rings, which true eels don't have.

Substrate

If a substrate is used, always use smooth small pebbles (also known as "water-worn" pebbles) as opposed to jagged, angular or sharp gravel. Some burrowing cecillians would appreciate fine sand, in lieu of mud, in which to burrow. (For terrestrial species for which you wish to include planted live vegetation, use only sterile potting soil.) Another substrate is dried sphagnum moss, available in pet shops. This should be discarded and replaced every few days, as it becomes fouled with excreta and becomes unhygienic in the process.

Water Quality

Although many species live in murky, sometimes even polluted waters, this is not the ideal situation. Home aquariums for aquatic amphibians should be filled with crystal-clear water that is filtered by at least two filter systems: an undergravel filter and either an outside power filter or a high-efficiency inside filter. Some use a combination of all three: inside or submersible, outside and undergravel.

Aeration is of prime concern. It not only prevents stagnation and pollution, it increases oxygen content of the water by lowering the surface tension and enables oxygen from the atmosphere to more effectively dissolve into solution. Aeration can be provided by a small air pump connected to an airstone or "Bubble-Wand"™. Cooler water holds more oxygen than warmer water. Strictly aquatic amphibians, for this reason, do well at temperatures slightly below those of most commonly kept tropical fish. Water temperatures between 60 and 70 degrees F are recommended. Air conditoning or an expensive water-chilling device may be required in non–air-conditioned homes during particularly hot weather or in homes that are kept particularly warm during the colder times of the year.

pH

The pH measurement is really a mathematically derived index of the acidity or alkalinity of a solution. Pure, distilled water or rainwater has a pH of 7.0, which is neutral. Any pH level below 7.0 indicates an acidic condition; above 7.0 indicates an alkaline condition. Most tap water in North America is adjusted to a pH of 7.0, but if you use well water or have any doubts, be sure and verify the water's pH before using to fill your aquarium.

As an alternative, you can buy purified, sterile spring water in multi-gallon containers at your food store. As an added bonus, spring waters have minerals that may benefit your amphibians nutritionally.

Most amphibians are apt to find a neutral (7.0) or slightly acidic (6.0 to 7.0) pH preferable to a highly alkaline environment. pH can be measured with simple test kits available in pet supply shops. Pet shops also sell chemical additives that can be used to chemically raise or lower the pH of your amphibian aquarium should a test result require it. After adjusting the pH with one of these additives, it is necessary to recheck your results to make sure you are on the mark. It is also important to raise and lower pH levels slowly rather than rapidly to avoid shock in your animals, so a series of additions/dilutions and testings may be required to achieve the best results. Bear in mind that excreta and urine will acidify the water. In short, keeping strictly aquatic amphibians can be as demanding and time-consuming as maintaining a tank full of delicate tropical fish, but millions of fish hobbyists do this every day—indeed, many fish-keepers have made the transition to amphibians, realizing that the equipment, knowledge and amount of work required is about the same.

Water Hardness

Water hardness, or the amount of dissolved minerals in water, is another water-quality concern. The only way to completely remove unwanted dissolved minerals is by distillation. On the other hand, chlorine in your tap water readily dissipates when left to stand for a day or two prior to using. You can hasten the process of getting the chlorine out of your tap water by either aerating it or using chemical additives sold in aquarium supply/pet shops. Note that if you use chlorinated water in a soaking dish for hardier species kept in terrestrial environments, the chlorine is of little consequence and may actually help kill germs that might lurk there. Some researchers have also allowed aquatic species with bacterial skin diseases to swim in chlorinated water as a temporary therapeutic option and have had good results in combatting infections.

Arboreal Habitats

Arboreal environments are obviously for climbing species, such as tree frogs and flying frogs. In addition to providing a sufficient base, these tanks need to be as high as possible. An arboreal habitat requires well-anchored branches or perches that are sturdy enough to support the weight of the tank's occupants. Although a few tree frogs exist on ground level, most require an arboreal habitat to be completely at home. Pet shops sell a variety of driftwood pieces and

Make your tree frogs feel at home by providing sturdy branches for climbing (Pine Barrens Tree Frog, *Hyla andersoni*).

artificial limbs and branches. You can also use wooden perches designed for bird cages or go out and collect your own branches, fashioning them to fit in your terrarium. Be sure that wood collected in the field is free of unwanted pests such as aphids, ants, termites and the like—although it is likely that if they are present, your frog will make quick work of them.

Fossorial Habitats

Fossorial means "from beneath the surface," and the term *fossil* is derived therefrom. In this case, it describes living species that like to burrow beneath the surface and some that actually spend most of their lives as "fossils" of a sort.

Obviously, you will need to provide such life forms with a substrate they can dig into and live in. This might include sterile potting soil or mixtures of sand and soil. Some fossorial species may be content to crawl under crumpled-up paper toweling. Clearly this is most hygienic because if it gets soiled, all you need to do is discard and replace. It is not visually aesthetic, however.

Semi-aquatic Environments

A semi-aquatic aquarium is roughly half land or dry area and half filtered water, sufficient in depth for your amphibians to completely submerge, breed or swim in. Such tanks need to be larger than you might expect. Perhaps a single pair of moderate-sized specimens (3 to 5 inches in length) could be comfortably housed in a 30-gallon-long tank with about 16 inches of landside and 20 inches of water to a depth of 4 or 5 inches. Such setups are constructed either by dividing the tank with the right-sized piece of plexiglass or plate glass, or by using styrofoam inserts.

As an alternative, you can create a land mass in a partially water-filled aquarium by including carefully landscaped rock formations that jut above the surface. The rocks provide beachheads for amphibians

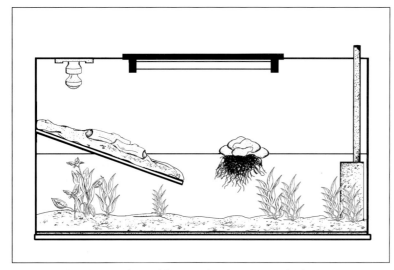

A semi-aquatic environment for amphibians needing some access to land.

Accessorizing

There are a number of commercially available accessories that can help you achieve your amphibian husbandry goals.

Floating Islands

Floating islands are made for semi-aquatic environments where the animals spend most of the time in the water but need to haul out occasionally. The same type of arrangement can be built using shale and other types of aquarium-safe rock you can either collect yourself or buy by the pound in a pet shop. In some areas, such as southern Florida, all such rock must be bought commercially, because the only rock that occurs naturally is calcareous stone, which would alkalinize the water.

to haul out on. Potted plants can even be situated between the rocks for a naturalistic appearance.

A third means of creating land is the use of pre-cut styrofoam or foam rubber forms, safety-dyed to resemble embankments. Styrofoam floats can be used as floating islands or can be cemented to the walls of the aquarium at water surface levels.

Terrestrial Setups

Terrestrial amphibians can be housed in a conventional, all-land-based terrarium that contains a small dish of water to serve as a pond for occasional soaking. The "pond" will also serve as a source of humidity. Such terrariums should include a base layer of pebbles, over which sterile sandy soil, potting

soil or loam, can be laid. It can be decorated with rocks, caves, pieces of rotted wood and green plants, either alive or artificial, to create a naturalistic appearance.

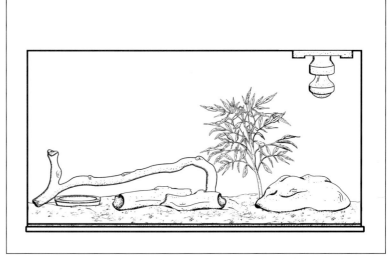

Mostly terrestrial frogs and salamanders will need a clean setup with just a small "pond" to soak in.

Branches

A wide variety of driftwood branches, artificial branches and logs, as well as a plastic corner hammock that can be hung off the top of your enclosure, are useful accessories for arboreal tree frogs. You can either purchase or build such items yourself.

Waterfalls

Several companies make "power" waterfalls that recirculate water from a pond-like storage container. A waterfall is often aesthetically preferable to a simple dish of water for mainly terrestrial frogs that need to douse themselves or soak on occasion. Of course, a waterfall is a bit problematic to tear down and clean, but it can be done. You may also want to consider buying a rock pool, a dish that is more attractive than a simple plastic food dish (which also works) to serve as your "pond."

Rainmaking

Yes, there is such a thing as rain-making equipment! (See Chapter 15). A rainmaker will periodically liberate a fine spray of water over the habitat. This is useful in not only providing much-needed humidity for some species, but in inducing or stimulating others to mate and breed. Alternatively, if you have the time, you can use a clean, never-used plant sprayer filled with distilled water and spray the habitat manually several times a day.

Fogging Equipment

Using miniaturized ultrasonic aerosol technology borrowed from the medical industry, at least one company makes a device that produces an exceptionally fine mist that looks like fog over the habitat. This is an awesome effect, and if you see it you're going to want it. Again, this is valuable to tropical rain-forest species that need liberal amounts of humidity. And it is visually stunning. Note, however, that the transducers of some of these devices become hot and have injured small frogs, so you should consider this possiblility before buying.

Humidity can also be maintained by using a screen cover in conjunction with a section of plate glass. By placing the plate glass over a *part* of the screen cover, you can maintain some humidity but be sure not to cover the entire top of the tank. A top that is totally covered will turn your habitat into a hothouse and you risk killing your amphibians. All terrestrial and semi-aquatic amphibians need the right amount—not too little and certainly not too much—of humidity. At the same time, they need good ventilation to prevent air stagnation and heat buildup. By judiciously using the glass in conjunction with the screen and by experimenting a bit, you can achieve the right mix. You can use an inside thermometer to make sure temperatures do not rise too high. If water begins to accumulate on the sides of the tank and you have difficulty seeing inside, the environment is too humid and it's time to allow the tank to air out— simply replace a solid glass or plex-iglass cover with a screen.

Live Plants

One must be cautious about the introduction of live plants into an environment for delicate-skinned amphibians, because they can absorb toxins so readily through their skin. Store- or nursery-bought plants need to be rinsed thoroughly to remove pesticides or chemical fertilizers that may be present, and some plants themselves may exude toxic substances.

For most smaller rain-forest frogs such as dendrobatids, mantel-lids and the like, a number of plants are safe. These include pothos, African violets and a variety of ferns. Air plants or bromeli-ads are popular additions to dendrobatid and tree frog terrariums, and in fact, some species of dendrobatid lay their eggs in water trapped in such plants, making them a useful as well as aesthetic choice if you are considering breeding such species. Plants also help to maintain humidity levels and keep the terrarium air fresh.

Decorating the enclosures of larger species might best be accomplished with sturdy artificial plants and strong pieces of driftwood, often anchored to pieces of slate.

Temperature Control Equipment

There are two aspects to controlling temperature: heating and cooling. Cooling off an environment can be infinitely more difficult than warming it up. For warming, use under-tank heat pads that are thermostatically controlled, perhaps in conjunction with an incandescent fixture. You can purchase bulbs that provide heat and light or only heat.

Hot rocks and heated caves and branches are potentially dangerous. I have tried a number of these devices and in spite of assurances otherwise, they caused hot spots that overheated, shocked and even burned some animals. Fellow hobbyists have reported similar incidents with this equipment—it

SAFE PLANTS FOR YOUR AMPHIBIAN'S HOME

Abelia	Bridal Veil	Hibiscus	Petunia
African Violet	Bougainvillea	Iceplant	Spineless Cacti
Areca Palm	Bromeliads	Impatiens	Swedish Ivy
Asparagus Fern	Camellia	Jasmine	Sweet Alyssum
Aster	Coleus	Lavender	Wandering Jew
Baby Tears	Dracaena	Marigold	
Bird's Nest Fern	Grass	Palms	

should not be considered an option for any kind of amphibian heating.

If your environment is too warm, either due to improper or malfunctioning thermostats or excessive environmental temperature, it should be moved to an air-conditioned location or placed in a cool, well-shaded corner. You might even consider setting up a household fan to cool it off or partly opening a window in cooler weather to achieve the same thing.

Overheating amphibians can cause their death. Making them too cold can kill them if they have no means to successfully hibernate. All amphibians have a range in which they function best, and this is known as their critical temperature. You can learn what your amphibian's critical temperature range is by knowing where it is found in nature and becoming familiar with temperature ranges in such geographic locations during times of the year when amphibians are most likely to breed or otherwise be active. If you are keeping an amphibian native to your area, this evaluation is relatively simple; but if you're keeping a species from a far-off place, some research is in order. And so, keeping amphibians is not only fun, it's educational too.

CHAPTER 7

Handling

Just like tropical fish, amphibians are primarily for display, study and exhibit purposes—they should not be handled any more than is absolutely necessary. Unless one is examining them for a scientific purpose, little or nothing is gained by excessive handling of amphibians and, in fact, it can be harmful to them. In addition, many species of amphibians exude or secrete toxic substances from glands in their skin. These substances can be dangerous to humans if ingested or if they find their way into the bloodstream through a cut or sore.

Small children, especially, should be taught to look but not touch—to observe and study amphibians, but to resist the temptation to play with or handle them. After all, they are not toys.

Obviously, the less slippery amphibians, such as some of the tree frogs, are the easiest to handle. White's Tree Frogs are likely to sit still in your hand—but you never know when your frog will decide to jump off! (adult and juvenile White's Tree Frogs, *Litoria caerulea*).

Handling at Home

Handling should be reserved for unavoidable situations like the need to retrieve an escapee, for close examination, for photographing or to remove a sick or dead specimen. To remove a sick or dead animal from the enclosure, a net should be used, and the net should be disinfected afterward in a net dip solution sold in pet shops. This should be followed by rinsing the net vigorously in scalding water and allowing it to dry naturally before using it again. Nets are inexpensive, and separate nets should be obtained if you have more than one tank full of amphibians. Do not use the net for one tank on specimens in another, or you risk moving infectious organisms from one part of your collection to another. Nylon nets, of varying sizes used either singly or in pairs

(to prevent an animal from jumping or crawling out while transferring), are the simplest and best handling tools you can acquire.

Bare-handed Handling

A few amphibians can be readily handled with the bare hands, such as dry-skinned and relatively less slippery types, including bufonid toads, some kinds of tree frogs and ranids. But some types are completely impossible to handle bare-handed, such as Sirens, Amphiumas and other slippery, eel-like aquatic amphibians. You have to learn how to net them or trap them in a portable container in order to move them or examine them closely.

Before you handle any amphibian, make sure your hands are

absolutely free of any soaps, detergents, disinfectants or chemicals. This means washing them and then rinsing them for several minutes until they are absolutely clean and free of any soap residue. Keep in mind that excessive handling of amphibians that have a slippery mucous coat disrupts that protective coating, and you need to keep such handling to a minimum. If you grab a frog, toad or salamander too tightly you are apt to cause it internal injury. It is important to be firm yet gentle. The best and safest place to handle a frog is from around its waist, pinning its legs together between the palm of your hands. This effectively immobilizes the frog without injuring it, provided you don't squeeze too hard. Smaller

Pick a frog up from around the waist (African Bullfrog, *Pyxiecephalus adsperus*).

species of frogs and toads, juveniles and salamanders can be cupped in the hands when being caught and then rapidly transferred to a transport or their regular housing.

Handling for Tank Cleaning

If you are tearing down and cleaning an aquatic, semi-aquatic or terrestrial enclosure, it may be necessary to temporarily move your animals to short-term housing and then back again. A clean, clear plastic shoe box or plastic food storage container suffices for this purpose. Afterward, be sure and wash it thoroughly with just hot water (no soap or disinfectant) if you intend to use it again for this purpose. Obviously, you should not use the container for your leftover lasagna. Wipe dry with a clean paper towel.

Handling Tiny Frogs

Extremely tiny, active frogs pose special handling challenges. Any

attempt to grab and restrain them is apt to result in injury, and netting them can be a problem, as they can easily escape from nets unless very expertly manipulated.

I have developed a special set of tools to handle, examine and move such frogs. It includes a 6-inch length of clear (1-inch diameter) plastic tubing with corks or caps fitted on both ends and a chopstick. One end of the tube is capped, and the open end is inserted into the frog tank near or on top

of the frog. Using a wooden or plastic chopstick or similar blunt-ended instrument, you can give the frog a gentle prod or poke in the behind up into the tube. As soon as it enters it will move forward (frogs don't walk backwards as a rule, especially when being prodded). As soon as it is well inside, cap the bottom or entranceway. Now you can examine the frog at closer range or move it, store it there temporarily while cleaning its enclosure or transfer it elsewhere. When you are ready to release it, uncap the top, then the bottom, and using the aforementioned prod, poke it so that it exits the other end. This technique is particularly useful for dart poison frogs, mantellas, peepers, rocket frogs and other tiny, nervous and highly active species. Similar tubes, even toilet paper rolls, can be used to transfer baby crickets from their holding tank to the frog tank for feeding.

It is extremely difficult to handle tiny frogs such as mantellas and dart poison frogs without hurting them. Use great caution (Harlequin Dart Poison Frog, *Dendrobates histrionicus*).

Biters

Handling amphibians that bite—and these include a few species of larger frog and salamanders—dictates the need, on occasion, of using protective hand gloves. Clean, inexpensive cotton gloves that can be rinsed are recommended. Under no circumstances should one handle an amphibian with oil-stained or contaminated work gloves, as such contaminants can easily be absorbed by the animal with disastrous results. If you find it necessary to handle an amphibian for the purpose of examining or treating an infectious skin disease (see Chapter 10, "Health Care"), you should resort to using clean, disposable unpowdered surgical gloves, which are readily available at any drugstore, surgical/medical or hair-dressing supply company.

Shipping

The United States Fish and Wildlife Service has proposed a set of regulatory guidelines for the packing, shipping and air transport of a wide range of amphibians and reptiles. Although not passed into law at the time this is being written, some of the amphibian regulations can be of interest and value to hobbyists and would-be commercial captive breeders. The proposed regulations follow:

As is evident, biters will test their teeth at an early age (Argentinian Ornate Horned Frog, *Ceratophrys ornata*).

"Specification for Amphibians (Urodela/Caudata, Anura/Salientia, and Gymniophiona/Apoda):

Design and Construction (of shipping containers):

(a) Shipper shall use expanded polystyrene, burlap, cloth, or clear plastic bags, water resistant chipboard, rigid plastics, water resistant fiberboard, and/or water resistant wood in the construction of the primary enclosures and inner enclosures.

(b) Principles of design. The shipper must meet the following principles of design [in addition to others omitted here].

(1) The shipper shall cover air holes with plastic mesh on the inside of the primary enclosure. The shipper shall make the air holes to provide adequate ventilation but shall punch them outwardly so that the animal will not be able to get its snout through the primary enclosure.

(2) The shipper may carry frogs, toads, and terrestrial salamanders in a shallow primary enclosure designed to prevent stacking of the animals, with the bottom lined with damp non-abrasive material.

(3) Large frogs that might jump at the lids of the primary enclosure and injure themselves require special packing. For these species, the shipper shall pad the inside of the covers of the primary enclosures with cotton of fine weave muslin, bubble wrap, or foam rubber unless the shipper has packed the animals in bags in the primary enclosure.

(4) In the case of small animals, the shipper may place up to four animals in the same compartmentalized container of the primary enclosure, provided that the animals are not toxic or aggressive to each other and will not be injured by stacking.

(5) The shipper may carry aquatic species of amphibians (such as

Necturus, Axolotls, Caecillians [Typhlonectes], Pipa and Xenopus) in a primary enclosure of two double-bagged sealed plastic bags a third full of water. The shipper shall fill the remainder with oxygen as specified by International Air Transport Association Live Animals Regulations Container Requirements for transporting fish.

Preparations before dispatch.

For those frogs, newts, salamanders, caecillians and toad species which require moisture, the shipper shall pack the animals in primary enclosures with sponges or balls of crushed blotting paper or foam rubber chips which the shipper shall moisten with water. The shipper may also use other dampened suitable material.

General care and loading.

(a) The shipper shall not mix or combine species with other species in a single bag or compartment within the primary enclosure.

(b) Temperature. The shipper and carrier shall take special care to avoid exposure to extreme temperatures, including the use of insulated shipping boxes. Particularly during cold weather, these animals lie dormant for prolonged periods and, therefore, neither the shipper nor the carrier shall presume the animals to be dead."

In a separate section of the rules, temperature ranges for the holding areas and transport conveyance are specified for amphibians:

"In the case of amphibians, neither the shipper nor the carrier shall allow ambient temperatures to fall below 15.6 degrees C (60 degrees F), nor to exceed 21.1 degrees C (70 degrees F)."

A veterinary inspection prior to shipment is required. In addition to being examined for signs of general illness, amphibians are also to be inspected for the presence of ecoparasites that may include ticks and leeches, plus overt or outward signs of infection such as external fungal and bacterial processes. In shipments of many animals, random samplings are allowed.

There are many other general provisions of the regulation that extend to amphibians, so any shipper of these animals is advised to obtain a copy of the regulations by requesting them from the U.S. Fish and Wildlife Service. These regulations apply to shipments reaching the United States, and importers may be liable if their shippers/ exporters do not comply with them, so foreign entities are well advised to become familiar with the regulations if they ship amphibians into the United States from any foreign port. The precise regulation is 50 CFR Part 14. The title is Humane and Healthful Transport of Wild Mammals, Birds, Reptiles and Amphibians to the United States.

Feeding

Most amphibians eat only live foods. A few exceptions have been mentioned previously, but they are by no means the norm. It is useful to learn some of the terminology of feeding habits.

Animals that eat vegetable matter, which include few amphibians, are known as herbivores. Virtually all adult-stage amphibians are carnivores, which means they eat animal matter. More specifically, most eat insects, and so are more properly known as insectivores. A few eat other types of invertebrates, such as crustaceans or other arthropods including spiders, and some larger species will eat small mammals such as juvenile or newborn mice. Insects, however, are the natural food of most amphibians. The most widely available of these foods are crickets. Mealworms (which are not really worms at all, but the larvae of a beetle) are also widely available. Any animal that habitually eats both animal and vegetable matter is referred to as omnivorous. Larval salamanders are basically carnivores; larval frogs and toads, on the other hand, may be herbivores, omnivores or carnivores, depending on species. Feeding amphibian larvae will be discussed separately below.

The ensuing discussion involves feeding only adult-stage amphibians.

Obtaining Live Foods

The easiest and most convenient source of live foods is one's pet shop, assuming it sells reptiles and amphibians. The shop staff not only need a stock of such foods to feed their own stock, but are under an unwritten commercial obligation

Termites and other pest species cannot be shipped, so you must collect them yourself if you want to include them in your amphibian's diet. These Dyeing Dart Poison Frogs (*Dendrobates tinctorius*) have gathered for a termite feast.

to help provide their customers with appropriate foods for the animals they sell them. This is also good business for the shops. One needs to seriously question the ethics and practices of any pet shop that sells amphibians and reptiles but has no food on hand for them.

Barring pet shop acquisition of such foods, the next best place is to order them by mail. Orders can be placed over the phone. Many suppliers ship COD or take credit cards, which saves valuable time in getting the order to you. Live foods in the warmer months can be shipped by two- or three-day air, whereas in the colder months they not only need to be specially packed but shipped overnight express as well. Live insects that arrive frozen are of little use.

Some states such as Arizona, California and Hawaii have restrictions on what types of live insects can be shipped into the state. Most shippers are aware of these limitations, but you should be familiar with such restrictions as well. In some cases, you can obtain a permit from the U.S. Department of Agriculture exempting certain varieties of insect from state restriction. For example, fruit flies are a dangerous pest species in California and Florida, where fruits are an important cash crop. However, fruit flies raised for lab use, or for feeding amphibians, are either a wingless or flightless (with attenuated wings) variety, which poses no threat to agricultural interests and can be exempted from regulations in states where a single fruit fly on the wing is often great cause for alarm. Chapter 16 lists a number of reliable, licensed or USDA-permitted mail-order suppliers.

You may want to collect your own live food when weather permits. If you do so, you must be absolutely certain such bugs have not been exposed to pesticides or other environmental contaminants. To collect your own insects, you need a good fine-mesh long-handled net, screen-ventilated containers to stow and transport the insects and someplace to keep them prior to feeding. For most people this is a time-consuming option that has little appeal, yet others love the opportunity of spending a few hours a week outdoors doing something practical for their amphibians. Because pest species such as ants, termites and aphids are not shipped interstate or internationally, it is necessary to collect these bugs yourself to feed small specimens. A final option is to culture your own live foods.

able in any pet shop that sells reptiles and amphibians. Some pet shops even carry several sizes of crickets. Pet shops usually charge a bit more than mail-order companies, but if you do not need many in a short period of time or don't wish to be bothered caring for a large colony, this may be your preferred source. Crickets are also available in bulk from mail-order dealers. Quantities of a thousand cost around 25 to 30 dollars, which includes overnight express delivery in the United States. If you are feeding small amphibians or amphibians that need one of the sub-adult stages, you may have to buy your crickets from a breeder, as not all pet shops carry the smaller crickets.

Selecting which cricket size to feed your amphibian depends mainly on the size of the amphibian. Fully grown adult crickets cannot be eaten by many smaller species of amphibians, so it is nec-

essary to feed them pinhead (newborn), one- or two-week-old or some intermediate-size crickets. Larger crickets that are not eaten may also attack some amphibians, as they are rather indiscriminate feeders themselves and when they do not have the right foods they will eat almost anything! Therefore, if you dump a batch of crickets into an amphibian enclosure and they are not all eaten, the remaining crickets should be removed and placed in an enclosure of their own to be held for feeding to your amphibian(s) another day.

Companies that sell crickets also sell equipment for their maintenance, care and keeping should you opt to buy the 1,000-plus minimum quantities sold by mail. Crickets can be kept in screened-top boxes such as plastic tubs. They should be maintained at temperatures between 70 and 80 degrees F. Warmth can be supplied either by

Foods for Terrestrial and Semi-aquatic Amphibians

Common Gray Cricket (Acheta domesticus)

Common gray crickets (*Acheta domesticus*) are, or should be, avail-

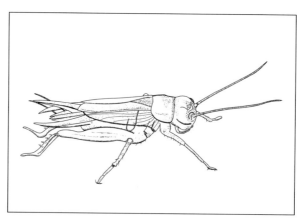

A cricket.

A horned frog enjoys a cricket (albino Cranwell's Horned Frog, *Ceratophrys cranwelli*).

an incandescent bulb over the enclosure, environmental heat or a heating pad beneath the container. In the light, crickets will hide. As they are nocturnal, you don't usually hear them chirping until after sunset under normal conditions.

You can purchase commercially made dry cricket chows or feed them cereals in combination with protein-based dog chows. "Gut-loading" crickets or other insects means feeding them vitamin-enriched protein chows prior to feeding them to your amphibians. The crickets, fed in this way, will be all the more nutritious to your animals. They can also be dusted with a fine-powdered calcium-and-vitamin supplement that is available at pet suppliers. Be careful not to oversupplement adult amphibians; dusting the crickets once a week should be enough.

Developing nonlarval amphibians should have their food supplemented several times a week. The best way to dust a group of crickets to be fed is to place them in a plastic bag with some of the powdered supplement already present and shake them around in it, sort of like shake and bake but without the "bake."

Special water dishes containing a sponge are used to water crickets, and these can be purchased inexpensively from cricket dealers. Never leave an open water dish in the cricket tank, as the crickets will climb in and drown—even if such dishes are relatively shallow. Crickets will also drown in a water dish in your amphibians' enclosure, so it is best to feed only the number that your amphibians will eat. Always remove dead, drowned

crickets quickly from your amphibian enclosure to prevent bacterial decomposition and contamination.

Mealworm Larvae

Mealworm larvae (*Tenebrio molitor*) are the larval form of the flour beetle. They are widely used as food for insectivorous cage birds, reptiles and amphibians, and can be maintained and stored in quantity rather easily. Because these larvae are apt to change into pupae, which then change into adult beetles, such worms should be refrigerated. Keeping them cool helps to retard their metamorphosis and maintain them in a larval state for much longer. The warmer they are kept, the faster they will grow. Keeping them at around 50 degrees F, however, restricts their growth and increases the longevity of their value as a food item. So unless you are intent on raising them to adult beetles for the purpose of breeding them yourself, it is best to keep them at low temperatures. The adult beetle is hard-shelled and difficult to digest, and is recommended as a food item only for the larger amphibians. Even for larger specimens, adult beetles should not be given as a staple item, but as part of a mix of other, softer-bodied foods. Even the chitinous outer skin of the larvae is credited with producing intestinal blockages in smaller

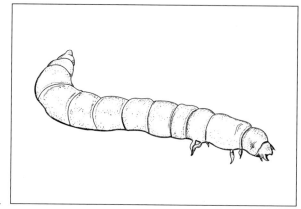

A mealworm.

amphibians when they are used as a sole source of food. This problem can be avoided by feeding freshly molted mealworms. Freshly molted specimens are creamy white in color and have a very soft body, whereas mealworms that are yellow, or a deep yellow color, will tend to have a hard outer skin.

Mealworms should be stored in a mixture of finely milled or crushed wheat bran or rolled oats. They are best kept in smooth-sided, high containers with the bran or oat mixture just covering the top of the mass. Keeping these worms in rough-sided, low-walled containers can result in their escape. They do not require actual water; moisture, instead, can be supplied by adding a cut-up piece of raw potato. The potato should be replaced every day or two, as it dries out or becomes the target of a potentially lethal mold. If a mold or fungus is noted, immediately remove the infected material and transfer the worms to a new, clean and well-ventilated container. Mold growth is usually the result of excessively warm and humid conditions. If the mold is pervasive, it is best to discard the entire lot and start anew with fresh larvae.

While mealworms can be simply dropped into your amphibians' enclosure, many will rapidly dig into the substrate while others may crawl to the water dish and drown in it. They should, therefore, be fed in a dry low-walled pan or dish to keep them herded, giving your amphibians a few moments to take notice of them. Once spotted, the amphibians will come to the "corral" and start feeding off them. If feeding only one or two larvae to a single amphibian, you can drop them in one at a time directly in front of the animal, but keep watch that the larva doesn't rapidly burrow into the substrate and escape.

Mealworms are also relatively inexpensive, selling for seven to 10 cents each in pet shops. They can be purchased (at lower prices) in quantities of hundreds or even thousands from mail-order dealers. They travel better than crickets, so unless you are in a hurry to get them you can settle for three- or four-day rather than overnight delivery.

You can dust mealworms with calcium and vitamin supplements using the technique described above for crickets or simply place them in a deli cup with the supplement for a few minutes prior to feeding. They are not capable of jumping away like crickets, so they don't need to be enclosed in a plastic bag as long as you keep the container in view and make sure none crawl up the sides and escape.

Waxworms and Wax Moths

Waxworms (larvae) and the adult wax moth (*Galleria mellonella*) both make ideal amphibian foods. The larvae and adults are both soft-bodied, easily digestible and move very little, but they wriggle enough to catch your amphibian's attention. The larvae of this moth feed on the wax of bee honeycombs, destroying them in the process, so they are serious pests to beekeepers and honey harvesting operations. Never allow any adult moths or larvae to escape, especially if there are apiaries in your area.

Waxworms and wax moths can be easily purchased at pet shops or ordered by mail. They live for

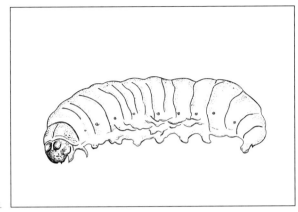

A waxworm.

weeks under refrigeration without food. These pale white, gray or yellowish worms may grow up to $^1/_2$ inch long. Dead larvae should be removed from containers and can be identified by their very dark, almost black color. Most keepers maintain these larvae in a simple substrate of sawdust. Because they are high in fat content, they should not be used as a sole food source but rather to supplement more high-protein bugs such as crickets and flies. They sell for about 10 for a dollar and are even less expensive if bought in quantity from mail-order suppliers. Given their cost and the relative infrequency with which they should be fed, it is probably not worth raising wax-worms yourself.

Super or King Mealworms (Zoophobus mario)

Super or king mealworms (*Zoophobus mario*) resemble meal-worms but are an altogether different species of giant beetle. They are advertised also as "zoophobus" and as "zoophobias," and one rancher says they look like mealworms on steroids. They are much softer-bodied than mealworms, are larger in diameter and are almost 2 inches in length. These insects are not commonly available in pet shops and need to be ordered from specialty dealers.

Super mealworms are of value in feeding larger ($3^1/_2$ to 5 or more inches in length) amphibians. Smaller animals will have a difficult time subduing and swallowing them. They too can be kept in a substrate of wheat bran with a slice or two of potato for moisture. However, they must be kept warm (at room temperature to 80 degrees) at all times and should never be refrigerated.

These worms are sold by the pound, with about 1,000 worms per pound. One pound from a mail-order dealer sells for 20 to 25 dollars plus packing and shipping, and the final price by mail order would be around .03 to .04 cents each. Pet shops that have them sell them for about 10 for a dollar, about the same price as regular mealworms. They are, however, a better buy because of their great size.

Amphibians that enjoy super mealworms include bullfrogs, giant toads, horned frogs and the larger ambystomaid salamanders.

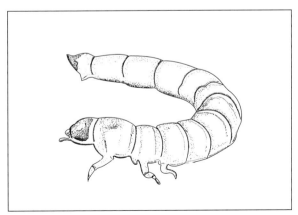

A super mealworm.

Fruit Flies

Flightless fruit flies *(Drosophia melanogaster)* are only about $1/10$ to $1/8$ inch in length, making them excellent food for a variety of small amphibians as well as newly metamorphosed frogs and salamanders. They are a staple for the small dart poison and mantella frogs. With a little bit of effort and research, you can culture them in your own home, thus assuring a steady supply of food for such amphibians, especially in the cold winter months when freezing temperatures make the delivery of pinhead crickets and other small bugs problematic.

Amphibians need to eat, at the very least, once and preferably two or three times a day. In nature, when they are not mating, their primary occupation is seeking and eating bugs. Many small, active species quickly wither and die, sometimes after the second or third day without sustenance.

Fruit fly starter cultures may be purchased from the sources listed in Chapter 16. These companies sell culture jars, covering material and culture medium. They also provide instruction manuals for keeping cultures going. On occasion such cultures may die out, in which case you have to discard them, clean your culture jars and start again with fresh starter cultures.

You should order your starter cultures about $1^1/2$ months before you plan to start using the flies as amphibian food. This will give you time to start a second generation to keep the culture going. As such cultures are inexpensive, you may opt to purchase several starter colonies at one time, feed one and try and keep the others going.

Fruit fly cultures are maintained in clean wide-mouthed glass jars with either special lids made of polyurethane foam that allow air in and out or a piece of cotton cloth or muslin tied over the top with a piece of string or a sturdy rubber band. A four-ounce jar is recommended.

Culture medium is placed in the bottom to a depth of about 1 inch. Add some flies from your existing culture to the new preparation to get it started. Keep repeating the process until you have a cycle of enough cultures to supply all the needs of your small amphibians.

Cultures should be kept in subdued lighting at between 68 to 75 degrees F. The most common cause of culture failure is mold. A mold inhibitor is available, but if mold does attack your cultures it is best to discard them and start over.

Culture medium that needn't be cooked can be purchased from suppliers, or you can brew your own mixture by bringing 1 cup of water to simmering and then adding 1 tablespoon of cornmeal, 1 teaspoon of sulfur-free molasses and $1/8$ teaspoon of calcium propionate (preservative/mold inhibitor supplied by Eastman Kodak Corp.). Also add 1 teaspoon of agar, a protein-rich seaweed powder available in health food stores. Boil for about three minutes and allow to cool off slightly, then pour directly into your culture jars. Add a few grains of brewer's yeast to each jar as well.

Using your starter culture, add a few flies to each of your new bottles. In about three weeks the new bottles should be teeming. After feeding most of the adult flies in

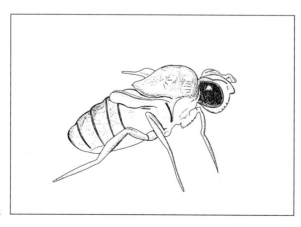

A fruit fly.

each bottle to your pets, allow the culture to renew itself. In a few days you should have a second batch ready for use.

The adult female fruit fly lives for several weeks, and during her short life span she produces about 500 eggs. The eggs are deposited in the culture medium, where they breathe through two snorkel-like "respiration tubes" that stick above the surface. They hatch into larvae in just one day. The larvae feed on yeast that is produced in the culture medium as it ferments. They molt twice and in about two weeks they harden, changing into pupae. This stage lasts about five days before they turn into flies. Adult female flies begin producing eggs at the ripe old age of two days. These fruit flies are strictly flightless but they do crawl and hop around quite effectively. Nonetheless, they cannot travel very far, so you needn't worry if an occasional one escapes—it won't be a threat to local fruit crops. There are both totally wingless forms and forms that have vestigial or attenuated wings that are practically useless for flying purposes. Some dealers are breeding a larger species of fruit fly for somewhat larger amphibians. Any amphibian over 2 inches in length can, however, be fed more economically.

Common Housefly

While we tend to think of the housefly (*Musca domestica*) as a

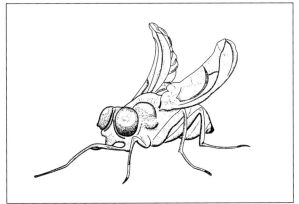

A housefly.

pest to be swatted and eliminated, a flightless variety is available for laboratory and amphibian feeding use. It is much larger than the fruit fly, so it is a more economical meal for larger amphibians. These genetically altered flies have wings that have been bred to occur in a twisted configuration, making them useless for flight. They are great walkers and hoppers, so care should still be taken to keep them confined. No pet stores carry them, and thus they must be obtained via mail-order suppliers. They are shipped as immobile pupae for security reasons and should be tightly confined as they transform into adult flies. You should feed them to your pets immediately after they turn into adults.

The pupae change to adult flies between one and two days after arrival, depending on what stage of development they're in. They should be placed in a 1-gallon glass jug with a cover containing air

holes. Adult flies should be fed a mixture of powdered milk and dry sugar (1:1 ratio). Water should be provided separately via a dampened sponge or cotton pads set in a shallow dish or ash tray.

Culturing your own houseflies can be difficult, so it is probably best to order the pupae as you need them. They are relatively inexpensive.

Blow-fly Larvae

Most of the fly larvae sold as live food for amphibians are from the blow-fly family (family Calliphoridae). These larvae are larger than ordinary housefly larvae, reaching about $1/2$ inch in length. They should be refrigerated down to 36 degrees F to retard metamorphosis if you intend to feed them as larvae. They can be stored in a tightly lidded plastic refrigerator/food dish with just a few small air holes drilled in the lid. Larvae kept at room temperature will quickly turn into pupae and a week later into flies. The larvae of the Calliphora are high in protein, have little indigestible chitin and are higher in calcium than mealworm larvae. They are slow-moving; larvae are normally legless and worm-like and are easily captured by small to moderate-sized amphibians, as well as larger animals. Nonetheless, they should be placed in the animals' enclosure in a shallow, dark-colored dish to prevent their dispersal in the habitat. Uneaten specimens should be returned to the refrigerator.

Earthworms

Earthworms (*Lumbricus terrestris*) or night crawlers and other members of the annelid clan are excellent amphibian food relished and habitually eaten by many species. Others disdain them because of their foul-tasting secretions. Prior to feeding earthworms it may be worthwhile to thoroughly rinse them in cool, running water for a minute or so to remove the nasty taste. They are inexpensive and readily available by mail order, as well as in bait shops in areas where fishing is popular. Earthworms are easy to keep and also easy to raise. Numerous people have been lulled into believing they can make a good living raising earthworms for the bait and amphibian food trade, and some have actually done so. There are hundreds of species, but the most commonly available is *Lumbricus terrestris.*

Two commonly available as bait are the dung (manure) worm and the red earthworm. The dung worm is less palatable and gives off a foul odor that repels amphibians, so the common red worm is a preferable choice.

Earthworms can be raised indoors in pans (such as kitty litter trays) measuring a mere 2 feet by 2 feet and 6 inches high. They can be kept at a wide range of room temperatures, between 50 and 75 degrees F. The pan should have a bottom layer of peat moss, covered by grass clippings and then sterile potting soil. The worms will eat about any kind of decaying organic material including chicken mash, cornmeal, animal manure and even discarded kitchen vegetable matter. Place food material on the surface and the worms will rise to the top to feed. The bed should be covered with a dampened piece of burlap to help hold moisture. Harvest as needed, and always wash the worms thoroughly before feeding.

Silkworm Larvae

Silkworm larvae (*Bombyx mori*) make excellent fodder for larger amphibians, including salamanders over 7 inches in length such as large Ambystomids, and the bigger frogs and toad species including bullfrogs, Cane Toads and horned frogs. The larvae of the silk moth or the silkworm reach 3 inches in length and could weigh as much as 4 grams. These insects have been cultured for millennia by the Chinese and are, in fact, extinct in the wild. They exist today only to produce silk and are among the very few insects that can truly be considered a domestic animal of sorts.

Silkworms are reared primarily in Asia, the Mediterranean and South America using modern technology to enable mass breeding. The eggs are processed under aseptic conditions by specially clothed workers.

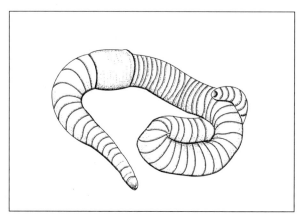

An earthworm.

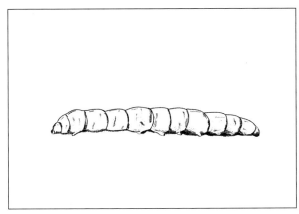

Silkworm larvae.

Upon hatching, the larvae are placed in special rearing trays where they are fed on a diet consisting exclusively of mulberry leaves. On reaching 3 inches in length, they spin a silken cocoon that is then placed in high-temperature drying ovens that kill the pupae ensconced within. The silken cocoons are then packaged and sent to a processor, where they are unwound and the spun material is turned into silken thread and woven into cloth. Nearly 2,000 pounds of mulberry leaves are needed to produce 12 pounds of silk.

A number of live food dealers handle the silkworm larvae, which must be fed only on the tender young leaves of the white mulberry tree. Such leaves need to be cleaned and specially processed as well. It is infinitely easier to buy silkworm larvae as you need them than to try and cultivate them yourself, as the process is lengthy and complicated and requires material that may be difficult to obtain. They can be kept refrigerated at around 50 degrees to retard cocoon and pupae formation and can be fed one at a time to larger amphibians.

Isopods
(Pillbugs and Sowbugs)

These small bugs are easy to collect in the wild and to culture in captivity. They make a good addition to any amphibian diet but are not a good sole source of nutrition, because they are hard-shelled with a significant percentage of their weight being composed of indigestible chitinous material.

Isopods are found worldwide and are actually crustaceans related to crayfish and lobsters. Terrestrial forms such as pillbugs and sowbugs can be found under rocks and pieces of wood or any similar material laid flat on the ground under which some moisture may also be present. This is where they hide during the day. At night they leave their hiding places to forage in the damp evening air. You can even draw them to you by laying down some flat rocks or small wooden boards and watering the area frequently. Within a few days you should find a congregation of these creatures ready to be scooped up.

They can also be easily cultured, and starter cultures can be purchased from some of the food suppliers listed in Chapter 16. A plastic-covered storage box with 3 to 4 inches of peat moss or even lawn

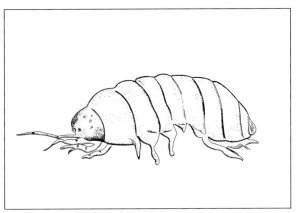

An isopod.

clippings can be used to begin your culture. Spray a mist over the substrate on occasion and keep it just slightly damp. These crustaceans will eat alfalfa pellets, coffee grinds or just about any decaying vegetable matter, so isopod cultures are a good way to dispose of fresh vegetables that have turned before you could eat them yourself. The cultures do not need much ventilation, so a few small holes drilled in the lid is all that is necessary.

Isopods should be fed to amphibians only once or twice a week, not as part of a regular diet. They should be presented to your animals in a shallow dish unless you want them to escape into your habitat and start a self-sustaining colony.

Feeding Larval and Strictly Aquatic Amphibians

Frog and toad tadpoles are herbivorous, carnivorous or omnivorous, and most are not above feeding on the bodies of their dead or dying siblings, making them cannibalistic as well. Larval salamanders are entirely carnivorous, and some are also cannibalistic. All adult-stage, strictly aquatic amphibians are carnivorous and eat only animal matter; any vegetable material ingested is usually done so incidentally when foraging among plant matter.

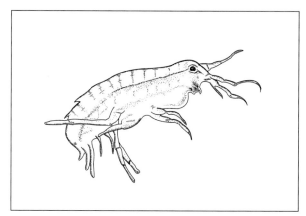

A scud.

Scuds

Scuds (*Grammarus sp.*) are a group of small crustaceans of the Order Amphiopoda. They are often eaten in the wild by salamanders and frogs in aquatic environments. They resemble tiny shrimp and are about $1/4$ inch in length. They can survive nicely in fresh, brackish and saltwater environments, but as food for amphibians they should be kept exclusively in fresh water.

Scuds are rather easy to breed, and one pair can produce tens of thousands of babies over a period of several months. They are easy to culture in larger indoor aquariums or outdoor ponds and pools. Scuds are best introduced into an environment of aged water with a good growth of green algae present. Chlorinated tap water will kill them. Duckweed, a small floating plant, also helps scud cultures, filtering impurities and providing shelter. They will feed on algae and other plant matter introduced into the aquarium.

Scuds should be fed to amphibian larvae and small aquatic species such as young Axolotls and Dwarf Clawed Frogs by collecting them in a brine shrimp net and then releasing them in your amphibian tank. Land-based semi-aquatic amphibians will feed on them if they are placed in a shallow dish such as an ashtray with a small amount of water present. Their movement will catch your amphibian's eye, and they will be quickly devoured.

Springtails

Springtails (Order Collembola) are primitive, wingless insects that are found virtually everywhere in the world save perhaps the Antarctic. They are called springtails because of their unusual method of locomotion. Springtails have a forked organ known as the furcula that is turned forward under the abdomen and grabbed by another structure called a tenaculum. On release, the tiny insect is propelled forward and

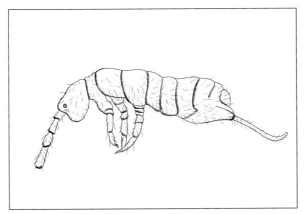

A springtail.

upward. Springtails are tiny (less than 5 millimeters in length) but are extremely abundant. A small section of damp soil, leaf mold and other detritus contains tens of millions of them, which can be extracted by shaking handfuls of such material over a fine netting stretched over a wide-mouthed funnel—much like panning for gold. Springtails are a plentiful and convenient food for the tiniest of frogs and salamanders, such as newly metamorphosed dart poison frogs and other small species.

FEEDING TIP FOR SMALL SPECIES

When feeding small aquatic organisms to aquatic species, be sure to temporarily turn off your aquarium filter. If you don't, there is a good chance that the food will be sucked into the filter system before your animals get an opportunity to eat it.

Aquatic Isopods

Aquatic isopods (*Assellus sp.*) are small (³/₄ inch maximum length) freshwater crustaceans found in streams and ponds, where they feed on decaying plant and animal matter. Their body shape is more cigar-like than that of their terrestrial counterparts, making them better equipped for an aquatic existence.

They can be easily cultured in a 10-gallon tank filled with aged water from an established aquarium. The tank need be fitted only

A WARNING ABOUT BRINE SHRIMP

Brine shrimp, a common live tropical fish food, are poor fodder for small aquatic amphibians. They have a high salt content (many amphibians will reject them) and must be rinsed before feeding. Because they consist largely of water and chitin, they provide little useable protein. Moreover, they cannot survive very long in a freshwater environment. They were first discovered in the Great Salt Lake at Salt Lake City, Utah, a lake with a higher salt concentration than sea water. It is so salty, in fact, that these small crustaceans (*Artemia salina*) are among a very few organisms that can even survive there.

with an airstone and good algae growth. Small bits of cooked spinach and oatmeal can be used to feed them. Allow the material to float to the bottom, where the

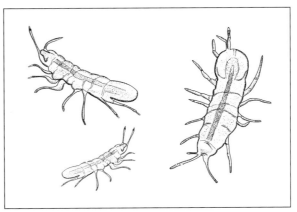

Aquatic isopods.

isopods will find it. They should be maintained at water temperatures of 60 to 65 degrees F and can be collected with a brine shrimp net to be fed to aquatic amphibians and carnivorous amphibian larvae.

Tubifex Worms

Tubifex worms, of the genus *Tubifex sp.*, are annelids, or segmented threadlike worms, that live in masses in mud and sewers. Clean, washed, cultured tubifex worms are available as live aquarium fish foods in many pet shops.

These worms constantly writhe or wriggle to extract what available oxygen is present in the waters that they occupy. They are useful food for almost all carnivorous aquatic amphibians, and some semi-aquatic species may even eat them out of the water when served in a small dish of shallow water on the land side of the tank. If you are going to just place them in the water, start by feeding only a pinch. You want

to make sure your amphibians accept them, as uneaten tubifex worms are apt to die and decay in the tank if they are placed in the aquarium in profusion. They can be stored in a clean glass container and should be rinsed under cool, filtered or unchlorinated water for several minutes to wash away dead worms and debris prior to feeding. Keep them in enough unchlorinated water to cover them completely, and store them in the refrigerator to retard spoilage and reduce metabolism and oxygen consumption. Tubifex worms are difficult to breed and culture in captivity, so buying them from a reliable source on a regular basis is often preferred. Commercially, they are raised in large silt-bottomed vats under a stream of constantly flowing cool water. It is difficult to miniaturize this type of an operation in the home environment.

Other live aquatic worms include bloodworms, which are

also available occasionally in some pet shops and can be used to feed aquatic amphibians.

Water Fleas, Daphnia or Phyllopods

Water fleas (*Daphnia sp.*), of the crustacean order Phyllopoda, are small aquatic organisms relished by fish, aquatic amphibians and carnivorous amphibian larvae. They are often available from pet shops and aquarium suppliers in small portions. They are ubiquitous in nature, found in almost any standing body of fresh water. In the warmer weather, you can net these and other small aquatic organisms from pristine, uncontaminated waters (if they are available to you) to feed your aquatic amphibians. They should not be fed as a sole source of food to aquatic amphibians and are required only for short periods of time to supplement the diet of larvae. Accordingly, you may prefer to buy portions as needed rather than try and culture them yourself.

Fresh Frozen Aquatic Foods

Tubifex worms, bloodworms, brine shrimp and daphnia are readily available as frozen slabs that are broken off in small chunks, defrosted and fed to tropical fish. It is unlikely amphibians would eat dead matter such as this, although fish do. However, in aquariums with vigorous aeration such dead

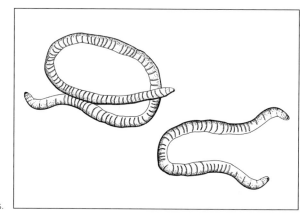
Tubifex worms.

matter may be made to swirl and move around, fooling some amphibians into attention at the "liveliness" of such prey, and they may actually eat them. Hobbyists are encouraged to experiment with such tricks because when they work, the use of such frozen foods can represent a great convenience for caretakers, especially when live foods are not available or are inconvenient to obtain.

Feeding Herbivorous and Omnivorous Frog and Toad Tadpoles

There are many species of frogs and toads that eat vegetable matter during the larval or tadpole stage. If you are breeding or collecting such tadpoles from the wild, their feeding habits should be researched beforehand. Because there are so many species that are herbivorous, omnivorous or carnivorous, it is beyond the scope of this volume to list them all by feeding habits— even if all were known!

Some few species of tadpole exist on their own yolk reserves, and some dendrobatid species have been known to feed on unfertilized eggs passed to them from the female frog. Tadpoles that metamorphose into froglets inside the vocal, dorsal pouch or stomachs of a few unique species feed by scrap-

AMPHIBIAN FEEDING TIPS

- If at all possible, remove any uneaten food, particularly larger crickets, pinky mice or fuzzy rodents. Also remove and discard insect matter that dies by drowning in the aquatic side of a terrarium or in a water bowl. When this occurs, change the water immediately.

- Almost all active amphibians (those that are not hibernating or estivating) need to eat at least once a day. Larger amphibians that eat larger food items such as small rodents or great quantities of larger insects probably can be fed less frequently, such as every two or three days. In some cases, a large animal may be fed only once or twice a week. You need to offer food at various intervals and, if accepted, follow the pattern established by your animal. Some small species eat large quantities of small insects many times in a single day. If such amphibians are deprived of food for more than a day or two, they quickly wither and die.

- Do not re-offer food that has been rejected or ignored by your amphibian.

- Amphibians that do not eat may be suffering from a health problem. Other common causes of inappetence in captive amphibians are inadequate or improper environmental conditions including those of temperature, substrate, humidity or hygiene. Another obvious cause is that the animal simply rejects the food matter as unappetizing. Of course, it is possible your amphibian is not hungry. Finally, your pet may be preoccupied with mating or territorial issues.

ing nutrient matter from the lining of their unusual wombs or subsist on yolk reserves they retain after hatching. In fact, many species of tadpoles carry such reserves for up to several days after hatching and may not feed on any extraneous matter until yolk reserves are used up. Frog species that bypass the tadpole stage and develop from egg to froglet also subsist by means of heavier-than-usual yolk reserves.

If you cannot find information on the feeding habits of your tadpoles, the next best thing is to experiment and research the subject yourself. Try feeding them

both vegetable and animal matter, observe which they prefer or eat exclusively, and perhaps you will make a new discovery about your particular species. In some cases, scientists can discern feeding habits by examining the mouth parts of tadpoles. The structure of the oral passage entrance can provide clues on preferred means of feeding and in some cases, preferred types of foods. If one of your tadpoles should die, examine its mouth parts under a hand lens and make a drawing of what you see, then compare it to mouth part types found in amphibian textbooks.

Sometimes the only way to know what type of tadpole you have is to compare mouth part structures.

Aquarium Plants

A number of small-leafed aquarium plants such as elodea, anachris and cabomba should be used in the tadpole tank, as herbivorous species feed on such matter.

Vegetables for Humans

Boiled leafy green spinach, rich in iron and calcium, can be fed occasionally and sparingly. It is relished by herbivorous tadpoles but contains certain potentially harmful oxalates. It should be fed only in small amounts every few days. You can also boil down collard greens, dandelion greens and small amounts of romaine lettuce to feed regularly. Cruciferous vegetables rich in oxalates, such as broccoli, cabbage and turnips, and carotenoids should be fed in small amounts if at all. Some colorful species may require carotenoids to maintain their coloration as adults. In nature, they undoubtedly obtain such nutrients from the gut of plant-eating bugs.

CHAPTER 9

Reproduction and Breeding

All species are under an imperative to reproduce, and thereby assure their future as a race. Amphibians are no exception and they do this by a bewildering array of means, far more diverse than any other group of animals where mating, breeding and the care of offspring are concerned. In fact, some of the strategies employed by amphibians are so bizarre that they border on the totally improbable—but exist they do. Although occasional references have been made in the previous family and species accounts, this chapter will discuss the various aspects of the reproductive imperative among the three orders of amphibians, describing the three essential ingredients in more detail:

1. **Mating:** in essence, finding a partner of the opposite sex.

2. **Breeding:** engaging in behavior that results in the fertilization of the egg, necessary for its development.

3. **Egg (ovum) deposition and development:** the change from egg into larvae or fully formed miniature versions of the adult parent, as the case may be.

Laid in a cattle trough, it's unlikely that these frog eggs will survive.

Cecillian Reproduction

Of the three orders of amphibians, least is known about cecillian breeding, and hobbyists who choose these animals as study subjects are apt to make the greatest contributions to the knowledge base in this area. Cecillians, as previously indicated, are not as avowedly popular as other amphibians as terrarium or aquarium animals, so interest in them is somewhat limited. Conservationists no doubt believe that this is a good thing for the cecillians and that they do well left alone in their subterranean existence to go about their business of propagating themselves unfettered.

While more visible species of amphibians enjoy great popularity, their very visibility and presence at the surface makes them more vulnerable than the cecillians to a variety of threats, both natural and man-made. One could speculate that because cecillians are the most primitive of all the amphibians, they have managed to survive in fairly substantial numbers for millions of years with their existence scarcely noticed by predators and, when they arrived, by humans as well. And when or if surface life forms, including mankind, disappear from the planet, it is likely they will leave behind such creatures, protected by their subterranean habitat, to begin the evolutionary process anew.

But in spite of their resistance to exposure and study, a few species of cecillians have been scrutinized by dedicated scientists, and what little is known about their reproductive methods will be briefly discussed. It is well known that the majority of cecillians are viviparous, or live-bearing, a fact that distinguishes them as more advanced, reproductively speaking, than egg-laying amphibians (in spite of their other primitive characteristics). Again, it is their fossorial existence that has probably been responsible for their failure to advance beyond their current evolutionary and geographic status.

Members of the genera *Ichythophis* (which means "fish-snake") and *Cecilia* (*var:* Caecilia) are egg layers, whereas the members of the Family

Typhlonectidae are live bearers. In comparison to frogs and salamanders, cecillian larvae hatch at a far more advanced stage of life; they differ from their parents only in their size and the presence of a gill slit and a fin that undergo metamorphosis to terrestrial cecillians. As opposed to frog and tadpole larvae, which become shorter at metamorphosis, the larvae of cecillians are shorter than those of their adult counterparts. They have long, filamentous gills, extremely thin permeable skin, a lateral line organ and the same sorts of teeth as adults. The tentacle is absent and appears only at metamorphosis.

The Mexican or Violet Cecillian (*Dermophis mexicanus*) is occasionally available in the pet trade and is viviparous, giving birth to live young. Thompson's Giant Cecillian (*Cecilia thompsoni*) is well named, as it reaches lengths of 4 to 5 feet. Due to export restrictions in its native Colombia, this animal is rarely available. Little is known of its courtship activity, and the only discernible or outward difference between males and females is a swelling near the cloacal region in males during the mating period. Females deposit from 20 to 50 eggs in a damp terrestrial nest close to water. Upon hatching, the larvae wriggle their way into the water. Hatching occurs in about 8 weeks and metamorphosis occurs 12 weeks after that. Larvae can be fed any of the aquatic organisms mentioned earlier, such as ispopods, Daphnia and brine shrimp.

The mostly commonly seen cecillians in the pet trade are members of the genus Ichthyophis (fish cecillians). They are frequently imported to the west from Asia along with tropical fish shipments and are often misidentified as some sort of "freshwater eel." They live in rice paddies as well as in dampened soil or shallow, muddy waters. They are roused into courtship activity by being kept in a damp soil substrate that is increasingly moistened until completely saturated, mimicking perhaps the monsoon rains of their region. Fish cecillians estivate, or become inactive, as the soil dries.

In nature, females deposit up to 30 heavily yolked eggs in shallow hole nests constructed near water. The female coils around her eggs, protectively maintaining their moisture content and viability by use of her own skin secretions. She will periodically enter the water and return re-wetted and coil around the eggs, thereby also adding to their moisture content.

Eggs hatch in about four months, at which time the larvae wriggle to the water and lead a strictly aquatic existence for up to eight weeks longer. They will eat small aquatic crustaceans and other tiny arthropods. Newly metamorphosed fish cecillians can be fed on small waxworm and mealworm larvae, chopped earthworms, tubifex and other tiny insects, gradually increasing in size as adulthood is reached. Burrowing insects such as earthworms and mealworms are ideal, because they can be located and eaten underground by these unusual amphibians.

Salamander Reproduction

Salamanders fall into one of three categories with respect to producing offspring:

1. **Oviparous**, which means they lay eggs externally, either in the water or in a moist terrestrial environment. Such eggs, if deposited on land, may develop into larvae that must find their way to water to complete their development, *or* they undergo direct development into adult, land-stage or semi-aquatic salamanders.

2. **Viviparous**, which means they produce live young after gestating their eggs internally. Such young may be larvae, which are deposited by the female in water, or in the case of very few species, such young may be fully developed land-stage salamanders. In viviparous reproduction, the eggs are retained long enough to exchange gases, excrete waste products and obtain nutrients from the maternal bloodstream.

3. **Ovoviparous**, which means that the eggs are retained within the female for a short period of time, hatching within the oviduct. In this case, the female always releases aquatic, larval-form salamanders.

Live bearing has evolved in many species of reptiles and amphibians because of inhospitable conditions for external egg development. It is a reason that is amply demonstrated in Alpine Salamanders (*Salamandra atra*), which live at cold, high altitudes where seasonal warmth is of such abbreviated duration that there is just no time for eggs and larvae to develop externally. This species produces between 20 and 30 eggs, of which only one or two are fertile and actually develop. When the fertilized eggs use up their yolk supply, they begin utilizing the yolk supply of the remaining unfertilized eggs. They do this for over a year and when the sustenance provided by these unfertile eggs is exhausted, the embryos begin eating cells scraped from the walls of the mother's reproductive tract, using specialized teeth. This goes on for two to four years, after which the female gives birth to one or two fully metamorphosed salamanders.

Unquestionably, this is the longest gestation period of any vertebrate, as it could conceivably last as long as five years! Thus, for animals in inhospitable and colder climates, live bearing and longer times for development are necessary. Viviparity, however, may occur for reasons other than climate, such as the availability or unavailability of water for sufficient periods to permit eggs and larvae to reach adulthood. Thus species that live in arid conditions or at locations where ponds and other pools of water are short-lived due to lack of replenishing rain and excessive heat may also evolve the need to produce their young through some type of viviparity or ovoviviparity.

Internal Fertilization

All salamanders reproduce by means of internal fertilization, as opposed to most of their frog and toad relatives. In all but a very few species, fertilization in frogs and toads is external: The male sheds his sperm atop or near the eggs as the female extrudes them during a mating embrace known as amplexus. In salamanders, the male deposits all of his sperm in the water, neatly wrapped in a packet known as the spermatophore. The female is manipulated by the male in such a way as to insure that she receives this packet of sperm, which is stored in a pouch-like receptacle inside her cloaca known as the spermatotheca, until such time that the eggs are ready to be fertilized.

Unlike frogs, therefore, mating and fertilization take place at different points in time as well as internally. On the one hand, this method is unreliable because females don't always receive the spermatophore when they should; on the other hand, it provides time for the female to hide or nest her eggs, sometimes in numerous different places, which helps assure that at least some of the progeny may escape predation or other hazards and survive to adulthood.

Egg Development

Salamanders and newts that lay eggs place them either singly or in clusters in one of three possible situations:

1. Eggs are left in open, still waters. This method is used by all European newts and many salamanders.

2. Eggs are secreted in hidden nests located in running water. This method is typical of the brook salamanders (*Eurycea sp.*).

3. Eggs are laid in a moist, terrestrial hiding place and undergo direct development into fully metamorphosed or developed salamanders, bypassing a free-living larval stage. This method is found only in the lungless salamanders (Plethodontidae) and European cave salamanders (*Hydromantes sp.*).

Egg development in salamanders is dependent on water temperature as well as the presence of an abundance of aquatic vegetation.

Members of the newt genus Triturus, for example, wrap each egg individually in the leaves of aquatic plants near the surface—because that's where dissolved oxygen levels tend to be greatest. If the eggs were allowed to sink into the bottom mud, they would die by suffocation.

Save for the direct-developing species mentioned above, all salamanders and newts tend to produce large numbers of eggs and larvae, which helps offset high mortality rates incurred during development. Other adaptations to improve survival also occur. Amphibians that lay eggs in open areas exposed to sunlight tend to have darkly pigmented eggs, whereas most (but not all) species that hide their eggs in nests or away from sunlight have nonpigmented eggs. Darkly pigmented eggs also absorb and retain heat more readily, and this can help them maintain a temperature that may be higher than that of surrounding waters and therefore help

to hasten development. Temperature is the most important factor in determining the rate of egg development. An increase of a mere 5 degrees C can cut about three weeks off the time it takes many species of newt to hatch.

Salamander Larvae

All salamander larvae can be divided into one of two types: those that live in quiet pond waters and stream dwellers. Temperature affects metamorphosis, with cooler temperatures prolonging the time needed for transformation. A constant decrease in temperature in studies of newt transformation indicated that larvae raised in colder waters required six times as long to metamorphose than those raised at temperatures some 8 to 10 degrees warmer.

All salamander and newt larvae are carnivorous. They are known as gape-limited predators because they will feed on anything they can get in their mouth and swallow.

Breeding Mole Salamanders
Axolotls
Among the mole salamanders, or family Ambystomidae, the most frequently captive-bred species is undoubtedly the Axolotl (*Ambystoma mexicanum*). Large laboratory colonies exist at some universities throughout the world, where researchers are engaged in a variety of genetic, hormone and related studies in which these salamanders can be of inestimable value.

The technique for breeding these neotenous, strictly aquatic salamanders is to first lower water temperature to between 45 and 50 degrees F for one month. After doing so, increasing the temperature to 70 degrees F stimulates the male to start luring the female. If she is so disposed, the male then produces spermatophores and manipulates her over them. The female lays about 200 eggs that adhere en masse to pebbles and rocks.

These rocks and pebbles should be carefully removed to a rearing tank or, if this is not feasible, the parents and any other animals should be removed to prevent the eggs from being eaten. The eggs should be incubated at 60 to 70 degrees F. They hatch in 12 to 20 days and take about a year to become sexually mature.

Tiger Salamanders
The Tiger Salamander (*Ambystoma tigrinum*) is a large (over a foot

---

TADPOLE TRIVIA

Salamander and newt larvae are frequently referred to as tadpoles, but this is a misuse of a word that should be reserved solely for describing the larvae of frogs and toads. In fact, the word *tadpole* is from two Middle English words that mean "toad" and "head," or "toad-head."

Frog and toad larvae undergo numerous developmental changes when transforming from aquatic larvae to adult form. Salamander larvae, on the other hand, possess the basic adult body structure, and metamorphosis for them is not as complicated as it is for frogs and toads.

To breed Tiger Salamanders, a large aquarium or outdoor pool is best (Tiger Salamander, *Ambystoma tigrinum*).

less than three weeks. Note, however, that quickly developed larvae incubated at higher temperatures are not as robust or healthy as those that spend a much longer time developing. They metamorphose at about four months of age and take up to five years to sexually mature. In the wild, the absence of iodine in some inland bodies of water may result in some populations remaining in their larval state for much longer, or indefinitely. Iodine deficiency results in thyroid deficiency, which in turn results in a lack of hormone production that is responsible for arrested development.

long when fully grown), long-lived (up to 18 years) semi-aquatic salamander. The numerous subspecies have different breeding requirements insofar as season and temperature are concerned, as they are found in different climatic zones throughout the United States. They are best bred in large aquariums or outdoor ponds. At the northern latitudes, a 10-week (38 degree F) period of hibernation precedes mating and breeding activity, and this needs to be duplicated if the salamanders are being bred indoors. Once temperatures exceed 40 degrees F, these salamanders become active and will mate and breed. They should be provided with deep water (30 to 40 inches).

The female deposits about 250 eggs, divided into as many as 15 small packets that she places in aquatic plants or pebbles. They need to be removed (or the adults removed) and incubated at 45 to 75 degrees F. The time to hatching depends on the temperature. At lower temperatures, eggs hatch in about 50 days, whereas at higher temperatures, they could develop in

Spotted Salamanders

The Spotted Salamander (*Ambystoma maculatum*) also requires a large, deep-water indoor aquarium with a land side or is better yet bred in an outdoor facility. In an indoor situation, misting or watering with warm water (using a rainmaker or similar device) after two to three

The larvae of Spotted Salamanders will eat each other if not provided sufficient food and space (Spotted Salamander, *Ambystoma maculatum*).

months of hibernation will stimulate mating behavior. This causes the salamanders to enter the cooler water, where mating and fertilization follows the standard salamander pattern. Spotted Salamanders produce two to three clumps of 20 to 75 eggs that must be separated from the adults for incubation and hatching. These long-lived (up to 18 years) salamanders may, as larvae, cannibalize each other if they are not kept well fed and in spacious surroundings. Overcrowding leads to increased contact, which is apt to elicit biting and feeding responses between the larvae.

Marbled Salamanders

The Marbled Salamander (*Ambystoma opacum*) departs from the standard ambystomid life history in that it deposits its eggs in a damp, terrestrial depression or nest in the fall. The female then guards her eggs (about 75) until rainfall creates a puddle in the nest. Shortly thereafter, the larvae hatch. If the nest remains dry, development still occurs, but it does so inside the egg capsule. Young then hatch during the following spring rains. Metamorphosis takes four to five months.

Other Ambystomid Salamanders

A few other ambystomid salamanders are worth mentioning as candidates for breeding. Certainly one of the most beautiful is the Ringed Salamander (*Ambystoma annulatum*). It is an elongated salamander that reaches only about 7 inches in length, with striking coloring of yellow rings on a black body. Breeding is stimulated by flooding the terrarium in the fall with warm water. Once stimulated, the female deposits about 50 eggs that hatch rapidly and metamorphose in six to eight weeks. The Blue-Spotted Salamander (*Ambystoma laterale*) is a hardy species that also breeds readily after a hibernation phase and deposits about 50 slowly developing eggs.

Breeding Lungless Salamanders

Dusky Salamanders

The lungless salamanders of the Family Plethodontidae include several species that have been bred successfully in captivity. The Dusky Salamanders (*Desmognathus fuscus*) hibernate from February to early April. Courtship and breeding occur when these salamanders emerge from dormancy. As do most lungless salamanders, Dusky Salamanders lay their eggs on land, in damp substrate close to the water's edge. The female coils around her clutch, usually numbering from 20 to 60 eggs, until they hatch. Her primary job is not only to defend them against predation, but to keep them moist, which she does by entering the water and dripping it on them when she emerges. The larvae remain in the egg capsule for up to seven months but if the fully developed eggs are placed in water, the larvae will emerge as free-living fully aquatic larvae.

Red-Backed Salamanders

The Red-Backed Salamander (*Plethodon cinerus*) is found throughout the northeastern United States, in the Great Lakes region and throughout most of southeastern Canada. They are among the most commonly kept salamanders in the United States and make an excellent starter salamander.

The Red-Backed is a cyclical breeder, induced to court in the

WHEN PATIENCE IS A NECESSITY

The Giant or Cope's Salamanders (*Dicamptodon sp.*) mate and breed in a manner similar to that of the ambystomids. They deposit their eggs in shallow, cool, slow-moving waters in late summer and autumn. They produce anywhere from 20 to 50 eggs that adhere to the undersides of underwater rocks. In colder waters, eggs may take two years to hatch. Simulating these conditions in captivity, while not impossible, is apt to be extremely complicated.

The larvae of the Red-Backed Salamander (*Plethodon cinerus*) immediately transform into miniature salamanders.

spring after a hibernation period lasting three to four months. Males are territorial and secure a small patch that they protect against other males. When a female enters, he begins courting her and produces a spermatophore. He then positions the female over it so as to pick up the cap containing the sperm. Up to 16 large eggs are produced and deposited under a piece of rotting log. The female remains with them, departing to secure food and to get wet so she can keep the eggs moistened. The larvae undergo direct transformation into miniature replicas of their parents. They should be raised separately in small containers lined with moss or a similar substrate. The young achieve maturity in one-and-one-half to two years.

Red Salamanders
Another interesting species of lungless salamander is the Red Salamander (*Pseudotriton ruber*).

Unlike other members of this family, the Red Salamanders of this genus breed in water. Their generic name, in fact, means "false newt." Following hibernation, they enter cold, still waters where they breed according to the standard salamander plan. Over 100 eggs are deposited; these should be main-

tained in cool, clear and well-oxygenated water. The eggs hatch in about six weeks. Larvae are best separated into small groups of 10 or so animals to prevent overcrowding and aggressive behavior. They may take between two and three years to metamorphose and then another two-and-a-half years longer to mature.

Breeding Fire Salamanders and Newts
Members of the Family Salamandridae—the fire salamanders and the newts—are commonly bred in captivity by hobbyists.

Eastern Newts
One of the most frequently available newts in the United States is the Eastern Newt (*Notophthalmus*

Unlike other lungless salamanders, Red Salamanders breed in the water (Red Salamander, *Pseudotriton ruber*).

viridescens), but care in handling is required, as it exudes a toxic skin secretion that can be fatal if ingested. Eastern Newts breed at relatively cool temperatures (50 degrees F) in heavily planted, well-filtered water. After hibernating for about three months, these animals mate and breed in the water, where they deposit more than 300 eggs that may either be wrapped in the leaves of the aquatic plants (*Elodea*) or deposited in clumps or groups along the plant stalks.

European Fire Salamanders

The European Fire Salamander is another exceedingly popular member of this family and is widely available in the pet trade from both wild-caught and captive-bred sources. There are more than a dozen subspecies, each with varying breeding seasons depending on their geographic location. Thus, some experimentation may be necessary with the specimens you obtain, although they are apt to conform and adjust to the temperature conditions imposed by their captivity rather than nature. After allowing them to hibernate for three months beginning in late autumn, they should be warmed to around 50 degrees F and then fed.

In nature, Fire Salamanders breed at night in mild, damp weather. Mating occurs on land, and fertilization is internal. In most areas, the eggs are retained internally, and when ready to hatch the female immerses her hindquarters in the water and releases between 10 and 30 fully formed larvae. Because the adult is fully terrestrial, provide the female with only a shallow pool of water, assuring that she does not drown in the process of releasing the larvae. You can move the larvae to a larger rearing tank after she completes her delivery. The larvae are vociferous feeders and are cannibalistic of smaller and weaker siblings, so separation by size or health status may be necessary if you hope to raise the majority of the clutch. The larvae need only about 3 to 5 inches of filtered water. When they begin to metamorphose, it is necessary to lower water levels to a mere inch to prevent them from drowning at this critical period between aquatic and terrestrial status. Be sure to provide rafts of floating vegetation and gently sloped rock formations

jutting above the surface so as to give them a place to haul out or hang above the surface if they need to breathe air before metamorphosis is completed. You can also add several pounds of smooth pebbles to form a gently sloping beachhead or mound that will serve a similar purpose.

Emperor (Mandarin) Newts

The Emperor or Mandarin Newt, which is also known as the Crocodile Newt (*Tylototriton verrucosus*), is a beautiful species with an unusual appearance. It is frequently available in the U.S. pet trade, exported along with tropical fish shipments from Burma, Thailand and elsewhere in southeast Asia. Because males are highly territorial and fight with each other, attempts at mating should include no more than one pair (male and female) per enclosure, unless the newts are mated in a large greenhouse or outdoor pond.

Territorial tendencies require Emperor Newts to be kept in pairs (Emperor Newt, *Tylototriton verrucosus*).

TO BREED, OR NOT TO BREED

Regrettably, many of the salamanders that appear in the pet trade or on animal dealer lists are wild-caught. This is due, no doubt, to a small market and little interest in these amphibians in comparison with frogs, toads and reptiles. Many aquatic species such as newts are increasingly being bred on tropical fish farms as a sideline occupation. Because salamander larvae are carnivorous and would eat up all the fish fry, it is necessary for such fish farmers to raise larvae separately from the fish. As a result, only a few fish farmers raise but a very few species of salamander for the trade.

If you are seriously interested in salamanders, then by all means acquire, study and breed them. You may, however, find a very small number of takers for your offspring. Under no circumstances should they be released in the wild, as they were raised in captivity and, moreover, they may not be native to your geographic locale. So if you can't sell your progeny, try and give them away. College and university biology departments, high schools and pet shops may be able to care for them, and the latter may be able to sell them for you. You may also find people willing to adopt a salamander by placing an ad in the newspaper or in the newsletter of your local herpetological society.

Following a two- to three-month period of hibernation, they emerge to feed, mate and breed in cool shallow waters. Females deposit up to 150 eggs on aquatic vegetation, which hatch in about four days. Larvae require cool temperatures (55 to 60 degrees F) and well-oxygenated water. Metamorphosis is completed in about one year.

Frog and Toad Reproduction

"The familiar progression from egg to tadpole is only one of many methods. Others include egg to froglet, egg brooding, and tadpoles in the mother's stomach."

—William E. Duellman, *Scientific American,* July 1992

The first major work to explore the standard life history of a common frog was published in 1758 by a German scientist, von Rosenhoft. In painstaking detail he illustrated the progression from egg to tadpole to four-legged froglet. Von Rosenhoft's discoveries and observations revealed the mysterious and unusual life history of a large number of the world's frogs (even though it was based on a study of a common European ranid: the Edible Frog, *Rana esculenta*).

Today, however, scientists have catalogued so many departures from this classic understanding that it is truly impossible to describe frog and toad reproduction from one viewpoint, as "classical" as it may be. More than 20 percent (over 800) of all the frog species bypass the larval tadpole stage and progress directly to the adult form from the egg—an adaptation known as "direct development." The adaptation occurs because these frogs have no safe, long-term body of water readily available to them for free-living aquatic larvae. This situation has not deterred them from reproducing, and direct development is the means by which they survive. Other frogs are viviparous and lay no eggs externally. They retain their eggs internally or hold them externally; brood them in pouches, their vocal sacs or, as in the case of two now extinct Australian species, in their stomachs; and then release either fully formed froglets or, if water is available for the larvae, fully formed tadpoles.

But regardless of life history or the means by which it is accomplished, it is the free-living larval stage of amphibians and its progression or metamorphosis to an adult form that has endeared amphibians to scientific researchers. This unusual chain of events enables students and scientists to study embryological development outside of the egg, as amphibian larvae are somewhat analogous to embryos (save for the fact that they are free-living and not dependent on the egg for their continued development). When a larval amphibian is about to change into the adult form, that period is known as the metamorphic climax. It is a short, ill-defined period of time when the aquatic larval form suddenly becomes an adult, air-breathing animal.

One of frogdom's favorite stories is that told by Professor William E. Duellman, one of America's premier and most noted amphibian biologists. Duellman discovered a most unusual frog life history in 1975 during a field expedition to Chile. He had happened upon a male Darwin's Frog just as it was giving birth. Yes, a male!

The male of this species takes the newly hatched tadpoles into the mouth, where they migrate into the vocal sacs and remain for several weeks until they metamorphose. They then pop out of the father's mouth as fully formed froglets. An amazing photo of a baby frog peering out of its father's mouth accompanied news of this exciting discovery. Duellman conveyed the news to a fellow frog scientist in Australia, Professor Michael Tyler. At around the same time, Tyler and colleagues had discovered the manner in which two Australian species, *Rheobatrachus sp.*, brood their young: They convert their stomachs into a womb and then release their young through the oral cavity as fully developed froglets. In this case, the

female actually swallows her own eggs but somehow shuts off all digestive processes while the eggs are in residence. Tyler calls this "oral-birth." On receipt of Duellman's observation, he sent back a copy of the paper describing his observation, inscribing it simply with one word: "Touché."

Males of other species (*Alytes sp.*) carry their eggs and tadpoles on their back; females of the aquatic genera *Pipa* do likewise. Another genus has pouches on its rear legs into which its eggs are brooded (*Asa sp.*). And a large group of South American tree frogs, the Marsupial Frogs (*Gastrotheca sp.*), brood their eggs in special pouches under the skin of their back and flank. When I first witnessed the live birth of tadpoles from *Gastrotheca*, I thought I was hallucinating (having just spent several months flat on my back with a serious illness). I had to call my father, mother and sister to verify what I was seeing. At that time (1957), high schools and colleges were teaching essentially the same life history of frogs and toads as first published back in 1758! Hardly anyone had yet discovered any of these unusual life histories, much less observed them in a controlled captive environment. The strange life histories of tropical species were considered oddities left to dedicated frog biologists, and there was little or no widespread popular

interest in them. However, today we know that there are more than 1,000 species of frogs that depart substantially from the classical example. And it is envisioned that new and perhaps even more improbable life histories are yet to be discovered.

With so many thousands of different frog and toad species, it is virtually impossible to describe the mating, breeding and reproductive characteristics of all of them. Therefore, a few of the more popular groups and species within these groups have been selected for discussion.

Breeding Oriental Fire-Bellied Toads and European Yellow-Bellied Toads

The Oriental Fire-Bellied and European Yellow-Bellied Toads (*Bombina sp.*) breed readily in captivity, and many specimens reaching the pet market are from captive-bred as well as wild-caught stocks. Attempts to breed these species require a large aqua-terrarium where there is a substantial area of shallow water.

Breeding occurs readily under bright light, spray misting or automated rain equipment after a four-month period of hibernation at 40 degrees F. The toads will call a mournful cry during this period that will both startle and delight the keeper. After one or two

Many of the Bombinids available to the pet trade have been bred in captivity (Oriental Fire-Bellied Toad, *Bombina orientalis*).

months of feeding and gradual warming (to 65 to 75 degrees F), they will begin to breed. The males readily engage in amplexus with other males as well as females that are "not ready." A release call, indicating that the eager male's attentions are not welcome, is commonly heard when this occurs. Because amplexus can go on for prolonged periods in the water, it is wise to lower water levels to 1 to 2 inches to prevent a the female from drowning, although this species is fairly aquatic and adept in the water even when in a mating embrace.

Up to 150 eggs are deposited, either singly or in clumps. They must be removed for rearing in a separate facility or the adults transferred if the eggs are left in place. Hatching occurs within one week or slightly less, and tadpoles metamorphose in four to eight weeks. Bombinid tadpoles are omnivorous and vociferously consume large amounts of both vegetable and animal matter. Vegetarian fish flakes and even tiny pieces of lean red meat can be fed. Transforming larvae and froglets should be raised in small, size-categorized groups in sweater- or shoe-box-sized plastic bins with only $1/2$ inch of water and a beach-head constructed of smooth pebbles or small, easy-to-climb rocks.

Because captive-born bombinids frequently lose their bright underbelly coloration, vitamin supplements containing beta-carotene should be dusted on pinhead crickets, fruit flies and other small bugs used as food.

Breeding Bufonid Toads
Harlequin Toads

The Bufonid toads contain a few species that are of interest to breeders. Among these are the Harlequin Toads of the genus *Atelopus,* colorful poisonous species that are the Bufonid version of the Central and South American dart poison frogs and Madagascar's mantella frogs. They are also known as "Stub-Foot Toads." Most popular species of *Atelopus* are protected by law, and their export is banned in many of the countries where they are known to occur. However, stocks of captive-bred animals exist in Europe; and with a few breeders in the United States, they are occasionally available from breeders and dealers. They are considered poor breeders in captivity, but some have succeeded with them. They are definitely a challenge.

For stimulating breeding, moving water is considered of paramount importance. Fortunately, a number of waterfall and moving stream accessories can be purchased to help meet this requirement. Breeding is also triggered by rainmaking equipment or frequent manual spraying of the toads' enclosure. Mating occurs at the water's edge, and the female attaches her eggs to the substrate just below the water's surface in shallow pools. In captive breeding reports of the Veragoa Harlequin Toad (*Atelopus varius*), tadpoles hatched within one-and-one-half days. These unusual larvae have flat bodies and an odd abdominal sucker that appears to help them move about without being carried off by the currents of the fast-moving streams that they inhabit in nature.

Under captive conditions, you may wish to move the larvae to an aquarium containing well-aerated and well-filtered warm water. They

Colorado River Toads are popular with amateur breeders (Colorado River Toad, *Bufo alvarius*).

Although there is some demand for the species enumerated above, most other local Bufo toads can be collected from the wild so long as they are neither protected by law nor under any danger of extinction or diminishing numbers. There is apt to be a very small market for such common locally collected species, and many of these are often sold as food animals for toad-eating snakes. Although troublesome extinctions of toad populations have occurred, these events have never been connected to over-collecting, but rather to a variety of environmental insults, pollution, disease and habitat destruction.

All temperate-zone Bufo toads breed after a winter hibernation period. They mate in the water, where the female extrudes her eggs and the male releases sperm in the general vicinity of the release.

Although the eggs of *Bufo* toads are apt to be highly toxic, they are still preyed upon and consumed

transform into froglets within a month.

Breeding Other Bufonids

There are a number of toads of the genus Bufo that attract attention because of their unusual coloration or large size. These include Cane or Marine Toads (*Bufo marinus),* Blomberg's Toad (*Bufo blombergi*), the Colorado River Toad (*Bufo alvarius),* the Red Spotted Toad (*Bufo punctatus),* the Green Toad (*Bufo debilis*) and the Black Spined Toad (*Bufo melanosticus*), to name but a few of this very large and widespread family.

All bufonid toads breed in the water and need a spacious aqua-terrarium. Like most anurans, they are stimulated by temperature changes, warmer weather and rain. They are apt to breed readily and most species

lay thousands of eggs, far too many to even consider raising. You can, of course, consider breeding them outdoors, but you run a serious risk of escape with any nonnative species you keep outdoors—there can be very negative environmental consequences should they thrive and become permanently established where they don't normally occur.

Bufo toads in amplexus (*Bufo valliceps*).

with impunity by a variety of aquatic organisms. Accordingly, out of the thousands of eggs laid, very few survive to adulthood. Nevertheless, their fecundity is well established, and they may be extremely populous in some areas and absent in others for no apparent reason. If breeding them indoors in enclosures or aquariums of a limited size, it may be necessary to cull a good many of the eggs and give special attention to a hundred or so that are retained (hoping they are fertilized, as not all the eggs produced may be fertile). The Marine or Cane Toad (*Bufo marinus*) lays up to 30,000 eggs—obviously an untenable number for any home hobbyist to consider rearing. For this reason, and its availability as a wild-caught pest species, there is no rationale in trying to captive breed this species.

Breeding Dart Poison Frogs

The dendrobatid or dart poison frogs (also known as arrow poison frogs) exist in an unbelievable array of wild colors and patterns that rival those of saltwater reef fish. It is their strikingly beautiful appearance that has made reef fish so enormously popular; and a similar band of enthusiasts breed, trade and sell these frogs for the same aesthetic reasons.

Although getting most dendrobatids to mate and breed is not particularly difficult, rearing the eggs

Most dart poison frogs will breed readily in captivity, but rearing the young can be challenging (Blue Dart Poison Frog, *Dendrobates azureus*).

and larvae is quite difficult for many species. Given healthy, well-fed adults and suitable temperatures (70 to 80 degrees F) and humidity conditions (including either frequent spray mistings or preprogrammed rainmaking events), females will swell with eggs and the males can be heard calling. It is important to remember that dendrobatids lay their eggs on land, on leaves or on bromeliad plants, conditions that must be provided in your terrarium. One or both of the adults watch over the eggs until they hatch, at which time the adults position themselves so that the larvae can wriggle up onto their backs. The carrying parent then proceeds to the nearest shallow pool of water (which you must also provide) and releases the tadpoles.

The Strawberry Dart Poison Frog (*Dendrobates pumilio*) deposits each of her eggs in an axil (vase or cupola of a bromeliad or air plant), one to a container. She then returns daily to each of her tadpoles, now housed separately, and extrudes an unfertilized egg into their water, which they use as food. Advanced and very astute breeders of this species in captivity find it difficult to duplicate this behavior in their female, so they draw up a tiny quantity of chicken egg yolk in an eyedropper and simulate the feedings that are provided by the mother in the wild. Great care must be taken not to place too much (but just the right amount) of the artificial feed in each nursery or uneaten material will quickly decompose, killing the tadpole.

In the case of all dendrobatids, it is important to provide suitable, secluded regions with a smooth, clean surface for egg laying. Many breeders use plastic petri dishes, an inverted half of a cleaned-out coconut shell or similar devices, which most dendrobatids will use to deposit their eggs. The egg mass is wetted by gently placing a dampened piece of unprinted paper toweling, gauze pads or capillary matting (used in horticulture) over the eggs to keep them moist. Some breeders remove the laying sites to an incubator tank and position them at hatching time so that the tadpoles can wriggle into a shallow pool of water, while others leave them under the parents' care. Because of problems with territoriality, it is wise to breed just one pair per enclosure. When artificially incubating the eggs in a separate enclosure, breeders of many of these species have found it worthwhile to dampen the eggs several times a day with about a millimeter of warm water, raising the water level as the eggs begin to hatch so that the tadpoles are safe in an aquatic milieu.

Once hatched, tadpoles can be scooped up individually in a spoon and transferred to individual rearing containers. Some breeders use large plastic ice-cube trays for this purpose. Separating the tadpoles precludes the possibility of cannibalism and also permits the breed-er to examine the progress of each specimen individually. Tadpoles can be fed ground fish flakes or dry food, brine shrimp and other tiny aquatic crustaceans (see the discussion of feeding tadpoles in Chapter 8). Strawberry Dart Poison Frog tadpoles must be reared on egg yolk, but it is necessary to supplement this at least once a week by adding a pinch of such preparations directly to the water. Uneaten food and the water should be pipetted out after a few hours and replaced with aged tap water at about the same temperature.

Breeders rearing a large number of tadpoles individually in containers such as ice-cube trays have added tiny holes at the bottom of each compartment so that water withdrawn at one end is pulled from each individual compartment. It is necessary to add the new water simultaneously. It is important not to injure the tadpoles during this process, so often the end drain compartment is not used to house a tadpole. Depending on the species and water temperature (around 75 to 80 degrees F is recommended), tadpoles change into froglets in two to three months. As soon as all four legs erupt, the tiny frogs should be transferred to a heavily planted rearing terrarium that can be seeded with aphids and springtails. It is a good idea to limit rearing groups to no more than five froglets per 10-gallon terrarium. A shallow water dish with $1/4$ inch of water should be provided. Finally, it is advised that should you start breeding these frogs, you try to find other breeders with whom to trade stock so that you can avoid potential problems with inbreeding that, in turn, can result in genetic defects in offspring. Joining the American, British or Dutch Dendrobatid Groups (see Chapter 14) or all three can help you connect with others in the hobby.

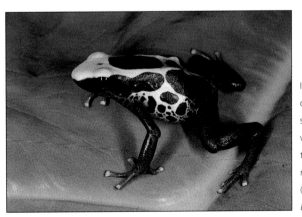

If you decide to breed dart poison frogs, you should try to trade stock with other breeders to avoid inbreeding and resulting genetic defects (Dyeing Dart Poison Frog, *Dendrobates tinctorius*).

A number of American zoos and universities have established breeding colonies of dendrobatid frogs. Although studies have not yet been published, it is instructive to follow the means by which they raise dendrobatid tadpoles individually and, in some cases, in small groups, in perforated plastic refrigerator dishes. The dishes are mounted on a screen platform that sits on bricks, the whole affair immersed in a larger well-filtered aquarium tank. This enables the breeders to control water quality and temperature for all the tadpoles while allowing each to have a separate enclosure (or in some cases, for several to be in a single enclosure). The results of these projects will help determine the best way of raising dart poison frog larvae.

Breeding Discoglossid Frogs
Midwife Toads

The Discoglossid frog in which breeding is most frequently attempted, particularly in its native Europe, is the aforementioned Midwife Toad. British experts say it is a difficult species to breed in captivity, but successful free-living outdoor breeding colonies have been established in several locations in Great Britain.

If breeding is attempted in an indoor vivarium, the enclosure should be as large as possible, kept at cool temperatures (50 to 60 degrees F) and kept moist, either by frequent spray misting or through use of a preprogrammed rainmaker. A three-month hibernation period in which the frogs are kept at 40 degrees F should precede any attempts at breeding this species.

The male engages the female in amplexus, and they remain in this embrace for up to one week before extruding up to 50 eggs, each with a hardened, water- and gas-permeable membrane. The male fertilizes them and then wraps the egg string around his legs. He must be given a shallow dish of water to periodically enter for the purpose of moistening the eggs. After about eight to 12 weeks, he sheds the eggs in the water, where the membranes disintegrate. The eggs hatch into free-living tadpoles, a process that could take several hours. They metamorphose into froglets in about four months. When all four legs start to appear, the water level must be lowered to about 1 inch and/or a mound of pebbles must be provided to prevent the transforming froglets from drowning.

Breeding Tree Frogs
Marsupial Frogs

Marsupial Frogs (*Gastrotheca sp.*) can be bred under relatively simple conditions. They are largely a high-altitude species that endure cool temperatures (55 to 65 degrees F) and are active at night, although some seem to be as diurnal as they are nocturnal.

Breeding takes place in the spring and is signaled by crawking and clucking vocalizations. Females ready to mate approach the males and amplexus takes place on land. As the eggs are laid, the male fertilizes them. Both male and female push the eggs into the female's dorsal pouch for incubation and hatching. Some species retain the eggs as larvae and deliver fully formed froglets, whereas others release the eggs as tadpoles into shallow water. The female uses her hind-leg toes to stretch open the pouch slit to release her young, often alternating with one foot and then the other in an attempt to empty the pouch from both sides. The tadpoles eat vegetarian fish flakes, boiled lettuce, spinach and other greens, aquatic plants and algae. Clutch size ranges from 90 to 150 eggs and varies with species and the size of the female. Froglets are carnivorous insectivores and eat a variety of suitably sized bugs.

White's Tree Frogs

White's Tree Frog (*Litoria caerulea*), an Australian species also found in Papua New Guinea and Indonesia, is an attractive subject for captive breeding. This is a highly popular species, and successful breeders should have no trouble finding homes for offspring.

However, breeding White's Tree Frogs involves some environmental alterations. First, well-fed adult

You don't need to worry that the young of your White's Tree Frogs will go homeless—there is strong demand for this popular species (White's Tree Frog, *Litoria caerulea*).

males and females should be selected. Males have grayer, more wrinkled throats than females and are smaller and less rounded in appearance. It is necessary to estivate them under dry conditions for about four weeks. In response to dehydration, they will develop a watertight cocoon made up of layers of shed epidermal tissue. After the dormancy period ends, they are roused by being showered with warm water for about one hour. A large water bowl should also be placed in the enclosure. After awakening from their stimulating shower the frogs will enter the water bowl, where they will begin to call until the female, if receptive, responds by permitting amplexus. The embrace can last for as long as 24 hours, during which time the female extrudes large clumps of eggs totaling about 100 to 150 in all.

The eggs should be carefully netted and placed in a 20-gallon (or larger) warm-water aquarium, where they will develop into tadpoles in about two or three days. They transform into froglets in less than three weeks when fed a steady diet of fish food, chopped earthworms and small strips of lean, raw red meat. At metamorphosis, water levels must be reduced and a land area should be provided so that the transforming tadpoles do not drown. As soon as they are transformed, they should be removed from the tadpole rearing tank and installed in raising containers or terrariums, with five to 10 frogs per 10-gallon tank. They continue to grow and reach a fairly large size within one to two years. After being started on insects as froglets, they should be quickly sold, traded or given to other hobbyists. However, some may be held back for future breeding projects with unrelated mates.

Piebald and white White's Tree Frogs are in great demand, and if you can cull out babies with these traits and back cross them to produce such specimens, they bring a greater price than standard frogs. This is true also of some members of this species that become completely blue rather than having the normal green or dark green coloration.

Red-Eyed Tree Frogs

Another extremely popular species, which is usually exported wild-caught from Nicaragua, is the Red-Eyed Tree Frog (*Agalychnis callidryas*). These frogs can be bred in captivity, and notable successes have occurred within the past few years. More captive breeders of this species are needed to help stem reliance on wild-caught specimens. A well-planted and well-landscaped terrarium is needed for this species, as they lay their eggs on the underside of broad leaves that overhang the water. Such plants, moreover, must be able to support the weight of two adult frogs, as mating occurs on these leaves as well.

During amplexus and fertilization, the female extrudes and

By breeding Red-Eyed Tree Frogs for the pet trade, you'll help to reduce the significant number taken from the wild (Red-Eyed Tree Frog, *Agalychnis callidryas*).

deposits about 75 jelly-covered, sticky eggs to the leaf. As the tadpoles hatch, they fall directly into the water below to begin their free-living aquatic larval stage. When this occurs, it is recommended that they be carefully netted and transferred to a well-planted 3-gallon rearing aquarium with about 8 inches of warmed, well-aerated and well-filtered water. The tadpoles are omnivorous and will eat fish flakes, parsley and lean, red, raw meat. Metamorphosis occurs approximately 45 days later, at which time water levels should be lowered and floating platforms and mats of vegetation added to enable the newly transformed froglets to haul out of the water. They should then be transferred to a terrestrial setup with a shallow ($^1/_4$-inch) pond of water and plenty of small plants and branches on which to climb. They should be fed a variety of small insects, dusted with a vitamin/mineral supplement. After being well started on terrestrial food they can be easily sold, traded or given away, as there is no shortage of people who desire these beautiful frogs.

Breeding Leptodactylidae Frogs
Horned Frogs

Unquestionably the most popular group of frogs in the Family Leptodactylidae are the horned or "Pac-Man" frogs of the genus *Ceratophrys*. Ornate or Argentinean Horned Frogs (*Ceratophrys ornata*) are currently being captive bred in large numbers and are widely available as hatchlings or well-started metamorphosed froglets. Males of the species can be identified by their bluish-gray tinted throats and the loose skin that accommodates their vocal sac. They also possess dark brown or blackish nuptial pads on the inner toes of the front feet.

A single pair consisting of an adult male and gravid female should be placed together in a large aqua-terrarium with the water side kept to about 3 inches to prevent drowning. One also needs to assure that there is little size difference between the members of the pair, because these frogs are cannibalistic and are not above eating each other if they feel so inclined. Amplexus lasts up to four hours and is accompanied by the deposit and external fertilization of anywhere from several hundred to

Horned frogs in amplexus (Argentinian Ornate Horned Frogs, *Ceratophrys ornata*).

1,000 eggs, many of which may escape fertilization and die. The eggs should then be dip-netted and transferred to a minimum 55- or 60-gallon aquarium filled to a height of 12 inches. The water should be well aerated and filtered, but filter returns need to be covered with fine mesh to prevent sucking the eggs up into the filter box. Fertile eggs will hatch within two days at a water temperature of 75 to 80 degrees F. Lower temperatures produce smaller hatch rates and deformities among tadpoles that do hatch.

Horned frog tadpoles are truly the piranhas of the frog world. They travel in packs and swarm in on larger aquatic prey, devouring it as a group. They will also feed off strips of lean, red meat dangled in the water. After about one month, metamorphosis will occur and water levels need to be lowered. Froglets should be immediately removed to individual plastic pint-sized deli containers or refrigerator dishes and housed separately from this time forward. In order to prevent accidental drowning, floating platforms, floating mats of vegetation and other structures should be added to the aquarium in the event metamorphosis occurs when you are not watching the frogs. The rearing containers are best positioned on a slight angle with a small puddle of water at one end. Baby frogs are fed chopped fish

Baby horned frogs have a good appetite— this frog is not much bigger than the cricket it's eating (Argentinian Ornate Horned Frog, *Ceratophrys ornata*).

with bones intact, earthworms, waxworms and other insects. Supplementing with a mineral/vitamin supplement helps prevent bone deformities. After being started this way by breeders, these small frogs are ready to be sold, traded or given away to new homes.

Budgett's Frogs

Another popular Leptodactylid frog is a large species (up to 6 inches) found in Argentina and Paraguay known as Budgett's Frog (*Lepidobatrachus laevis*). This frog is almost cartoonish in appearance, with a fat, fleshy body, wide mouth and white eyes with small black pupils that look almost as if they were drawn on. It is easily bred in captivity.

The procedure for breeding this species is to first replace its pool of water with dry sand, into which it will burrow, forming a cocoon. After two-and-one-half months, the sand should be heavily saturat-

ed with water to awaken the estivating frogs. Amplexus occurs in shallow water accompanied by the deposit of as many as 2,000 eggs, which attach to aquatic plants. The eggs should be transferred to a large aquarium filled with warm water (80 degrees F) and numerous aquatic plants. The eggs hatch in about five days. The tadpoles are voracious carnivores, swallowing anything they can suck into their tube-like mouths; they grow rapidly, reaching maximum lengths of about 3 inches before beginning metamorphosis, which occurs in about three to four weeks. At metamorphic climax, water levels should be lowered to about 3 inches and mats of floating vegetation, platforms or sand or pebble mounds should be provided for the transforming frogs. On completion of metamorphosis they should be removed to individual rearing cups and fed any bug small enough to swallow. Their large mouths allow them to ingest insects that would be too large for most newly transformed froglets.

Breeding Microhylidae Frogs

Among the family Microhylidae, a number of species are popular subjects for captive care and breeding.

Madagascar Tomato Frogs

One of the most colorful members of this family is the Madagascar Tomato Frog (*Dyscophus sp.*). These rotund red frogs reach lengths of about 3 inches. Export is largely banned now from Madagascar, so all specimens coming into the pet and hobby trade are from captive-bred stocks that trace their ancestry to specimens imported before the legal prohibition.

Mating, fertilization and the deposit of eggs occur in warm shallow water with rafts of vegetation present. Females deposit up to 3,000 eggs but, of course, not all are fertile. The eggs should be removed after being laid to a large, well-aerated warm-water (80 degrees F) aquarium, where they will hatch in about three days. Tadpoles are primarily herbivorous and will feed on algae and vegetarian fish flakes. They transform into froglets in about two months.

These frogs are prized for their color. The species that is the brightest red of all is the Northern Tomato Frog (*Dyscophis antongili*), but it is extremely scarce. Its numbers are reduced in the wild, which has been attributed to a combination of habitat destruction and

overcollecting for the hobby trade. The most commonly available captive-bred species is the Southern Tomato Frog (*Dyscophus guineti*). Unlike most newly transformed froglets, which look just like miniature versions of their parents, the colors of the young depart markedly from those they develop as adults. As juveniles, they are brownish above and dark blue below. Adults are an orange-red, but not nearly as brightly hued as the northern form.

Breeding Malayan Painted Toads

The Malayan Painted Toad (*Kaloula pulchra*) is a commonly seen import that has been bred in captivity. These plump brown and tan frogs reach lengths of 4 inches when sexually mature. They are difficult to sex save for the fact that adult males appear smaller than females. No special stimulating factors cause this species to breed in captivity other than higher temperatures and increased humidity and rainfall (simulated by spray misting).

Because of their obesity, it is difficult for the males to grasp the females in amplexus, so they secrete a sticky substance from glands on their bellies that hardens, bonding the pair together. They can remain like this for a month, perhaps longer, until the female decides to spawn and enters shallow water that is permeated with

Prized for its bright color, the Northern Tomato Frog is quite scarce—don't hesitate to breed this species (Northern tomato frog, *Dyscophus antongili*).

floating vegetation. After depositing her eggs, which the male fertilizes, she sheds her skin, which, coupled with the water, helps to release the male. Any manual attempt to pry the male off the female will injure both frogs, perhaps fatally. (A number of other species also bond to the female using mucoid glue-like secretions, and frog hobbyists are forewarned not to attempt to separate them for the same reason.)

Tadpoles hatch after four or five days and live on their yolk sac reserves for another week. They remain motionless during this period, so don't think they are dead and don't attempt to feed them. Tadpoles are carnivorous, eating raw meat, trout pellets and other animal-based foods once yolk reserves are gone and they become mobile. Newly metamorphosed froglets are delicate. After metamorphosis they should be kept in small containers with a moist substrate, as they can dry out easily. Small insects must be provided up to several times a day, or the froglets will die within a day or so.

Breeding Pipid Frogs

The family Pipidae is a strictly aquatic group that is frequently bred in captivity, primarily for the aquarium trade and for scientific research. Among the species commonly encountered are the common African Clawed Frog (*Xenopus*

The tiny tadpoles of the gigantic African Clawed Frog are likely to be eaten by their parents, so be sure to remove the adults from the tank (African Clawed Frog, *Pyxicephalus adspersa*).

laevis), the West African Dwarf Clawed Frog (*Hymenochirus boettgeri*) and the South American Surinam Toad (*Pipa pipa*).

African Clawed Frogs

African Clawed Frogs are easily bred in large aquariums following hormone administration, but hobbyist breeders can also breed them without the benefit of hormones. Females begin to ovulate in warm (85 degree F) shallow water; then, by adding ice, water temperature is suddenly decreased and water levels restored. If the female is receptive, she allows the male to embrace her in amplexus and the frogs begin doing somersaults in the water, releasing up to a dozen eggs with each turn while the male liberates sperm to fertilize them. Some 500 eggs are produced, which settle on the substrate—this should consist of smooth pebbles and rocks. The eggs hatch in several days. The parents should be

removed from the tank, as they are likely to eat the tiny tadpoles. Fry fish food should be offered at first, although up to 80 percent of the tiny larvae are likely to die before metamorphosis, which occurs within three months.

West African Dwarf Clawed Frogs

The procedures for inducing mating and breeding in West African Dwarf Clawed Frogs (*Hymenochirus boettgeri*) are similar to those applicable to their larger cousins, except that water temperature should be maintained at about 85 degrees F for several weeks. Initially, water level should be shallow (about 3 inches); then it should be increased suddenly to 8 to 10 inches by rapidly adding warm water.

Once the female becomes gravid, the male will embrace her and begin a spawning display similar to that of *Xenopus*. As the adults will eat the eggs, they should be removed immediately after spawning is complete. The eggs hatch into tadpoles within a few days and are carnivorous from the outset. They feed readily on microscopic aquatic organisms, gradually consuming larger and larger aquatic invertebrates.

Surinam Toads

Breeding the Surinam Toad is somewhat more problematic than breeding its African relatives. Spawning can be induced by cooling water down to as little as 45 degrees for several days and then increasing it suddenly to around 85 degrees F. The frogs should be well fed at this time. Eggs rapidly develop, and the male embraces the female in amplexus around the waist. The pair, now bound to each other, swim off doing somersaults. The female's back begins to swell. The male squeezes her violently to expel the eggs, fertilizes them and then maneuvers as many as he can onto her back, where they stick. After doing this up to ten times, the pair separate and the eggs remain embedded in chambers or pockmarks all over the female's dorsum. The eggs undergo direct development into froglets while being carried by the female and after nearly five months, fully formed Surinam "toadlets" (strictly speaking these frogs are not toads) appear. The adults will try and eat

the baby frogs, so the young should be removed to rearing tanks that are well filtered and aerated and fed a diet of daphnia, small aquatic worms (tubifex) and fish fry or tiny feeder guppies.

Breeding Ranid Frogs

The family Ranidae, or true frogs, contain several genera that are much in demand by hobbyists and are definitely worth captive breeding.

Mantella Frogs

A very popular group in this family are the mantella frogs of Madagascar, brightly colored ranids similar in appearance to the Dendrobatid or dart poison frogs. Like the dart poison frogs, they contain poisonous skin secretions;

however, those of the mantella frogs are not nearly as toxic. The Golden Mantella (*Mantella aurantiaca*), Cowan's Multicolored Mantella (*Mantella cowani*) and the Green Mantella (*Mantella viridis*) are among the most popular. These frogs have also suffered serious declines in their native Madagascar and export is prohibited. However, there are examples of these frogs in the hands of breeders, and some continue to be available as captive-bred rather than as wild-caught.

Golden Mantella Frogs

Once Golden Mantellas settle in, they can breed regularly. They are often maintained in breeding colonies of eight or so animals. Courtship, mating and egg laying

Golden mantellas are relatively easy to breed in captivity (Golden Mantella in red phase, left; Golden Mantella in gold phase, right, *Mantella auranticaca*).

occur out of the water. Lowering daytime temperatures to around 72 degrees F for about three weeks (so they can be less active) and increasing the temperature to 80 degrees F at night, along with heavy misting or rainmaking cycles, helps stimulate female ovulation. After the females become gravid, the males can be heard calling from their hides during the day. After the eggs are laid by the female beneath damp wood or in sphagnum moss, they are fertilized by one or several males in the group. Up to 80 eggs are deposited, and both the male and female tend their nest by secreting fluid over the eggs to keep them moist and viable as the tadpoles develop within. As in other terrestrial laying species, the eggs undergo direct development. However, in the mantella frogs, development occurs not within the egg, but in the gelatinous outer egg casing. The tadpoles change into froglets in about three months. Each female may clutch 10 times per year, and the young frogs are placed in individual plastic rearing containers where they are fed tiny insects until sold or traded. The Golden Mantella departs substantially from the standard ranid form of aquatic mating, egg-laying and free-living tadpole stage.

The tadpoles of the striking Cowan's Mantella Frogs will develop in or out of the water, depending on where the eggs were laid (Cowan's Mantella Frog, *Mantella cowani*).

REPRODUCTIVE SYNERGY

Frogs of the genus *Xenopus* ovulate readily in response to injections of human chorionic gonadotropin (HCG), a hormone that is found in the urine of pregnant women. This discovery has made these frogs unusually popular for reproductive and related research, as their ova can practically be obtained on demand. And until the advent of simpler chemical indicator tests, these frogs were also often used in pregnancy testing.

Cowan's Multicolored Mantella Frogs

Breeding groups of *Mantella cowani* deposit their eggs close to or actually in shallow water. The tadpoles, on hatching, continue their development within the egg case or, on occasion, as free-living aquatic larvae if they were deposited as eggs in water.

Other Ranid Frogs

The Matang Frog or Malayan Painted Frog (*Rana signata*) is beautifully "painted" with orange and yellow bars over a dark black background color. Little is known of its reproductive behavior, but it is occasionally available as an import. Ranids such as Leopard Frogs, American Bullfrogs and the African Bullfrog require enormously spacious, preferably outdoor, enclosures. Both American Bullfrogs and Leopard Frogs are raised commercially on frog farms for the frog leg trade and as lab animals, respectively. These are easily and inexpensively diverted to the hobbyist trade, so there is no need to invest in the in-home captive breeding of these species.

CHAPTER 10

Health Care

Veterinarians who look after the health care of captive amphibians, as well as field biologists who must discern whether a disease is affecting wild populations, all agree that the study of amphibian health care is in its infancy. The likelihood of finding a veterinarian with any meaningful experience in amphibian medicine is slim. In addition, veterinary care is often expensive, and many hobbyists without access to expert professional advice are often forced to go it alone when handling amphibian health care problems. If you are lucky, you may have a veterinary expert not far from you; you can write the Association of Reptile and Amphibian Veterinarians (see Chapter 14) to obtain a list of experts in your general vicinity. You should do this today—well in advance of any medical emergency that may befall your animals.

And while amphibians suffer the same sorts of illnesses that afflict reptiles and other animals, there is little scientific basis for making a firm diagnosis and instituting treatment. There are no studies, for example, of what doses of antibiotic or parasitic medications to use. Thus, even if your veterinarian or you discover that your animal has a particular internal parasite and the drug of choice to kill it is apparent, there is little or nothing known of how much of the medication to give, how often it should be given, and which route of administration is apt to be most effective in amphibian patients. Nor can anyone be certain if the indicated drug is safe to use in amphibians or at what doses it may be harmful.

In spite of this lamentable situation, it still pays hobbyists to have a rudimentary knowledge of amphibian health care problems. Determining the existence of such problems and trying to alleviate them are better than doing nothing at all. Such efforts may result in a satisfactory outcome that can be shared with other hobbyists through hobbyist newsletters or amphibian/reptile magazines, even if only in a letter to the editor.

Categories of Disease

Amphibians are known to suffer the following types of health problems:

Developmental disorders. Developmental disorders are related to poor nutrition as tadpoles or as developing adults, but of course poor nutrition can have a serious impact on your amphibian's health at any time of its life.

Infectious diseases. These include diseases caused by bacteria, viruses, unicellular and multicellular parasites (both internal and external) and fungi.

Traumas. Traumas are problems related to injuries such as broken bones or wounds.

Environmental diseases. Amphibians are in intimate contact with their environment. Captive environments that are too wet, too dry, too cold, too hot, too light or too dark can all result in stress, decreased immunity and constitutional problems.

Toxic diseases. These are diseases caused by poison, venom or other toxins.

Zoonoses. Zoonoses are infectious diseases that are contagious to humans from animals. There are about 300 such infectious diseases in the world, and a number of them can originate in amphibians.

Symptoms of Disease

Your amphibians should be examined regularly for the signs and

Examine your frog or salamander often for signs of poor health. Skin should be free of lesions or fungi (Green Mantella Frog, *Mantella viridis*).

symptoms of health-related problems. In some cases signs may be so obvious—such as a broken leg, skin lesion, external parasite (e.g., leech) or external fungal or bacterial infection (blisters and odd-looking lesions)—that you can be fairly certain you have identified a problem. In other cases, such as when an amphibian refuses to eat, no longer jumps or moves as it did previously or appears strange (e.g., if its color darkens or lightens or it has excessive skin secretions), the underlying internal causes may not be easy to discern. Unfortunately, many amphibians die without their caretakers ever learning why.

Giving Medications

If you plan on treating your amphibian with medication, you must own a precision electronic or balance scale that reads in grams, centigrams and milligrams. It is important to know your amphibian's accurate weight, as this allows you to precisely dose it with the medication you're giving. Generally, an amphibian owner is advised to dose the animal with a drug in terms of milligrams per kilogram (1,000 grams). This means, simply, that for every 1,000 grams of your animal's body weight, x number of milligrams of medication must be given. Because few amphibians weigh 1,000 grams (2.2 pounds), a calculator is also

helpful. If a tiny frog weighs but a few grams, the dose given needs to be extremely small and it is difficult for home hobbyists to achieve this kind of precision.

It is easiest if you obtain such medications in liquid form pre-adjusted by the manufacturer to contain x number of milligrams of medication per milliliter or cc. Thus, if you determine that your animal needs 1 milligram of medication and the medication comes in a liquid form at 5 milligrams per cubic centimeter, you need to give $^1/_5$ of a cubic centimeter of the medicine to provide the desired dose, or to dilute a 1 cc dose to create 1 milligram.

Viral Diseases

Amphibians are susceptible to a number of viral diseases deriving from several groups of viruses: the iridoviruses, paromyxoviruses and herpes viruses. Viruses are highly specific as to target and rarely cross species lines, but some do. The rabies virus is an example of one that crosses from one species to another and from animals to humans. However, no fish, amphibian or reptile can be infected with rabies.

Bacterial Infections

Probably the most common bacterial infections affecting amphibians is a condition in frogs and toads

commonly referred to as "Red-Leg" infection. Unfortunately, scientists have been unable to determine how or why this condition occurs. Its earliest symptom is, indeed, a red rash-like discoloration of the lighter undersides of the hind legs. But this is just an early warning sign of much worse to come. The disease rapidly enters the bloodstream, becoming what is known as a septicemia, and it attacks internal organs including the liver, kidneys and spleen, soon killing the animal. It is caused by a pathogenic (disease-causing) bacterium known as *Aeromonas hydrophila* and, on occasion, by a bacterium called *Pseudomonas aeruginosa*.

For most delicate, small- and moderate-sized frogs the outlook for successfully treating this disease

Red-Leg infection takes a toll on any frog, but small, delicate frogs have a particularly hard time recovering (Red-Eyed Tree Frog, *Agalychnis callidyas*).

is bleak, and if it is not caught early it is invariably fatal. At its early stages, before it attacks the animal internally, baths with chlorinated water laced with antibiotics may be helpful in stopping the disease. Some experts recommend copper sulfate solution washes, and oral injections of tetracycline dissolved in water may also be helpful. Veterinary advice should always be obtained. Hobbyists using antibiotics without professional guidance run the risk of using too little or too much—too small a dose may cause the growth of resistant bacteria, while too large a dose can be toxic to the animal. Whole colonies and collections of frogs have been wiped out by Red-Leg. Following such debacles it is necessary to hygienically discard every-

thing inside your frogs' enclosures, sterilize them with weak bleach or ammonium solutions such as Nolvasan™ and rinse them thoroughly and repeatedly in hot water before using them for new, unaffected frogs.

Although Red-Leg infection has been documented only in captive

animals, there is belief that it or some related disease may also infect wild populations of frogs.

Other extremely serious bacterial diseases of amphibians are *Mycobacterium marinum* and *Mycobacterium fortuitum*—forms of cutaneous tuberculosis that are also contagious to humans. These diseases first appear as an unusual, rough-surfaced growth on the skin known as a granuloma but can also attack internal organs. In humans, *M. marinum* is called "Swimming Pool Granuloma" and "Fishermen's Granuloma." Nonchlorinated swimming pools were once a frequent source of the condition, and fishermen contract it on their hands and arms from handling infected fish. Mycobacterium, the same type of bacterium that causes tuberculosis and leprosy in humans, is extremely difficult to treat. Humans may require over a year of heavy doses of two or more antibiotics.

WHERE HAVE ALL THE TOADS GONE?

Several years ago it was theorized that populations of the Western or Boreal Toad (*Bufo boreas*), which became extinct for no obvious reason, had in fact succumbed to some sort of bacterial or viral epidemic including, quite possibly, Red-Leg. Their habitat was considered quite pristine, and environmental causes for their deaths seemed highly improbable. Because there were no toads left to examine when their disappearance was first discovered, it was impossible for field workers to determine the cause of the extinction. All they knew was that the toads were there a few years before and then, when they returned to the same locations, they were gone.

For this reason, veterinarians often recommend euthanizing an infected animal, as upsetting as this may be. Realistically, it is not logical to spend thousands of dollars on drugs for a frog that might not get well in any case and to permit the frog's illness to pose a serious risk to human health. Releasing that sick frog into the wild is also an extremely poor (and illegal) idea, as it can infect other, healthy frogs or fish with which it might come in contact before it dies. Dealing with death and disease is never pleasant, but it is a part of keeping pets (and a part of life) with which we must come to terms.

The insect prey of amphibians carry many bacteria on their bodies; thankfully, for the most part amphibians are resistant to these organisms. In some cases, however, amphibians may act as nonsymptomatic carriers. This often occurs with *Salmonella*, a bacterial organism that is pathogenic in mammals and humans. It is useless, dangerous and unnecessary to try and treat the problem in amphibians or reptiles. In these animals, the bacteria cause no problems and are almost considered a "normal" finding—in random samplings, 90 to 95 percent of the herps carry them.

Free-living amphibians in close association with human housing, plumbing and sewerage seem to be especially prone to carrying *Salmonella*. In one study in Panama, at least seven different kinds of *Salmonella* were found in Marine or Cane Toads *(Bufo marinus)* where these toads lived in close proximity to human dwellings. The risk presented to people can be minimized by following the guidelines set forth below in the discussion of zoonoses.

Amphibians are also susceptible to mouth or jaw rot, which is occasionally seen in Bufonid toads, Plethodontid salamanders and Salamandrids (newts and salamanders). It is often caused by *Pseudomonas aeruginosa, Aeromonas hydrophila* and, quite possibly, several other necrotizing or flesh-destroying types of pathogens. These types of bacteria are virtually everywhere, but in the wrong place and at the wrong time they could become pathogenic. This is not only true of amphibians but of people as well. Thus if a person has a sore or cut that is not properly disinfected and at the same time happens to come into contact with one of these bacteria, he or she runs the risk of contracting a serious infection. Those with immunodeficiencies are particularly susceptible. If your resistance is strong and your is skin intact, you have nothing to fear. Handling animals with such infections, however, puts you at greater risk, and such animals should be clinically isolated. If you handle an amphibian with one of these bacterial infections, you should wear gloves and wash your hands thoroughly with soap and hot water afterward.

If the specimen that develops this condition is particularly dear

Some amphibians, such as *Bufo* toads, will occasionally contract mouth rot (*Bufo typhonius*).

to you, be forewarned that veterinary treatment (because of the high cost of antibiotics needed) is apt to be expensive. If the infection spreads, it is often better to euthanize the animal.

Aquatic amphibians such as African Clawed Frogs occasionally develop a bacterial infection frequently seen in tropical fish known as "cotton mouth" disease. It is caused by a bacterium called *Columnaris,* which attacks an animal through broken skin, via the gill network, or through the membranous lining of the mouth. An obstructing mass of white fluffy material will form, which is actually stacks of the bacterium itself. If the lesions are external, hobbyists can try dipping the animal in a quarternary ammonium compound such as zephiran chloride. Infected animals can also be housed temporarily in fresh, chlorinated tap water for 24 hours.

This organism is usually susceptible to sulfa drugs, and the treatment should be prescribed by a veterinarian. Because very small doses are required, it is best to get professional help rather than trying to dose amphibians with these drugs yourself. Don't be deceived by the fact that you can purchase these drugs over the counter for use with tropical fish. Dosing an amphibian is significantly more complex than simply adding the medication to aquarium water.

Parasites

There are essentially four different types of parasites: internal, external, unicellular (one-celled organisms) and multicellular. External parasites are exclusively of the multicellular type. Internal parasites may be either unicellular or multicellular.

Parasites are found in or on both aquatic and terrestrial amphibians, and in or on their larvae. Some types of insects and their larvae parasitize adult amphibians as well as their eggs. Other insects use amphibian eggs or the bodies of adults to deposit and nurture their own eggs.

By definition, parasites that live in or on their host basically do so at the expense of the host. They derive nutrition (e.g., blood, tissue and bodily fluids) from their hosts and use the hosts to perpetuate themselves by adapting to conditions in the host that are suitable for initiating or completing their life cycles. Although some few parasites may exist outside a host for short periods, almost all are dependent on their hosts in order to survive and reproduce.

Amphibians are very much a part of the parasite world, serving as hosts for a number of organisms. Many of these parasites can seriously impair and ultimately kill their hosts, although this is ultimately self-defeating for the para-

site as well. The smartest kind of parasite uses its host's resources to its own benefit without overtaxing the host.

Protozoa

Protozoa are unicellular organisms (amoebas, opalina, trypansoma and others), and almost all wild-caught (and many captive-bred) amphibians have some sort of unicellular organisms on board with which they comfortably coexist—a condition known as symbiosis, which describes the "smart parasite." On the other hand, massive infections by some parasites completely overwhelm their amphibian hosts, and this can cause catastrophic declines or even the extinction of amphibian populations in the wild, as well as wipe out entire captive collections. In southern England, a sporozoan known as *Pleistophora* (found normally in insects and fish) eradicated entire populations of European Toads (*Bufo bufo*) about 30 years ago. Another sporozoan, *Charchesium*, clogs the gill slits of tadpoles, causing brain damage and death.

Entamoeba sp. and the flagellate (a parasite with a whip-like tail) *Opalina* are often found in the digestive tract of free-living amphibians. Much of the time the unicellular digestive system parasites exist in amphibians as harmless commensals. *Trypansoma sp.*

are blood-borne parasites, probably transmitted by bloodsucking leeches. *Hemogregarines* are another type of blood parasite that are transmitted by bloodsucking insects such as mosquitoes. A species of Malaria parasite, *Plasmodium*, may also occur in the blood of amphibians, as anopheles mosquitoes are known to bite them. Whether the types of *Plasmodium* dangerous to humans also occur in amphibians is unknown, but is not considered likely.

Blood-borne parasites such as trypanosomes are transmitted to amphibians through the bite of bloodsucking flies, but how seriously ill amphibians may become from these parasites is unknown. In people, trypanosomes transmitted from the bite of tsetse flies are the cause of African sleeping sickness and a variant of the disease in South America known as Chagas' disease.

Veterinary treatment of unicellular parasites depends on accurate identification of the offending organism. *Entamoeba invadens*, a common amoebic parasite of amphibians and reptiles, is treated effectively with Flagyl™ (metronidazole). It is given to reptiles every two weeks until stool smears are negative. *Coccidia* is treated with sulfa drugs such as Albon™, and *Cryptosporidia* resists any known antiparasite drug, although various antibiotics have been used with some success.

Multicellular Parasites

Most of the time, multicellulars (also known as metazoans) can be seen with the naked eye and can be examined in detail under relatively low-power magnification (such as with a 10X hand-held magnifier). Protozoans or unicellular parasites are microscopic and can be seen only with the aid of a microscope at 25X to 100X (or more) magnification power.

Among the multicellular parasites to look out for are helminths, worms or similar-looking organisms from a variety of different families and orders. The most common helminth parasites of amphibians are intestinal worms. They are known as nematodes, cestodes and trematodes. There are hundreds of such parasite species, which, worldwide, are found in amphibians. Amphibians become infected by eating the intermediate hosts of many of these organisms, such as insects and small crustaceans. The parasites should be treated only if they are causing a problem. In one type of nematode, a lung worm, treatment may cause the worm to rupture the lung as it tries to escape medication, killing the animal in the process. Left alone, the animal may have lived for a much longer time. Many species of frogs and salamanders may also serve as hosts in the life cycle of tapeworms, hookworms and other deleterious parasites. Humans have been infected with tapeworms by eating improperly cooked frogs' legs.

The annelids (from the same family as earthworms) also parasitize amphibians in the form of external, bloodsucking leeches. While one or two leeches never seem to cause much of a problem, attack by numerous leeches can cause the death of the animal from hemorrhage. Leeches inject their hosts near where they attach with an anticoagulant (hirudin). Amphibians can be overdosed on this

Mosquitoes carry disease and can pass parasites to an amphibian through a bite (Green Tree Frog, *Hyla cinerea*).

This dart poison frog has a tiny tick on its rear leg (Yellow-Banded Dart Poison Frog, *Dendrobates leucomelas*).

substance and bleed to death if numerous leeches are present on a single animal. In any case, leeches should always be removed from your pet. They can be carefully peeled off with tweezers or painted with a disinfectant (using a cotton-tipped swab) and then removed. The underlying mark where the leech was attached can be disinfected with an application of Betadine™ ointment. Some leeches can enter their hosts internally and remain there, feeding on blood from the liver or heart.

Insect and other arthropod parasites are also known to attack amphibians, their eggs and larvae. A number of tiny spiders attack land-living amphibians, including chigger mites and ticks (which are also bloodsuckers). Aquatic amphibians

may fall prey to the parasitic copepod *Argulus* (fish mite), which has been reported in both aquatic salamanders and frogs. The Diptera is the only group of insect parasites that afflict amphibians. These flies lay their eggs on terrestrial or semi-aquatic amphibians and on amphibian eggs deposited on land.

A number of small fly larvae will also live off frogs and their embryos. One type of fly larvae (*Lucilia*) migrates to the head of various European frogs and toads, where it enters the body through the eyes or nostrils and proceeds to eat its host from the inside out. Infection with this insect larva is invariably fatal to amphibians. Internal metazoan or multicellular parasites such as worms and flukes are often treated with Panacur™

and Flagyl™, although accurate dosing regimens for amphibians have not been developed.

Fungal Infection

Because the warm and often damp environments of amphibians are highly conducive to the growth of fungi, amphibians are particularly susceptible to fungal infections. Most fungi enter an amphibian's body through minor abrasions or wounds, but some also enter through the nostrils and, on occasion, through the mouth.

Systemic fungal infections are extremely difficult to counter and are invariably fatal. It is sometimes possible, if a fungus is noticed early on an external surface, to treat it successfully with applications of antibiotics and antifungal cremes, solutions and gels. One can try swabbing fungal patches with mercurochrome, Betadine or hydrogen peroxide as well as antifungal dyes such as malachite green. Antifungal ointments designed for human use and available over the counter may also be worth trying. The fungal species most often attacking amphibians include *Saprolegnia*, *Basidiobolus* and *Cladoaporium*, although many other types can and will take advantage of amphibians. *Candida* has been identified on the tadpoles of the Green Frog (*Rana clamitans*), and many species of fungi will invade and kill masses of amphibian eggs both in the water and when deposited in warm, damp locations on land.

Trauma

Injuries due to trauma are not uncommon in amphibians, and most trauma befalling captive amphibians can be attributed to management errors made on the part of human caretakers. Trauma includes cuts and abrasions, broken bones, damaged eyes and burned skin. Most cuts and abrasions in a captive amphibian occur because of sharp, jagged and otherwise hazardous caging "furniture" in the form of rocks, gravel and glass. Some amphibians will climb or jump to the top of their enclosure, constantly rubbing their snouts on the screening. Abrasions due to this can be avoided by using screen covers made of soft plastic netting instead of hardwire metal. Broken bones are often caused by falls from great heights, usually in animals escaping, limbs accidentally becoming crushed between rock formations and similar hazards. Rough handling of amphibians by humans unfamiliar with the correct, gentle but firm way that they need to be held or restrained can also result in such trauma. Burns are often incurred by carelessly placing overhead lights where they can come in contact with animals. Animals are also burned by

The tan areas on this Monkey Frog show the result of rough handling; the frog's back should be green (Monkey Frog, *Phyllomedusa hypochondrialis*).

hot rocks, an accessory that should be banned from all amphibian enclosures, not only as a burn hazard but as an electrical shock hazard as well.

Surface abrasions, cuts and wounds should be rapidly treated with a disinfectant ointment such as Betadine, Neosporin or Triple Antibiotic Ointment. This treatment will help promote healing and help to avoid secondary bacterial or fungal infection. Broken bones in amphibians can be more problematic, particularly in active species of frogs that do a lot of jumping and climbing. Applying a splint to and setting such breaks is a challenge to any veterinarian, and often the bones are left to heal by themselves. Unfortunately, a deformity and/or disability is the lasting consequence.

Developmental Problems

Nutritional problems are common in captive amphibians. A condition known as spindly-leg affects metamorphosing tadpoles, especially of the precious Dendrobatid clan, and this affliction has been attributed to mineral and vitamin deficiencies. It is usually fatal.

Metabolic bone disease, a very prevalent condition in reptiles, can also occur in developing amphibians. Nutritional disorders are easily prevented by supplementing "monotonous" captive diets with insects that have been dusted with vitamin/mineral supplement powders designed for amphibians and reptiles. You can also gut load the insects with nutritious vegetation

Dart poison frogs are particularly susceptible to spindly-leg, if deprived of sufficient vitamins and minerals while they develop (Green and Black Dart Poison Frog in blue phase, *Dendrobates auratus*).

that has been similarly treated. Frogs, toads and salamanders that have red or orange skin colors in the wild often appear washed out or discolored in captivity due to a lack of beta-carotene in their diets. Such animals should be fed bugs that are supplemented with mixtures that contain this essential nutrient. Beta-carotene also helps promote good eyesight and healthy skin.

Finally, although not technically a nutritional disorder, intestinal blockage is related to diet and feeding. A steady diet of hard-shelled insects or insect larvae such as mealworms, or the frequent accidental ingestion of gravel or pebbles, can completely block the intestinal tract. If the problem is discovered early, it might be treatable with tube feeds of lubricants such as mineral oil or, if the amphibian is particularly dear or valuable, by surgery. Unfortunately, by the time this silent condition is discovered it is usually too late to treat. Judging from its most common causes, it is eminently preventable.

Nutritional disorders of tadpoles and other amphibian larvae are well known. The best way to counter these problems is to offer varied diets that are not heavily dependent on one item. Sources of protein for tadpoles include liver, egg yolk and even tiny amounts of liverwurst and dried, crumbled hard-boiled egg yolk. Tadpoles also eat algae, so its growth should be encouraged in rearing containers or tanks.

Vary the diet with vegetarian and protein-based fish flakes, powdered rabbit chow for herbivorous species or dog chow for carnivorous or omnivorous species. Thawed frozen vegetables are a good choice, because freezing breaks down the cell walls of vegetable matter, thereby simplifying digestion. In a study of Dendrobatid frog tadpoles, researchers found those that were fed tropical fish-flake foods fared the best and those that ate boiled greens fared the worst. However, in another study of Marsupial Frog tadpoles fed algae, boiled spinach and leaf lettuce, only seven tadpoles out of 92 were lost. Clearly, further research needs to be done on the subject of tadpole diet and nutritional problems. There are no hard and fast rules, save perhaps for the need to feed egg yolk to the tadpoles of the Strawberry Dart Poison Frog

A study of dart poison frog tadpoles indicated that they fared well when fed tropical fish-flake foods (Harlequin Dart Poison Frog, *Dendrobates histrionicus*).

(*D. pumilio*). It has been clearly established in nature that these tadpoles feed on the eggs offered by their mother.

Toxic Dangers to Amphibians

Both the Canadian Environmental Agency (Environment Canada) and the U.S. Environmental Protection Agency have issued lengthy reports cataloging chemicals in the environment that are harmful specifically to amphibians. The list contains not only a substantial number of organophosphates, organochlorines and other petroleum-distillate-based substances, but also metals such as copper, mercury, lead and silver. Among the most toxic substances in the wild are the salts of metals. Insecticides, herbicides and industrial effluents all affect amphibian populations.

By reason of their thin, permeable skin, amphibians are basically delicate creatures. They act as early warning mechanisms that pollution may be present. Therefore, hazards such as these in captive environments must be studiously avoided. In fact, it is best to keep their enclosures as far away as possible from polluted areas. It behooves all of us, as well, to work toward preventing the proliferation and buildup of such noxious substances in the environment.

The symptoms of poisoning from either petroleum distillates or metals can be subtle or painfully obvious. They might include seizure-like activity, twitching, unusual behaviors and poor appetite. There is just no satisfactory remedy to reverse such toxic exposures in amphibians, which almost always result in death. What's worse, they also result in the extinction of entire populations of amphibians.

Zoonotic Diseases

Zoonoses, or zoonotic diseases, are infectious diseases that are transmitted from animals to humans by ingestion (e.g., *Salmonella*), through physical contact or as a result of a bite, such as in rabies. Because amphibians are not cuddly, kissy-feely or frequently handled animals, the incidence of contracting zoonotic diseases from them is far lower than it is from reptiles, birds and mammals. Amphibians are display animals, not animals that should undergo a lot of handling. Nevertheless zoonotic diseases can occur.

Preventing the contraction of a zoonotic disease requires the maintenance of absolutely hygienic conditions, for the benefit of both the amphibian and its human caretakers. In some cases, such as those involving the presence of tubercular lesions (*Mycobacteria*), euthanasia is often the only solution.

The following guidelines have been promulgated by a number of authorities including the U.S. Centers for Disease Control:

1. Contact between amphibians and reptiles and children under the

KEEP YOURSELF AND YOUR LOVED ONES SAFE

Young children, infants, the immunocompromised and the elderly are at greater risk than others of serious consequences from any infection that could possibly be transmitted between an amphibian or reptile and humans. Amphibians and reptiles should not be kept in day care centers, kindergartens or classrooms of children under eight years of age. Teaching children about reptiles and amphibians should be achieved by bringing the animals in and then removing them. Touching the animals should not be permitted except under stringent supervision. Hand disinfectant products or hot-water/soap hand-washing facilities should be readily accessible.

Direct contact may not be necessary for someone to become ill. Amphibian and reptile zoonoses can be present on surfaces or carried on the hands or clothing of one person to another.

age of eight should be prohibited. Older children should be carefully supervised. If contact between herps and younger children is unavoidable, be sure that thorough, hot-water-and-soap hand washing or hand disinfection is accomplished immediately thereafter.

2. Thorough hand washing, for at least 30 seconds, under hot water using a disinfectant soap should follow the handling of any amphibian or reptile, their enclosures or caging or after handling materials and food. In the absence of a sink, soap and hot water, portable disinfectant hand sprays and lotions should be used. Carry them to swap meets, to herp society meetings or on field trips to zoos or the great outdoors.

3. Under no circumstances should a person prepare, serve or eat food after handling any amphibian or reptile or related material without first disinfecting their hands. Children especially need to be supervised so that they do NOT put fingers in their mouth or eat sweets or sandwiches without hand washing as above first.

4. Pregnant women should avoid all contact with amphibians due to fetal risk.

5. People who are immunocompromised for any reason, be it HIV, some other medical condition or as a result of any medication or treatment, should avoid all contact.

6. Amphibian- or reptile-related cleaning and maintenance chores should not be done in proximity to eating utensils (near kitchen sink) or articles of personal hygiene (around bathroom sink) without those articles first being removed and stowed. Surface disinfection should occur prior to returning such articles.

PART III

The World of Amphibians and People

Amphibians in Fact and Fiction • Conservation and Legal Protection • Herpetological Education

CHAPTER 11

Amphibians in Fact and Fiction

"Sweet are the uses of adversity. Which, like the toad, ugly and venomous,/Wears yet a precious jewel in his head."

—*William Shakespeare, "As You Like It"*

Did Shakespeare refer to the frogs' beautiful golden eyes? Perhaps. (White-Lipped Tree Frog, *Litoria infrafrenata*).

Shakespeare makes frequent use of toad metaphors in his plays. Literary scholars have interpreted the jewel in the above line from "As You Like It" as a toad's gold-flecked eye, and while this seems to make a certain amount of sense, other conflicting explanations are often given. Ever since human primates appeared on earth, they have been interacting with amphibians in strange and often mystical ways. Early man no doubt discovered the hallucinogenic and, on occasion, fatal effects of ingestion of amphibians, glandular secretions and all.

Amphibians in Fiction

Medieval sorcerers and witches learned to extract these poisons and used them to accomplish what was portrayed to the uninformed as mystical powers.

Although traceable back to ancient Africa, more recently zombification of humans by Haitian sorcerers (bakus) has been exposed in an article published in the prestigious British medical journal *The Lancet*. Part of the zombie recipe is the secretion of the Marine or Cane Toad (*Bufo marinus*). Containing digitalis-like properties, such bufo poisons are clearly capable of slowing the heart rate to such imperceptibly low levels that the victims were often considered dead. Knowing otherwise, the baku would retrieve and revive these souls, who often suffered serious neurological deficit as a result of their ordeal. The victims were then used to perpetrate their zombie myths. Thus, people previously thought to be dead and buried are occasionally seen wandering around, neurologically impaired, and are then believed to be members of the oxymoronic "living dead."

However, amphibian glandular secretions are not just used by sorcerers, witch doctors and voodoo priests but by conventional scientists and medical researchers as well. Scientists are discovering a mind-boggling number of novel substances contained in and produced by amphibians with possible medical use.

Frogs and toads are enormously popular in fairy tales and other fictional literature. Few children don't know of the prince turned into a frog or toad by a wicked witch, only to be restored by the kiss of a beautiful princess. Many of you are familiar with Michigan J. Frog, the cartoon character who entertains his owner but refuses to sing and dance for anyone else. A whole generation of children has been raised on the television hi-jinks of the late Jim Henson's Kermit the Frog, probably the best-known celebrity frog in the world. And not to be left behind in the race for frog recognition (or "frognition," as some call it), the famous Budweiser frogs and their unique "bud, bud" call are so popular that their frog call is now repeated by people for no apparent reason at all.

One of the most enduring myths of all concerns that of the salamander's legendary resistance to fire. When man first discovered fire, he would gather wood to burn and salamanders, hidden in the rotted wood, would scamper out of the flames to avoid being burned. People witnessing this truly believed that the salamander was born of fire and was resistant to the

Early man believed that fire salamanders were born within the flames of his fire (Barred Fire Salamander, *Salamandra t. terrestris*).

effects of the flames. The fire salamander earned its common name as a result of this occurrence.

Amphibian Contributions to Mankind

Every freshman biology student at one time had the opportunity to learn basic anatomy by dissecting a frog. More advanced students often graduated to Mudpuppies, as well as other animals.

While there is vocal opposition to frog dissection, it may be the only way those students who are going to proceed in the sciences to become medical professionals or biologists can properly begin their education. For those to whom sci-

ence has no attraction and who also are opposed to learning their anatomy this way, a number of computer programs or virtual frog dissection programs are available on-line. No child should be forced to dissect an animal that was once alive who objects to it on moral or psychological grounds. Since such

protests made the media years ago, it has also been learned that some of the population extinctions of the common Leopard Frog in the United States may be due to the collection of the millions of such animals from the wild for the purpose of student dissections. Such a valuable resource, therefore, should not be sacrificed, particularly when virtual dissections on-line, models and drawings in a lab manual can provide the basic information just as easily and perhaps even more completely.

In the early 1990s, scientists at the National Institute of Health (NIH) working on the skin secretions of dendrobatid or dart poison frogs discovered a substance in the Phantasmal Dart Poison Frog (*Epidobates tricolor*) that they named epibatidine. This substance was found to be an effective painkiller—on a weight-for-weight basis, it is 200 times stronger than morphine but is nonsedating and

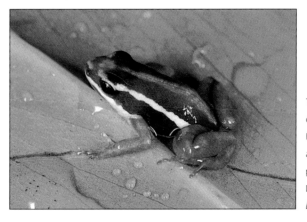

The skin secretions of the Phantasmal Dart Poison Frog are an amazingly effective pain killer (Phantasmal Dart Poison Frog, *Epidobates tricolor*).

nonaddictive. It works on nicotine instead of opiate receptors. Several pharmaceutical companies have succeeded in making a synthetic version of it, so they don't need a steady stream of frogs and a frog press in the back room to manufacture this drug. One company has announced that they received FDA approval to begin testing the drug. Other painkillers from dendrobatid frogs include a group of peptides (small proteins) known as dermorphins, also under study for possible medical use. Dermorphin has produced extremely potent and long-lasting pain relief when injected into mice. Scientists say morphine is 752 times *less* potent than some of these substances.

A secretion of the White's Tree Frog has been found to be of help to those suffering from severe intestinal dysfunction (White's Tree Frog, *Litoria caerulea*).

In addition, Russian studies indicate dermorphin may be a novel treatment for alcoholism. In studies of alcohol-dependent rats, dermorphin significantly reduced voluntary alcohol intake.

The White's Tree Frog (*Litoria caerulea*) produces a secretion known as caeruletide. It was discovered that this stimulates pancreatic enzyme secretion, causes gallbladder contraction and gastric emptying, but stimulates intestinal activity. Versions of it are already available for medical and medical/diagnostic use with trade names like Cerulex™, Ceusunin™ and Tymtran™. These are used in diagnostic imaging of the gallbladder and intestines and for testing pancreatic function. They have also been used for the treatment of an extremely serious and potentially fatal human disorder known as paralytic ileus and intestinal atony, in which the intestines contract and fail to move their contents on their way. Caeruletide and related compounds are also being studied as antipsychotic agents for patients with schizophrenia, as well as specialized pain killers, alleviating excruciatingly painful symptoms of biliary colic.

Bombinin and bombesin, the first vertebrate peptides ever discovered (in Oriental Fire-Bellied Toads), are being studied for their possible antibiotic effects, as are peptides from various other amphibians.

And the scientists in Australia who first discovered the now believed-to-be extinct Gastric Brooding Frogs say that medical science lost an important finding when this frog disappeared before they could definitely find out how it changed its stomach into a uterus—suspending acid production and peristalsis and going without food until its young hatched out into froglets and were released.

Another group of scientists also working under the auspices of the NIH were puzzled by the fact that the African Clawed Frogs (*Xenopus laevis*) used in experimental procedures that involved cuts or needle punctures through the skin never seemed to get infected, even when they returned to abysmally dirty holding-tank waters. Such wounds would scar over without any sign of infection, swelling or inflammation. It wasn't long before scientists discovered the reason for this amazing occurrence: a skin secretion that acted like an antibiotic and killed bacteria. These substances were named xenopsins and magainins (derived from the Hebrew word *magainin*, which means "shield"). They became part of a new era of antibiotic treatment: peptide antibiotics. A pharmaceutical company was organized by researchers to further test and exploit these substances that they were also able to synthesize in the laboratory. Thus far, only external uses are envisioned for these drugs, such as in the healing of diabetic foot or leg ulcers, bed sores and other wound infections, in healing burns, as an antibacterial mouthwash and, amazingly, because these chemicals kill sperm while also killing germs, as part of a barrier contraceptive that could do double duty: prevent conception and venereal disease simultaneously!

A group of enzymes dubbed onconases found in the egg jelly of developing frog eggs have been found to fight certain types of cancer. Bombesins, found in fire-bellied frogs, are being studied for their role in the inhibition of small-cell carcinoma of the lungs, a difficult-to-treat disease that kills hundreds of thousands of people annually.

Another group of substances found in frogs also have potent coronary vasodilator effects, working their magic apparently in the inner wall of the blood vessels rather than the smooth muscles that cause them to constrict. As long ago as 1966, scientists studied the effects of some of these substances in humans by administering them to patients suffering from arteriosclerosis of the leg vessels. Although the results were promising, the experiments were not carried forward.

But new drugs are not the only benefits conferred on humans by frogs. They are great exterminators

Bombesins, produced by Fire-Bellied Toads, may be a key to treating a form of lung cancer (Oriental Fire-Bellied Toad, *Bombina orientalis*).

as well. Insects are among the most populous pest- and disease-spreading species on earth, and amphibians gobble up billions of them daily. Although it is impossible to know if amphibian consumption truly makes a difference, it would appear certain that amphibians do help hold insect populations down to reasonable levels.

Amphibians also provide food for native peoples as well as gourmets dining in fine French restaurants. And many environmental scientists hold them out as proverbial miner's canaries—giving mankind early warning of impending toxic or other catastrophic environmental events. Studies of developing frogs eggs in the Pacific northwestern United States demonstrated that increased ultraviolet radiation from the sun (as a result of the well-publicized ozone layer hole) kills eggs deposited in the open, whereas those deposited in the shade survive. As was mentioned previously in the

discussion of amphibian health care, these animals are also unusually sensitive to toxic substances in the environment, such as pesticides and heavy metals. There is an enormous body of literature demonstrating interaction between amphibians and these pollutants and their effect on amphibian populations. More recently, amphibians with unusual limb deformities and extra legs have been appearing. One theory is that these are the result of nematode infestation around limb buds in developing amphibians. But where do all these extra nematodes come from? They bloom as a result of a process known as eutrophication, whereby excessive amounts of matter upon which they thrive enter the water supply. Such substances include cattle manure and phosphate- and nitrate-based fertilizers from agricultural runoff, a not-so-harmless form of pollution that farmers are now learning how to manage.

Conservation and Legal Protection

Everyone involved with amphibians wants to know "Is there really a declining amphibian crisis? If so, why and what can be done about it?"

There are vast differences of opinion on these issues. Some scientists say amphibians

disappear and then reappear, sometimes a decade later, and that this is natural. Others say this is hogwash. Amphibian populations, including whole species that have disappeared, are not hiding somewhere but have become extinct. The 1990 List of Threatened Animals prepared by the International Union for the Conservation of Nature includes 63 species of amphibians.

A few very well publicized disappearances include:

1. The beautiful Costa Rican Golden Toad (*Bufo periglenes*).
2. Two species of the Gastric Brooding Frog (*Rheobatrachus sp.*) in Australia.
3. The tree frogs of the genus *Hylodes* in Brazil.
4. Populations of the Boreal or Western Toad in North America (*Bufo boreas*).
5. Populations of what was once our most common species (and subspecies) of North American frog: the Leopard Frog (*Rana pipiens sp*).

There have also been a host of other less well publicized disappearances or declines.

Protected Species

In the United States alone, the following states list amphibian species as endangered:

Arizona—Huachuca Tiger Salamander, Barking Frog, Tarahumara Frog and the Plains Leopard Frog.
California—protects some 10 species of salamanders and three species of frogs.
Colorado—Western Toad.
Connecticut—Eastern Spadefoot Toad.
Delaware—Barking Frog and Cope's Gray Tree Frog.
Illinois—three species of salamanders including Hellbenders.

Indiana—the Hellbender and the Northern Red Salamander.
Iowa—Blue-Spot Salamander, Central Newt, Mudpuppy and Crawfish Frog.
Kansas—three species of salamanders.
Kentucky—Amphiumas and a species of lungless salamander.
Maryland—three species of salamander and the Narrow-Mouth Toad.
Michigan—Small-Mouth Salamander.
Mississippi—three species of salamander and the Dusky Gopher Frog.
New Jersey—three species of salamander and two species of tree frogs.
New Mexico—four species of frogs.
New York—the Tiger Salamander.
North Carolina—the Green Salamander, plus 16 other amphibians listed as threatened or of special concern.
Ohio—requires a special permit for the taking of five species of listed amphibians.
Oklahoma—10 salamander species that can be collected only with a special scientific permit.
Oregon—protects 10 species of endangered salamanders and eight species of frogs, including the Tailed Frog (*Ascaphus truei*); also prohibits all species of Xenopus and hybrids (albinos) from entering the state.

The Eastern Spadefoot Toad is considered an endangered species in Connecticut (Eastern Spadefoot Toad, *Scaphiopus holbrooki*).

Pennsylvania—protects two species of salamanders and two species of frogs.

South Carolina—protects three species of salamanders including the Dwarf Siren and the Pine Barrens Tree Frog (*Hyla andersoni*).

Texas—protects seven species of salamanders and five species of frogs, including the endangered Houston Toad (*Bufo houstoni*).

Utah—protects seven species of frogs.

Vermont—protects the Western Chorus Frog (*Pseudacris triseriata*).

Virginia—protects three species of salamanders.

Washington—protects one species of salamander.

West Virginia—protects one species of salamander.

Wisconsin—protects one species of frog.

Wyoming—protects the Wyoming Toad (*Bufo baxteri*). Probably extinct in the wild.

Regardless of what state you live in, you should check with your local fish and game department regarding any protected amphibians before you decide to go out and try and collect them. The above is an example of some states that protect amphibian species legally. Fines, arrest and prosecution could be the result of illegal collecting activities. And even more states list numerous amphibian species as threatened or of special concern. Literally hundreds of amphibians in North America are imperiled, and state legislatures, on the advice of environmental scientists, have seen fit to add such animals to the lists of protected species. Generally, this means that collecting or disturbing these animals is illegal and any activity that destroys or disturbs their habitat is also illegal. Developers often hire teams of lawyers and special lobbyists to represent them when a construction or other development project intrudes upon territory inhabited by an endangered species. Hearings are held, deals are struck, compensation is paid or mitigation (e.g., set aside of other land for the species) is proposed. Sometimes the developers get what they want (often at a price), and sometimes they don't.

Moving an endangered species interstate (whether the species is listed as endangered by state or Federal authorities) can result in Federal prosecution under a law known as the Lacy Act. This Federal law covers any interstate transport of protected species and international movement into the United States of any endangered species if said species is prohibited from export in its country of origin or is on a list of species created by an international treaty known as CITES (Convention on International Trade in Endangered Species of Wild Fauna and Flora). As of the end of 1997, 137 countries were signatories to the Washington Treaty, as the CITES convention is also known.

Along with several salamanders, the Pine Barrens Tree Frog is protected under regulations in South Carolina (Pine Barrens Tree Frog, *Hyla andersoni*).

Many countries are working to save their wildlife. Madagascar has banned the export of its stunning mantella frogs (Painted Mantella Frog, *Mantella madagascariensis*).

The Lacy Act is broad enough so that it can be invoked by law enforcement in a number of situations where either the letter or spirit of the law is violated. It can be applied by Federal prosecutors when a species that is legal to possess in one state is transported to another where its possession is illegal. Permits and waivers can be obtained for certain types of scientific, exhibition and educational research, as well as for the interstate sale of endangered species that have been certifiably captive bred and born.

While collecting avowedly popular and colorful species for the hobby trade does cause declines and puts pressure on wild populations of some amphibian species, others are declining for a variety of environmental reasons. Some of these include:

1. Excessive UV radiation from the sun (ozone layer hole) that harms amphibian eggs

2. The greenhouse effect (global warming)

3. Acid rain and acidification of waters occupied by amphibians or used for their eggs

4. Saltwater incursion into amphibian waters in coastal areas, usually the result of poorly planned nearby development, road building, sewer installation and similar projects

5. Pollution of land and water occupied by amphibians by nonspecific toxic wastes

6. Pollution of land and water occupied by amphibians by pesticides and herbicides

7. Pollution of land and water occupied by amphibians by heavy metals

8. Pollution of land and water by ionizing radiation from known (and unknown) sources

9. Outright habitat destruction, such as the drainage and filling of wetlands for the purpose of residential or commercial construction projects, roads and similar projects

10. Other incursions by man, such as garbage dumps and landfills

11. Introduction of microorganisms and fungi pathogenic to amphibians from natural or unnatural sources

12. Introduction of nonnative species to areas occupied by native amphibians that result in either excessive predation of amphibians by the introduced species or competition for food resources and territory by the introduced species

13. Natural disasters including drought, excessive rainfall, climate changes, soil erosion, plant blights that diminish insects (thereby diminishing amphibian foods), floods, hurricanes and other weather-related phenomena

14. Unknown causes or causes that cannot be proven or identified scientifically

15. Overcollecting for biological supply companies for research or school dissection use

16. Overcollecting for use as food, for scientific research and for sport (e.g., frog "giging")

Thus the cause of amphibian declines is not a simple, black-and-white issue. The causes can be myriad, and obviously more than one can be at work. A cause that is unknown and can never be discovered could be a solitary culprit, or an unknown cause could be to blame in conjunction with others.

Beautiful amphibian habitats are being destroyed by both pollution and natural disasters.

many scientists are fond of saying this or that species disappeared from wilderness that appeared pristine and untouched and that no natural disaster could be ascertained, obviously the amphibians did not see it the same way! The Costa Rican Golden Toad (*Bufo periglenes*) was last seen in 1989, and subsequent searches have failed to turn up a single specimen. The two species of Gastric Brooding Frog have not been found since 1979 (*R. silus*) and 1985 (*R. vitellinus*). No amount of searching has unearthed a single specimen since those years. Another Australian frog, the Mt.

As a result of amphibian declines and extinctions, various regional and international task forces on amphibian decline have been organized to study the problem. These groups conduct census studies, determine whether amphibians present before have been imperiled or made extinct and try to discern what cause or causes may be present. Looking at the above list is depressing for those who are interested in trying to do something about this problem. It is, in fact, overwhelming. However, environmental activists have made significant contributions in trying to eliminate some of these causes on a local level.

Many of today's amphibian declines are believed to have started back in the 1970s. And while

U.S. AMPHIBIANS IN TROUBLE

Some seven salamanders and five frogs found in the United States are on the Federal list of Endangered and Threatened species, and it is reliably believed at least one of these, the Wyoming Toad, is already extinct in nature. On the state lists, the number is much higher.

Salamanders include:

Santa Cruz Long-Toed Salamander, *Ambystoma macrodactylus croceum*
Desert Slender Salamander, *Batrachoseps aridus*
San Marcos Salamander, *Eurycea nanar*
Red Hills Salamander, *Phaeognathus hubrichti*
Cheat Mountain Salamander, *Plethodon nettingi*
Shenandoah Salamander, *Plethodon shenandoah*
Texas Blind Salamander, *Typhlomolge rathburni*

Endangered frogs include:

Wyoming Toad, *Bufo baxteri*
Arroyo Toad, *Bufo californicus*
Houston Toad, *Bufo houstonensis*
Puerto Rican Crested Toad, *Peltophryne lemur*
California Red-Legged Frog, *Rana aurora draytonii*

Glorious (diurnal) Torrent Frog, *Taudactylus diurnis,* once abundant in the same area as the Gastric Brooding Frog, hasn't been seen since 1979. Is this a coincidence? Australian scientists don't think so. Although these three species are the only Australian frogs believed to have recently become extinct, more than 25 others are on the Australian list of threatened, vulnerable and endangered species. Reasons range from habitat loss, fatal diseases and "indeterminate" to the introduction of the cane toad, which either eats or outcompetes native species for food and territory.

Worldwide, the following genera of amphibians appear on CITES lists. If a species is listed on Appendix I, it is all but impossible to export and import, as this is the most stringent category and consists of the most imperiled or endangered species. In fact, a few of the species on Appendix I are already believed extinct, but remain listed in the unlikely event they appear once again. Appendix II lists species whose future may be threatened by trade, which is therefore regulated. Permits are needed to export and import Appendix II species, and the data from such documents enable scientists to determine whether the volume of trade could be harmful to the animal. Some of the most important CITES-listed amphibians, with their Appendix Number after their name, follow:

Panamanian Golden Frog, *Atelopus varius zeteki* (I).
Costa Rican Golden (Monte Verde) Toad, *Bufo periglenes* (I), believed to now be extinct.
Sonoran Green Toad, *Bufo retiformis* (II).
Cameroon Toad, *Bufo superciliaris* (I).
All species of African viviparous toads, *Nectophrynoides sp.*(II).
West African Goliath Frog, *Conrau goliath* (II).
Dendrobatidae—All 175 or so species are listed in Appendix II.
Gastric Brooding Frogs, *Rheobatrachus sp.* (I). (If they were not extinct, which they probably are, these species would still be legally impossible to export from Australia because of Australian laws. Their presence on this list may be as much sentimental as it is practical.)

Tomato Frog, *Dyscophus antongilii* (I).
Israeli Painted Frog, *Dyscophus nigriventer* (I). This species is believed to be extinct in nature.
Asian Bullfrog, *Rana hexadactyla* (II).
Indian (Tiger) Bullfrog, *Rana tigerina* (II). (This, and the Asian Bullfrog, are on Appendix II because of concerted widespread harvesting of wild populations for the frog leg trade. Millions of pounds of frogs' legs from these two species have been exported to Europe, thus causing the fear of significant declines.)
Lake Patzcuaro Salamander, *Ambystoma dumerilii* (II).
Axolotl, *Ambystoma mexicanum* (II).

Approximately 100 other amphibians appear under various CITES categories as species of special concern because they are considered vulnerable, threatened or

The beautiful Northern Tomato Frog of Madagascar is listed on CITES Appendix I and is considered highly endangered (Northern Tomato Frog, *Dyscopyhus antongili*).

critically endangered in parts of their natural or historical range. These animals are listed in a volume known as the Red-Book, which is issued by the United Nations World Conservation Monitoring Center and is also available on the Internet.

All CITES-listed fauna or plants require permits to export and import. Export permits must be issued by the CITES authority in the country of origin, and permits to import must be issued by the CITES authority in the destination country. In the United States, the U.S. Fish and Wildlife Service operates a special branch that manages CITES issues and permitting. The CITES Authority is divided into two offices: the office of Scientific Authority, which addresses scientific issues such as species identification, and an office of Management Authority, which manages legal and paperwork requirements.

Other Legal Issues

In addition to the legal protections offered by Federal and state laws and international treaties, the air transport of amphibians is governed by rules enforced by the International Air Transport Association (IATA) and perhaps at some point in the near future, by new U.S. Fish and Wildlife regulations as well. States, counties and

If you have other pets or children, you may want to steer clear of highly poisonous species such as the dendrobatids and the bufonids (Dyeing Dart Poison Frog, *Dendrobates tinctorius*).

municipalities may also enforce laws regarding humane handling and housing of amphibians, and some jurisdictions may prohibit the possession of certain species because they are an environmental threat (should they accidentally escape—Marine Toads, bullfrogs and African Clawed Frogs have proven that this can be a serious problem).

There has been some talk of local health departments enforcing dangerous animal laws as they relate to highly poisonous amphibians. Irrespective of how poisonous some species of amphibians may be, they are infinitely safer and less unpredictable than venomous snakes, which strike, bite and deliver their venom actively. A poisonous frog or salamander is truly a threat only if it escapes and a pet or child picks the animal up and puts it in its mouth. If you have small children or other pets in the house, you may not want to become involved with such highly

poisonous species as the dendrobatids, mantellas, atelopids or bufonid toads. All enclosures should be well away from any possible access by either pets or small children, and covers to enclosures should be secured. This is not only for your other pets' and children's safety but for the security of the resident amphibian as well.

In many U.S. states, it is against the law to hunt frogs except during special times of the year, to exceed daily or per-person bag limits or to take frogs without a special sort of fishing or hunting license. At one time, hundreds of thousands of Leopard Frogs were collected by biological supply companies. Because of the radical declines experienced by this once common species, it is now illegal for such companies to obtain and resell wild-caught Leopard Frogs, and they must rely solely on frogs that are frog farm (captive)-bred for this purpose.

CHAPTER 13

Herpetological Education

Herpetology is the branch of zoology that deals with amphibians and reptiles; zoology is a branch of biology that deals with animals. The word *herpetology* derives from two words: the Greek *herpeton* or *herpes,* which means "to creep or crawl," and *-ology,* which means "the study of." So herpetology is the study of animals that creep or crawl. While that describes most reptiles and amphibians, it also includes other life forms, and frogs and toads, at least, also walk, hop and leap and, on occasion, fly. The words *herps* and *herptiles* are shorthand for all amphibians and reptiles and are frequently used conversationally, but neither word can be found in the dictionary.

Herpetology is a bio-science that is divided into a professional and an amateur sector. So while there are really no such people as "amateur surgeons" or "amateur dentists," there are plenty of amateur herpetologists. There are also amateur ornithologists or bird watchers, ichthyologists or fish keepers and entomologists or people interested in insects.

This state of affairs is often a result of the fact that job opportunities to work in herpetology or ornithology and the like tend to be rather limited, and people interested in these fields often have to find other ways to make a living while pursuing such studies. Herpetology is also a great self-educating hobby and from that point of view, serious adherents have plenty to learn, more so than stamp collectors, photography buffs or comic book collectors. At best, it might be compared to the serious marine fish hobbyist, but is even more diverse than that.

A serious study of herpetology involves in-depth knowledge of geography, climate, environmental conditions, reptile and amphibian biology, venoms and poisons (toxinology), reptile/amphibian veterinary care (or the ability to recognize veterinary medical problems), Latin and Greek word origins, taxonomy, systematics or classification, reproduction, water chemistry and conditions, botany/horticulture (to provide safe plants for your animals), entomology (to understand what your animals eat: insects) and nutrition. The list of disciplines allied to herpetology is enormous, and the serious hobbyist needs to know something about all of them.

Is it any wonder that parents would want to encourage this hobby for their children (and themselves as well)? Imagine how smart your kids will grow up to be when they get involved with herpetology. How do you get this kind of information? The answer is through self-study, attending local herpetological society meetings, subscribing to popular herpetology magazines as well as scientific journals and buying and reading books such as this one. A self-educated herper's (a word that is shorthand for "herpetology hobbyist") greatest asset is his or her library.

Amphibians on the Net

You can gather an enormous wealth of information over the Internet.

"Herp" and "herptile" are the vernacular for reptiles and amphibians. Many reptiles, like amphibians, are endangered, such as the Fiji Island Iguana (Fiji Island "Blue" Iguana, *Brachylophus fasciatus*). Possession of this species is prohibited by U.S. and international law.

Keeping amphibians as pets is a great way for children and adults to learn more about nature and ecology (Squirrel Tree Frog calling, *Hyla squirrela*).

Using search engines such as Yahoo!, Infoseek, Hotbot and Alta Vista, you can find amphibian sites all over the world, but you need to enter one or more key words for each search. Key words regarding amphibians include:

amphibia
amphibian(s)
frog(s)
toad(s)
salamanders(s)
newt(s)
anura
salientia
caudata
urodela
amphibian decline
amphibian conservation
apoda
gymniophiona
cecillians
(*var:* caecilians, caecillians)

plus any other subject related to the above in which you are interested.

Keep trying different key words and combinations until you find what you are looking for. You should be rewarded with sizable lists of Website links containing all kinds of valuable information. As part of the Internet tradition, such links will also contain nested within them more links, carrying you on an endless journey through amphibian and herpetological cyberspace. I have established a special gateway Website link that lists some of my favorite amphibian Website links. It is located at: http://www.xmission.com/~gastown/herpmed/amphibia.htm. The World Wide Web is a particularly valuable resource, as it often contains full-color photos of various species.

One of the most problematic issues facing inexperienced or even moderately experienced amphibian keepers is identification, particularly of foreign species unfamiliar to the hobbyist and for which he or she has no readily available reference guide. On "frognet" recently, a number of people started talking about the Green and Golden Bell Tree Frog (*Litoria aurea*), a threatened Australian species in serious decline, and a number of folks said they were widely available in pet shops in the United States. After some discussion of the likelihood that these animals had made their way to the United States, one member went to his field guides of Australian frogs and posted color, size and characteristics of Green and Golden Bell Tree Frogs. Two froggers wrote back to say this was not the frog that they had seen in the shops!

Properly identifying species based on common names that are used by pet shop managers or wholesale suppliers is a specious (no pun intended) exercise at best. Unless it is a familiar species over which there can be no dispute, don't take for granted the common name label put on any animal. While it may not seem to make a difference, it does. Knowing the origins and habits of the frogs you own can be quite helpful, but first you've got to know the identity of the frogs you own. There are so many frogs, and at any moment a species you've never heard of could show up on a dealer's or pet shop's doorstep. If the shop isn't sure what it is, the staff will place any good old name on the tank along with the price.

There are so many fascinating (not to mention strange) amphibians in the world! Studying herps teaches us about other environments, other countries (Foxface Tree Frog, *Scinax sugillata*).

Internet Forums

There are also two Internet forums devoted to the discussion of frogs, toads and other amphibians. You subscribe by e-mail; in return, every day you will receive e-mail messages with questions, discussion topics and answers to questions (yours and others) from people who have (or think they have) the answer. Erroneous information is soon corrected by a host of other members who jump into the fray. There is no fee to get on these lists. There are plenty of arguments, debates and, on occasion, even name calling, a practice called "flaming" that is *not* a nice thing to do no matter how you might feel. It is definitely against Internet etiquette (also called "netiquette"). Always try to be polite, regardless of the situation. To subscribe to these forums, all you need to do is send an e-mail message addressed to: majordomo@bb-elec.com, and in the body of your message write on the first line: subscribe frognet, followed by your e-mail address, and on the second line: subscribe anuran, then enter your e-mail address (such as "joedoe@internet.com"). If you have trouble subscribing, send a message to the above majordomo address and simply write in the body of the message one word: HELP. By return you will get a package of information that will point out where you are going wrong.

If you are interested in declining amphibians, you can subscribe to a discussion forum on this subject as well. Send an e-mail message to: listproc@ucdavis.edu, and in the body of the message write: subscribe amphibiandecline (note: "amphibiandecline" is all one word).

On USENET news groups there are two open (nonsubscribed) forums concerning reptiles and amphibians to which anyone can post. One is called sci.bio.herp and is for more serious, scientific questions regarding amphibians and reptiles. Questions on captive care, husbandry, diseases of herps and issues related to the hobby can be found on rec.pets.herp. You can automatically load the latest postings from these news groups by using a program called a news reader, which your Internet provider can supply. Check whether your provider has news groups available and how to access these two forums. If you do not have news access via your Internet account, you can still access newsgroups via the World Wide Web by using your Web browser and going to: http://www.dejanews.com. Enter the name of either of the two newsgroups in their opening search page and a list of the latest postings will be returned on screen. You can then read them, discard them or reply to them if you are inclined to do so. You can register your e-mail address with dejanews so you can avoid going through their authorization procedure every time you post to a newsgroup. This too is a free service.

If you are interested in dart poison frogs, there are groups devoted to the care and keeping of these species (Harlequin Dart Poison Frog, *Dendrobates histrionicus*).

Herpetological Societies

If you are lucky enough to have a local herpetological society that holds regular educational meetings nearby, this is another excellent way of pursuing your self-study of herpetology. A list of herpetological societies by geographic location can be found in Appendix I or in the Semi-Annual Herpetological Directory published by *Reptile and Amphibian* magazine. In addition, there are a few specialist groups for amphibian enthusiasts (see Appendix I for more information) that are inexpensive to join. They issue monthly newsletters convey-

ing very valuable information that is not available elsewhere on the care and breeding of delicate and unusual species such as dart poison frogs and mantella frogs. In fact, if you are going to keep either of these two groups, it is recommended that you buy every back-issue newsletter of the American and British Dendrobatid Groups and pour over them carefully.

Careers in Herpetology

If you are going to college in the near future it may not be too late to embark on a formal, profession-

al career in herpetology. Many universities and colleges in the United States and throughout the world have concentrations and special programs on herpetology as part of their general biology or environmental sciences curriculum.

There is so much to learn about herpetology that it is necessary, however, to select a narrower subject area in which to specialize. Some scientists study only amphibians. Others study the herpetology of one country, or even a small area inside a country. And a few make a single genus their life's work. I spent five years reviewing the published literature concerning the relationship between amphibians, reptiles and human medicine, which culminated in the publication of a monographic review on this important subject area.

There are plenty of interesting and unexplored areas in herpetology in which the new student can become involved. American colleges and universities that offer herpetology programs can be found in the Directory published by *Reptile and Amphibian* magazine as well.

Amphibian Resources Worldwide

Study Groups and Herpetological Societies

Amphibian Groups

The following groups specialize in amphibians. Write for membership information.

American Dendrobatid Group
2932 Sunburst Drive
San Jose, CA 95111

Amphibian Conservation and Research Center
International Hylid (Treefrog) Society
1423 Alabama Street
Lafayette, IN 47905

Amphibian Information Exchange
P.O. Box 441
Lake Grove, NY 11755

British Dendrobatid Group
5 Richards Road
Standish, Wigan WN-6 0-QU
England

Dendrobatidae Nederland
De Heer J. Zwoferink
Roelf Bosmastraat 62
7462 ME Rijssen
The Netherlands

International Society of Batrachology
Laboratoire des Reptiles et Amphibians
Museum National d'Histoire Naturelle
25 rue Cuvier
75005 Paris, France

**International Society for the Study and
Conservation of Amphibians**
Department of Biological Sciences
Louisiana State University
Lake Charles, LA 70605-2000

Xenopus Society
De Heer J. Vredenbregt
Mons Nolenslaan 618
3119 ER Schiedam
The Netherlands

Herpetological Societies

The following are national groups with a scientific orientation that publish English-language journals, reviews and newsletters of interest to all reptile and amphibian enthusiasts and scientists. These organizations are staffed by volunteers and don't accept phone calls as a rule, so it is necessary to write and request information on membership and benefits.

**American Association of Medical
Herpetologists/Medical Herpetology Foundation
(AAMH)**
57 Clay Pit Road
Staten Island, NY 10309

**American Society of Ichthyiologists and
Herpetologists (ASIH)**
Florida State Museum
University of Florida
Gainesville, FL 32611

Australian Herpetological Society
P.O. Box R-79
Royal Exchange
Sydney, New South Wales 2000
Australia

British Herpetological Society
c/o Zoological Society of London
Regent's Park
London, NW-1 4-RY
England

The Herpetologists' League
c/o Dr. Rebbecca Pyles
Department of Biological Sciences
Box 70726
East Tennessee State University
Johnson City, TN 37614

Society for the Study of
Amphibians and Reptiles (SSAR)
c/o Karen Toepfer
POB 626
Hays, KS 67601

In the United States, there are state and
local Herpetological Societies that cater
to the interests of hobbyists:

Fairbanks Herpetocultural Society
Taryn Merdes
P.O. Box 71309
Fairbanks, AK 99707

Arizona Herpetological Association
P.O. Box 39127
Phoenix, AZ 85069-9127

Arkansas Herpetological Association
Glyn Turnipseed
418 N. Fairbanks
Russelville, AR 72801

Northern California Herpetological Society
P.O. Box 1363
Davis, CA 95616-1363

Southern California Herpetology Association
P.O. Box 2932
Santa Fe Springs, CA 90607

Colorado Herpetological Society
P.O. Box 15381
Denver, CO 80215

Southern New England Herpetological Association
470 Durham Road
Madison, CT 06443-2060

Delaware Herpetological Society
Ashland Nature Center
Brackenville and Barley Mill Road
Hockessin, DE 19707

Central Florida Herpetological Society
P.O. Box 3277
Winter Haven, FL 33881

West Florida Herpetological Society
3055 Panama Road
Pensacola, FL 32526

Georgia Herpetological Society
Department of Herpetology, Atlanta Zoo
800 Cherokee Avenue SE
Atlanta, GA 30315

Idaho Herpetological Society
P.O. Box 6329
Boise, ID 83707

Central Illinois Herpetological Society
1125 W. Lake Avenue
Peoria, IL 61614

Hoosier Herpetological Society
P.O. Box 40544
Indianapolis, IN 46204

Iowa Herpetological Society
P.O. Box 166
Norwalk, IA 50211

Kansas Herpetological Society
Museum of Natural History, Dyche Hall
University of Kansas
Lawrence, KS 66045

Central Kentucky Herpetological Society
P.O. Box 12227
Lexington, KY 40581-2227

Louisiana Herpetological Society
Museum of Natural History
Foster Hall, LSU
Baton Rouge, LA 70803

Maryland Herpetological Society
Natural History Society
2643 N. Charles Street
Baltimore, MD 21218

New England Herpetological Society
P.O. Box 1082
Boston, MA 02103

Michigan Society of Herpetologists
321 W. Oakland
Lansing, MI 48906

Minnesota Herpetological Society
Bell Museum of Natural History
10 Church Street SE
Minneapolis, MN 55455-0104

Southern Mississippi Herpetological Society
P.O. Box 1685
Ocean Springs, MS 39564

St. Louis Herpetological Society
Harry Steinmann
P.O. Box 220153
Kirkwood, MO 63122

Northern Nevada Herpetological Society
Don Bloomer
P.O. Box 21282
Reno, NV 89502-1282

New Mexico Herpetological Society
University of New Mexico
Department of Biology
Albuquerque, NM 87131

New York Herpetological Society
P.O. Box 1245
Grand Central Station
New York, NY 10163-1245

North Carolina Herpetological Society
State Museum
P.O. Box 29555
Raleigh, NC 27626

Central Ohio Herpetological Society
217 E. New England Avenue
Worthington, OH 43085

Northern Ohio Association of Herpetologists
Department of Biology
Case Western Reserve University
Cleveland, OH 44106

Oklahoma Herpetological Society
Tulsa Chapter
5701 E. 36th Street N.
Tulsa, OK 74115

Oklahoma Herpetological Society
Oklahoma City Chapter
Oklahoma Zoo
2101 NE 50th
Oklahoma City, OK 73111

Oregon Herpetological Society
WISTEC
P.O. Box 1518
Eugene, OR 97440

Lehigh Valley Herpetological Society
Rich Rosevear
P.O. Box 9171
Allentown, PA 18105-9171

Philadelphia Herpetological Society
Mark Miller
P.O. Box 52261
Philadelphia, PA 19115

Pittsburgh Herpetological Society
Pittsburgh Zoo
1 Hill Road
Pittsburgh, PA 15206

Rhode Island Herpetological Association
30 Metropolitan Road
Providence, RI 02909

South Carolina Herpetological Society
James L. Knight
P.O. Box 100107
Columbia, SC 29230

Texas Herpetological Society
Hutchinson Hall of Science
31st at Canton
Lubbock, TX 79410

Utah Herpetological Society
Hogle Zoo
P.O. Box 8475
Salt Lake City, UT 84108

Washington Herpetological Society
12420 Rock Ridge Road
Herndon, VA 22070

Pacific Northwest Herpetological Society
P.O. Box 70231
Bellevue, WA 98008

Wisconsin Herpetological Society
P.O. Box 366
Germantown, WI 53022

FINDING AN AMPHIBIAN VETERINARIAN

Most veterinarians treat dogs, cats, birds, horses, cows and other domestic animals. However, you can find out if there is a herp veterinarian in your area by contacting the following organization:

Association of Reptile and Amphibian Veterinarians
POB 605
Chester Heights, PA 19017
Tel: 1-610-892-4812

Housing and Environmental Controls

Although the most common housing for amphibians starts with an ordinary all-glass aquarium tank that can be obtained in any pet shop or aquarium store, the following dealers have specialized items that are not readily available in pet shops:

ATV Habitats
1000 Asmore Way
Chester Springs, PA 19425
Tel: 1-610-524-1941
Manufactures vivariums/terrariums designed for amphibians.

Black Jungle Terrarium Supply
2160 W. Charleston, Suite L-33D
Las Vegas, NV 89102
Tel: 1-800-268-1813
Markets a variety of hard-to-find exotic plants (such as bromeliads/epiphytes) and other natural decor for terrariums.

EcoLogic Technologies
P.O. Box 1038
Pasadena, MD 21122
Tel: 1-410-255-8486
Manufactures rainmaking equipment.

Helix Controls
8535 Commerce Avenue
San Diego, CA 92121
Tel: 1-619-566-8335
Manufactures environmental temperature/humidity
control and monitoring equipment.

Reptronics
170 Creek Road
Bangor, PA 18013
Tel: 1-610-588-6011
Manufactures light and heating equipment
and controllers.

Live Food Providers

The following dealers accept credit card, phone or mail-in pre-paid orders for a variety of live feeder insects. Some may be willing to ship COD, although remittance fees make this option more expensive. Contact them first for availability and prices. Budget for your food sources before you obtain your first amphibian, especially if your local pet shop cannot supply you with such items.

Arbico
POB 4247
Tucson, AZ 85738
Tel: 1-800-827-2847

Armstrong's Cricket Farm
POB 745
Glennville, GA 30427
Tel: 1-800-658-3408

Drosophila (Live Fruit Fly Cultures)
POB 8301
Coral Springs, FL 33075
Tel: 1-800-545-2303

Fluker Farms
POB 378
Baton Rouge, LA 70821
Tel: 1-800-735-8537

Ghann's Cricket Farm
POB 211840
Augusta, GA 30917
Tel: 1-800-476-2248

Golden West Cricket
4608 E. Compton Blvd.
Compton, CA 90221
Tel: 1-213-634-7488

Grubco
POB 15001
Hamilton, OH 45015
Tel: 1-800-222-3563

Hurst Cricket Farm
POB 212
Savannah, TN 38372
Tel: 1-800-669-7304

Jimeny Cricket Farm Inc.
8508-C Glazebrook Avenue
Richmond, VA 23228
Tel: 1-804-262-8902

King and Company
7503 Lima Drive
Nampa, ID 83686
Tel: 1-208-466-4187

Nature's Way
POB 7268
Hamilton, OH 45013
Tel: 1-800-318-2611

Rainbow Mealworms
126 E. Spruce Street
Compton, CA 90220
Tel: 1-800-777-9676

Rock Bottom Bait Company
1660 Drum Street
Winter Park, FL 32789

Selph Cricket Ranch
POB 36
Mineral Wells, MS 38648
Tel: 1-800-238-7322

Timberline
201 E. Timberline Road
Marion, IL 62959
Tel: 1-800-423-2248

Top Hat Cricket Farm
1919 Forest Drive
Kalamazoo, MI 49002
Tel: 1-800-638-2555

Triple R Cricket Ranch
31585 RD 68
Visalia, CA 93291
Tel: 1-800-526-4410

Wabash Valley Bait Company
RR 1, Box 32
West Union, IL 62477
Tel: 1-800-262-6547

**Walker Brothers Cricket
Farm, Inc.**
POB 5002
North Little Rock, AR 72119
Tel: 1-501-945-2718

(Note: The majority of feeder mice dealers ship frozen mice only. Amphibians that take feeder mice require newborn or very young live mice that should be obtained locally. The above dealers sell not only crickets; many handle a variety of other insects such as mealworms, earthworms, flies, super mealworms and more. It is best to contact as many as you can and request their price lists.)

Additional Reading

Amphibian and Reptile Hobbyist Magazines

Reptile and Amphibian Magazine
RD#3, Box 3709A
Pottsville, PA 17901
Tel: 1-717-622-6050

Reptiles
POB 58700
Boulder, CO 80322
Tel: 1-303-786-7306

Reptilian
c/o ZooMed Labs
3100 McMillan Road
San Luis Obispo, CA 93401
Tel: 1-805-542-9988

The Vivarium
POB 3000067
Escondido, CA 92030
Tel: 1-619-747-4948

Amphibian and Reptile Book Dealers

As theirs is a truly self-educating hobby, amphibian and reptile keepers need reliable (and multiple) sources of out-of-print specialized books and other publications. The following dealers issue price lists and/or place them on the World Wide Web:

Bibliomania
195 West 200 North
Logan, UT 84321
Tel: 1-801-752-0297

Herpetological Search Service
117 E Santa Barbara Road
Lindenhurst, NY 11757
Tel: 1-516-957-3624

Herptitles
16 Idlewild Road
Levittown, PA 19057

Paul Gritis
POB 4298
Bethlehem, PA 18018
Tel: 1-610-867-9723

Maryland Reptile Farm
109 West Cherry Hill Road
Reistertown, MD 21136
Tel: 1-410-526-4186

K. Nunam
57 Clay Pit Road
Staten Island, NY 10309

Serpent's Tale
POB 405
Lanesboro, MN 55949
Tel: 1-507-467-8734

Books

Bishop, S. *Handbook of Salamanders (United States, Canada and Lower California).* Ithaca: Cornell University Press, 1994.

Conant, R. and Collins, J. *Reptiles and Amphibians: Eastern/Central North America.* Boston: Houghton Mifflin Co., 3rd ed., 1993.

Duellman, W. and Trueb, L. *Biology of Amphibians.* Baltimore: Johns Hopkins University Press, 1994.

Frank, N. and Ramus, E. *A Complete Guide to Scientific and Common Names of Reptiles and Amphibians of the World.* Pottsville, PA: Reptile and Amphibian Magazine, 1995.

Grenard, S. *Frogs and Toads: An Owner's Guide to a Happy Healthy Pet.* New York: Howell House, 1998.

Grenard, S. *Medical Herpetology: Amphibians and Reptiles and Human Medicine.* Pottsville, PA: Reptile and Amphibian Magazine, 1994.

Griffiths, R. *Newts and Salamanders of Europe.* New York: Academic Press, 1996.

Levell, J. *A Field Guide to Reptiles and the Law.* Lanesboro, MN: Serpent's Tale, 2nd Edition. 1997. (Includes amphibians.)

1998-1999 Herpetology Directory. Pottsville, PA: Reptile and Amphibian Magazine,1998.

Stebbins, R. *Western Reptiles and Amphibians.* Boston: Houghton Mifflin Co., 1987.

Stebbins, R. and Cohen, N. *A Natural History of Amphibians.* Princeton, NJ: Princeton University Press, 1995.

Tyler, M. *Australian Frogs: A Natural History.* Ithaca, NY: Cornell University Press, 1998.

Wright, A.H. and Wright, A.A. *Handbook of Frogs of the United States and Canada.* Ithaca, NY: Cornell University Press, 1995.

Index